Transgender **Care**

Transgender **Care**

Recommended Guidelines,
Practical Information,
and Personal Accounts

Written by and Essays Compiled by
Gianna E. Israel and
Donald E. Tarver II, M.D.

Foreword by **Joy Diane Shaffer, M.D.**

Temple University Press
Philadelphia

Temple University Press, Philadelphia 19122
Copyright © 1997 by Temple University
All rights reserved
Published 1997
Printed in the United States of America

Text design by Elizabeth Anne O'Donnell

♾ The paper used in this publication meets the requirements of American National Standard for Information Sciences—Permanence of Paper for Printed Library Materials, ANSI Z39.48–1984

Library of Congress Cataloging-in-Publication Data

Israel, Gianna E., 1963–
    Transgender care : recommended guidelines, practical information, and personal accounts / written by and essays compiled by Gianna E. Israel and Donald E. Tarver II ; foreword by Joy Diane Shaffer.
       p.   cm.
    Includes index.
    ISBN 1-56639-571-2 (alk. paper)
    1. Transsexuals—Medical care. 2. Transsexuals—Mental health services. I. Tarver, Donald E., 1960–   . II. Title.
RA564.9.T73I87   1997
362.1'086'6—dc21   97-17280

To the health and well-being of all transgender individuals in pursuit of self-determination and full human rights

Contents

Part I
Recommended Guidelines

Foreword

In 1966 Harry Benjamin, M.D., published the pioneering book *The Transsexual Phenomenon*. For three decades Benjamin's work continued to be the best medical and psychological reference book available for transsexuals, their friends and families, and the professionals who treated them. Benjamin's work sparked a short-lived era of academic interest in transsexuals. From the late 1960s to the late 1970s, many medical schools sponsored gender clinics for the study and treatment of transsexuals.

Unfortunately, the university gender clinics came to be universally unpopular. Transsexuals correctly felt put upon by having the access to their medical care controlled by opinionated researchers. Academic physicians and psychologists were often more interested in validating their own theories of the etiology of transsexualism than in helping transsexuals to live happier lives. Transsexuals learned to alter their own life stories to better match the pathologic model favored by the institution to which they were applying for their medical care. The research produced under these circumstances is highly suspect and of questionable value.

Gender researchers were usually conservative, and always nontranssexual. They did not mind having transsexuals as research subjects or patients, but they did not view us as social equals. Few would have been pleased to see a transsexual marry into their family. One example of this mindset: Robert J. Stoller, M.D., wrote me a letter in 1977 advising me not to even consider applying to medical school. The late Dr. Stoller was a UCLA psychiatrist, professor, and author of early gender studies based on psychiatric theory. He considered transsexualism to be a mental illness caused by poor childrearing practices. He felt that no medical school in the country would admit a known transsexual, whether pretransition, preoperative, or postoperative. This is not surprising, given his beliefs. If medical schools had a negative opinion of transsexuals, Stoller was among those who contributed significantly to this attitude.

Many physicians involved with gender-reassignment programs required their applicants to promise to be exclusively heterosexual following their reassignments. Not surprisingly, gay rights activists became suspicious that the practice of gender reassignment was a heterosexist plot to eliminate homosexual behavior. Some went so far as to assert that transsexualism was not a distinct entity at all, but merely a manifestation of homosexuality with internalized homophobia. Other scholars, especially feminists, asserted that gender roles were a cultural artifact. Feminists would argue that gender reassignment was in conflict with their goal of altering culture to produce a nonsexist society. Lesbian feminists were especially unhappy that some postoperative male-to-female transsexuals would adopt lesbian identities and seek entry into the lesbian subculture. Ironically, although transsexuals were often unwelcome in gay and lesbian circles, the organized anti-gay movement that emerged around 1977 considered transsexuals to be especially abominable. Transsexuals were an anathema to both the left and right in this politically charged environment.

In 1979 a highly flawed academic paper was published that suggested that transsexuals did not even benefit from gender reassignment. Finally, the consequences of the often poor quality of psychological and surgical work being done by university-based gender clinics became evident. Transsexuals sued their academically based health care providers for malpractice and sometimes won. Medical schools came to be embarrassed by the presence of these controversial gender clinics. One after another, the clinics, now economic and political liabilities, were closed.

For the past decade and a half, most medical and psychological care of transsexuals in the United States has been provided outside the university system. Transsexuals and other transgender consumers have benefited in several ways. Private practitioners have been much more flexible in accepting diverse individuals for gender-reassignment treatment. The free market has helped eliminate many of the practitioners who consider gender-identity issues as pathologic and who treat those with such issues in a denigrating or patronizing manner. The quality of surgical care has improved considerably, and the vast majority of gender operations are now done by a handful of surgeons, each of whom performs more than a hundred such operations a year.

Unfortunately, the free market has also had its downside. Funding for research into the care of transsexualism has vanished. Academic publications about transsexualism and other gender issues have been few. Transsexualism itself does not exist as a defined entity in medical textbooks or medical school curriculums. In the absence of medical advocacy for transsexuals, insurance companies frequently exclude medical coverage for genital reassignment with impunity. Imagine the uproar from hematologists if insurance companies chose to exclude medical coverage for leukemia. Concerning transsexualism, there is a deafening silence.

To fill this vacuum, a new generation of writers about transsexualism and other gender-identity issues emerged in the mid-1990s. Many, including my friend and colleague Gianna E. Israel, are transgender persons themselves. Ms. Israel is one of several of us who developed the professional skills to treat transsexuals and other transgender persons after undergoing gender reassignment herself. Her counseling practice grew, not from any arid academic theory, but from a heartfelt desire to help other transsexuals find happiness in their lives. This project, which gave her the opportunity to collaborate with a prominent gay African American psychiatrist, Donald Tarver, M.D., has been a labor of love, bringing cultural sensitivity to the treatment needs of transgender men and women. The work involved in publishing a book of this breadth and magnitude is enormous, and Ms. Israel did not have the luxury of being supported by an academic salary in undertaking her role as principal author.

Ms. Israel's sacrifices and Dr. Tarver's contributions are much needed. Most transsexuals do not have the benefit of living in the San Francisco area, where knowledgeable gender counselors and physicians are plentiful. Many transsexuals find themselves in the awkward position of being the first transsexual their counselor or physician has treated. Likewise, many transgender persons may not even realize that treatment plans exist for their needs. It is for the benefit of these persons that this book is intended. The Guidelines comprehensively cover the essentials of transsexual and transgender care. In addition, other important topics, such as human immunodeficiency virus (HIV) infection in transgender persons, are covered for the first time in any such volume.

Gianna Israel has contributed significantly to the burgeoning movement to depathologize transsexualism and transgenderism, and to improve the quality of care. Her efforts form a bridge to the longed-for day when transsexualism is a standard subject in medical school and in medical texts. Dr. Harry Benjamin would be proud; I certainly am. May this book grace every library.

Joy Diane Shaffer, M.D.
San Jose, California
January 1997

Review Committee

Each person selected for participation on this independent review committee was chosen because of her or his specialized experience and knowledge about gender-identity issues and expertise in a concurrent support specialty. This selection process included professionals and consumers, many of whom self-identify as both. Many members of the committee have contributed essays in Part II. Biographical sketches of these individuals, may be found in the About the Reviewers and Contributors section.

Barbara F. Anderson, Ph.D, L.C.S.W.
Mildred L. Brown, Ph.D.
Donna Colvin
Jason Cromwell, Ph.D.
Alexis Belinda Dinno
Sister Mary Elizabeth
Donna and Julie Freeman
Ayme Michelle Kantz
Stephanie Anne Lloyd
Victoria Lynn
Lisa Middleton, M.P.A.

Douglas K. Ousterhout, D.D.S., M.D.
Rachel Pollack, M.A.
Eugene A. Schrang, M.D.
Gail Sondegaard
Susan Stryker, Ph.D.
Sharon Ann Stuart
Delia van Maris, M.D.
Anne Vitale, Ph.D.
Sheri Webb
Kiki Whitlock

Preface and Acknowledgments

Transgender Care is a comprehensive resource providing background information as well as formal recommendations for professionals and consumers concerning the psychological, hormonal, surgical, and social support of transgender-identified individuals: transsexuals, transgenderists, transvestites and androgynes. The material contained in this resource has been authored by two gender-specializing care providers whose combined experiences encompass clinical and practical expertise. This resource has been peer reviewed by an independent committee composed of specializing professionals and transgender consumers, and thus has drawn upon their professional and community wisdom.

Cautionary Statement

The Recommended Guidelines for Transgender Care that appear at the ends of chapters in Part I are offered as a resource for professional care providers and consumers to be used with the understanding that they are based on current knowledge of this ever-growing support field. Because critical information about transgender support issues, gender-confirmation procedures, and professional precautions is continuously developing, this resource cannot be perfectly up-to-date. Care providers and consumers are advised that additional medical, psychological and gender-specialized information is available through the American Medical Association, the American Psychiatric Association, a variety of sexology, psychology and social work organizations, the American Educational Gender Information Service, the International Foundation for Gender Education, and other resources. Care providers may also find information about gender issues on the Internet, Medline, and other online service providers.

The proper use of these Guidelines requires a specialized body of knowledge and clinical experience in support of the transgender individual. Experienced Gender Specialists recognize that each transgender individual's circumstances are unique and that the provision of professional support, evaluation, and recommendations may require specialized consultation that goes beyond the issues covered in the Guidelines. Professionals in medicine, psychotherapy, and mental health who specialize in the care of transgender people are strongly advised to follow local, state or provincial, and national professional licensing laws and to maintain appropriate continuing education credits. Professionals, government agencies, and legal entities are welcome to use the Recommended Guidelines for Transgender Care as a resource in the support, evaluation, and care of transgender individuals.

Acknowledgments

This book is the product of a long organizational, authoring, review, and editing process. Finishing this book would have been impossible without the insights from our Review Committee, and the editorial commitments and special contributions of Larry Brinken; Donna Colvin; Dallas Denny, MA.; Alexis Belinda Dinno; Markisha Greaney; Gale E. S. Honeyman; Ayme Michelle Kantz; Heather Lamborn; Victoria Lynn; Lisa Middleton, M.P.A.; Rachel Pollack, M.A.; and Max Wolf Valerio. We also appreciate the support and encouragement we have received from Thomas Bodenheimer, M.D.; Greg Bortolussi; David Fillipello, O.M.D.; Rinna Flohr, L.C.S.W.; Jerome Franz, M.D.; Rik Isensee, L.C.S.W; Herb Leung, Pharm. D.; JoAnn Roberts, Ph.D.; Jean-Marie Stein; Alice Webb, L.C.S.W., Ph.D.(c.); Christine Wild; AEGIS Board of Directors; and LYRIC (San Francisco). Special thanks go to Larry Burton Sr.; Randy Daron, Ph.D.(c); Willie Leorn Dixon; Darlene Angela Hall, Ph.D.; Alys Claire Herring; Ron Hypolite, J.D.; Paul Fresina; Kevin Pedretti, Ph.D.; Marilyn Robinson; Monica Lynne Tarver; Tom Robertson, Ph.D.; Diana Weilliver, and Barry Zevin, M.D.

Part I

Recommended Guidelines

Introduction

Chapter 1

Uncovering current educational resources, assessment tools, and recommendations in support of the many different types of transgender individuals has been difficult for professionals as well as for consumers who are experiencing gender concerns. In 1979 the Harry Benjamin International Gender Dysphoria Association (HBIGDA) drafted its "Standards of Care for Gender Dysphoric Persons," which consists primarily of recommendations for hormonal and surgical treatment for transsexuals. Over the years that document and its subsequent revisions have come under sharp criticism for being too narrow in scope and pathologizing to transgender individuals. We would, however, like to commend those founding professionals who initiated safety measures where no formal precautions previously existed and that undoubtedly prevented a variety of psychological and surgical mishaps.

As we approach the new millennium, providing professional transgender support services has become all the more complex as the special needs of multiple populations come to the surface. As an example, over the years the staff at the Tom Wadell Medical Clinic in San Francisco noted the plight endured by transgender individuals surviving in the city's Tenderloin district, a zone of high poverty, violent crime, and drug addiction. Not only were these individuals underserved with regard to basic medical and psychological support services, they were frequently resorting to self-medication with black-market hormones or visiting irresponsible practitioners who promoted hormone administration and silicone treatments without appropriate medical follow-up. Clearly, few resources existed that addressed these individuals' special needs, or provided necessary consumer education and regular medical follow-up.

The cases of *transgenderist* individuals who are unable to obtain support services provide yet another example of how complex providing transgender support services has become. (Transgenderist individuals are those who live "in role," that is, as a member of the opposite gender, part or full time, yet are not interested in Genital Reassignment Surgery.) These individuals have been routinely turned away from mental health services or denied hormone administration and associated gender-confirmation surgeries. Since these individuals are not transsexuals, no resources have existed that define this subpopulation and its specialized needs or provide recommendations for its support and care.

The Guidelines provided herein do *not* supplement any existing literature or resources. Rather, they refine existing knowledge by addressing the uncertainties many professionals and consumers face in this rapidly evolving specialty field. Questions such as these are answered: How does one support the transgenderist's specialized needs? Can transgender HIV-positive individuals be referred for hormones and surgery? What options are available to transgender youth? How can mental health and social service providers best offer residential placement for transgender individuals, including the homeless? How do novice care providers distinguish between true mental disorders and a transgender identity? In addition, current recommendations for hormone administration and surgical treatment are presented. The latter subjects have been addressed in such a manner as to respect the individual's right for self-determination while promoting realistic models for medical follow-up and consumer self-protection.

The Guidelines provide the framework for further development of professional support of transgender individuals. Newly introduced is the concept of the Gender Specialist, a care provider who possesses a distinct body of knowledge gained within the context of support for transgender individuals and through professional peer consultation. Although no such specialty certification exists within larger professional organizations, the introduction of this concept herein provides not only the validation of such need but also gives consumers an easy-to-understand framework for determining which professionals are qualified to support their unique needs.

The development of the Guidelines from concept to authorship, then through the review and editing processes, has not occurred without obstacles. It has been an ongoing growth process in which the chief difficulties have been promoting nonpathologizing support models that protect the individual's right for self-identification while preserving and further defining medical, psychological, social support, and consumer protections. Language usage itself also presented some difficulty, as we endeavored to illustrate the support needs of *all* transgender populations—transsexuals, transvestites, transgenderists, androgynes, and including even the intersex and hermaphrodite individuals who sometimes self-identify as transgender.

One such question about language arose around so-called *cross-* words, that is, those beginning with the prefix *cross,* for example, crossdress, crosslive, crossgender. Several individuals on the Review Committee voiced objection to the application of *cross-* words, which they felt were inappropriate to use when describing transsexual-oriented behavior. In response, we searched the entire manuscript while asking whether *cross-* words were in fact being utilized in areas solely dedicated to transsexual individuals or were being used as an instrument to provide a broader frame of reference so as to be inclusive of other transgender populations. More information on *cross-* words may be found in the vocabulary section below.

The healthy process of asking questions such as these directly mirrors the developmental pathways encountered by transgender individuals, the transgender community, and supporting care providers. The whole process begins when a person asks, "What gender am I?" The process continues with professionals and transgender support organization leaders asking themselves, "How can we best provide resources and educational options so that transgender individuals can make informed choices?" Nationally, this has taken shape in many forms. Some of the results include passage of a city ordinance in San Francisco as well as similar legislation elsewhere that provides antidiscrimination protection for transgender individuals. In upstate New York one transgender social-educational organization is developing a health collective of physicians, psychologists, and other care providers interested in making support accessible for transgender individuals.

One of the singular difficulties faced by these endeavors and by transgender individuals nationwide is the hesitancy with which medical, psychological, and mental health providers approach transgender issues. Their hesitancy is due for the most part to a lack of resources that would demystify the support process. The Guidelines address those needs; they constitute a resource that begins by answering basic questions and continues by covering issues not addressed in current literature. *Transgender Care* is the first resource of its kind, and it addresses some very current issues; thus, it should not be misconstrued as the "final word" regarding transgender support, but, rather, as a catalyst encouraging further inquiry, growth, and change by consumers and care providers alike.

Several members of the Review Committee raised the question as to why transgender individuals need psychotherapy support services or guidelines at all, when in fact most transgender individuals are emotionally balanced and mature enough to make responsible decisions. We hope that this resource reflects that very sentiment while concurrently promoting recommendations for the provision of necessary consumer education and safeguards, as well as for dialogue between care providers and consumers. Recognized guidelines are necessary, and not solely for consumer protection. Both care providers and insurance companies need recognized guidelines in order to establish standards for professional services and insurance coverage. This is particularly true in the case of care providers who are unfamiliar with transgender needs. The Guidelines should prove a useful resource as care providers and consumers maintain dialogue regarding services and their insurance coverage. However, as practicing Gender Specialists, we believe that, with the exception that they may require medical intervention to bring their body in line with self-image, transgender consumers are in fact not unlike their nontransgender counterparts: Most individuals are emotionally balanced and mature, and so they can easily do without unnecessary mental health and medical interference. Some, however, may need to utilize professional services in order to gain the tools to improve their quality of life.

The Review Committee that helped develop the Guidelines is as unique as the resource itself. This independent body is composed of a balanced selection of specializing care providers and knowledgeable transgender consumers, many of whom are both. Each brought to this project invaluable insights based on his or her academic, clinical, social, and life experiences. Review Committee participants and several guest authors were offered an opportunity to contribute by submitting essays, which can be found in Part II. The inclusion of an essay does not constitute an endorsement of the particular psychotherapeutic, surgical, or theoretical model expressed by the writer of that essay. A list of resources can also be found in the Appendix. Biographical information on each contributing participant is provided in a concluding section.

The Vocabulary and the Issues

This important reference section will help the reader understand the terminology and concepts that are essential to a discussion of the support of transgender individuals and their special needs, and to an understanding of the Guidelines themselves. Some of the terminology presented reflects the stability of what might be considered common knowledge, and thus is an excellent starting point for newcomers to this specialty field. Other terms reflect the evolutionary process language undergoes as it responds to various growth processes, in this case, that of the development of fuller understanding of transgender individuals, of their needs, and of this specialty field. Some terms introduce new concepts; one example is *Gender Specialist,* a term designating those who have long labored in this specialty field without recognition.

The terminology used throughout the text has been chosen to reflect the transgender individual's right of self-identification as well as the need to promote better education of consumers and improved consumer-professional interaction.

Gender Identity

Gender identity refers to an individual's innate sense of maleness (masculinity) or femaleness (femininity), or both, as well as to how those feelings and needs are internalized and how they are presented to others. Rather than being fixed opposites, masculinity and femininity may gradate markedly, depending on individual and social interpretation. Biological sex is established by a medical assessment of genitalia in utero or at birth; subsequently, individuals are typically reared in their biological sex, with little additional thought given to an individual's psychological and behavioral self-identification. Many transgender individuals report having experienced conflict over such gender assignment throughout childhood and puberty, and it is not unknown for conflict to arise later in life.

Gender Pronouns—He, She or . . . ?

"How do I refer to *this* individual?" is typically the first question nontransgender professionals and other interested people ask. Following the premise that transgender individuals (like their nontransgender counterparts) have the human right to individually explore and determine self-identification, one should refer to transgender individuals on the basis their current presentation or their specified pronoun preference. If unsure, ask!

MTF and FTM

MTF and FTM are acronyms that refer, respectively, to "male-to-female" and "female-to-male" transitions. These designations identify which direction of transition or which established identity a transgender individual has chosen. Thus, a biologically determined male who self-identifies as female would be known as an MTF transsexual, crossdresser, or transgenderist. The acronym FTM is seen more often in print because MTF issues have largely dominated professional and transgender consumer resources, with the result that readers frequently assume that materials referring to transgender individuals or concerns refer to MTF individuals or concerns, when not otherwise specified.

Sexual Orientation

The term *sexual orientation* refers to the gender(s) of persons to whom an individual is sexually attracted. This could be the same or the opposite gender, or both. There are also transgender men and women who are attracted to other transgender persons, as well as those who are asexual or not attracted to anyone. Detailed information on how to refer to a transgender individual's sexual orientation is provided in the sexual orientation section of Chapter 2.

Gender Dysphoria

Gender dysphoria is a discomfort characterized by a feeling of incongruity with the physical gender assigned to one at birth. Frequently misunderstood by the individual, these feelings can remain suppressed and hidden from others. Unhealthy coping mechanisms include self-abuse, addictions, relationship difficulties, and suicidality, and they may mask gender dysphoria, making it difficult for care providers to detect. When conflict with one's gender identity is triggered (such as by a life change or personal crisis), the discomfort for many persons may reach crisis proportions. Gender dysphoria may be experienced by genetic males or females of any cultural, ethnic, or socioeconomic background.

The term *gender dysphoria* is often misapplied to individuals with self-actualized and stable transgender identities. It is most applicable to individuals who are in the beginning stages of transition and who yet may be unaware that they have a transgender identity. Once an individual has self-identified transition goals or has established a self-defined transgender identity, she or he is no longer considered to be gender dysphoric.

> Once an individual has self-identified transition goals or has established a self-defined transgender identity, she or he is no longer considered to be gender dysphoric.

This self-actualization process or exploration of gender (and of sexual and self-identification developmental pathways), though more sharply defined where pretransition transgender individuals are concerned with gender identity, is a natural, life-long developmental process that is experienced by all individuals of all genetic, cultural, ethnic, and socioeconomic backgrounds. These processes, including delayed gender-identity development, are not considered pathologic. Professionals wishing to classify an individual for medical or mental health treatment are encouraged to utilize a medical or mental health diagnosis appropriate to actual symptoms. (See the discussion of psychiatric diagnosis in Chapter 2.)

The key factors that help Gender Specialists determine whether an individual has successfully moved beyond gender dysphoria into self-identifying as a transgender individual are these:

- The ability to accurately describe in his or her own wording the difference between gender identity and sexual orientation, and how those constructs apply to his or her own experience.
- The ability to provide an easy-to-understand explanation of why he or she has self-identified as transgender.
- The ability to describe how his or her presentation fits in with a perceived sense of gender identity and self-defined goals.
- The ability to stay consistently within one's chosen presentation.

For more detail, see the Gender Identity Profile in Chapter 9.

Transgender Identity

Transgender identity is a term used to describe a number of groups of people: transvestites, transgenderists, those with androgynous presentations, or the intersexed. Any such individual may self-identify or be described as being transgender or having a transgender identity. A person may self-identify and be referred to as a "transgender individual" or having a "transgender identity" even if he or she has not yet found permanent roots within a specific transgender subpopulation. Once someone is self-identified as a transgender individual, it is inappropriate to refer to her or him as gender dysphoric. Although the individual is experiencing gender-identity concerns, has subsequently self-identified as transgender, and thus may no longer be considered gender dysphoric, there does exist the likelihood that he or she may still encounter some feelings of discomfort over gender-identity issues as he or she further explores his or her needs and moves toward self-identification with a particular subpopulation.

The term *transgender* has quickly become the word of choice for both professionals and consumers when referring to individuals or the community as a whole. Bringing individuals together under a common label is not without consequences. Potentially this may encourage people to overlook the unique traits and needs that distinguish various subpopulations. Additionally, some individuals abhor the thought of being associated with other subpopulations under a transgender label. They may feel that such an inclusion may be misperceived as pathologizing by others, or they may think inclusion inapplicable as a result of personal ideology.

The Guidelines advise that no agency, organization, or professional discriminate against any transgender individual or deny her or him services on the basis of ethnicity, sexual orientation, marital status, or social status. Transgender individuals exist in all ethnicities and social classes. The transgender population embraces a host of subpopulations affirming various gender and sexual identities; these include those who identify as lesbian women or gay men, as well as bisexual and heterosexual individuals.

> The Guidelines advise that no agency, organization, or professional discriminate against any transgender individual or deny her or him services on the basis of ethnicity, sexual orientation, marital status, or social status.

Crossgender, Crossliving, and Crossdressing

The *cross-* terms are grouped together for clarity. Each represents a transitional state within the framework of gender identification. To an extent, these terms help to perpetuate the misconception that gender is strictly a polar or binary state. Therefore, their usage, when referring to individuals who have permanently self-identified as living in role, may be inappropriate.

Crossgender is a self-identification commonly associated with transgenderist individuals (see the section below on transgender populations), bi-gendered individuals, and, to a lesser extent, other transgender populations such as transsexual individuals.

The terms *crossliving* and *living in role* are not exactly synonymous. The term *crossliving* is more appropriately used to refer to transgenderist individuals who maintain strong associations with both masculine and feminine presentations. Occasionally, *crossliving* is used to describe transsexuals early in their transition processes. Once an individual has strong associations with and self-identification as a transgender woman (MTF) or transgender man (FTM), then *living in role* more accurately describes her or his self-identification, actions, and processes.

Crossdressing is most appropriately assigned to crossdressers and transgenderists. After permanently self-identifying as a transgender man (FTM) or woman (MTF), transsexuals rarely self-identify with or describe themselves as crossdressing. To describe a permanently self-identified transgender man or woman's activities as "crossdressing" may be perceived as misinformed, inaccurate, and condescending.

Real-Life Test

Real-life test is a primary assessment term used to describe the period from the time a transsexual individual begins living in role to the time when he or she has been doing so long enough to be considered an appropriate candidate for aesthetic or Genital Reassignment Surgery. Primarily, the real-life test is thought to apply to Genital Reassignment Surgery; however, it also has been applied to breast procedures and hormone administration. Regrettably, we believe that the disparate uses of the term *real-life test* have confused professionals and consumers, undermining professional support services utilized by transgender individuals.

Regardless of the standards by which a real-life test protocol is defined, we believe that care providers and transgender individuals place far too much emphasis on the amount of time one must spend living in role prior to receiving recommendations for surgery. As a consequence, individuals often believe that all they have to do is conform to a stereotypical label, and, after a set period of time, they will receive the sought-after procedure. Furthermore, many feel that they will be punished or denied the procedure if they do not conform exactly to a real-life test as established by a care provider or program protocol. Because standards and protocols are typically written to protect care providers against malpractice suits as well as protect consumers from making harmful choices, rarely is emphasis placed on the individual's need to explore and define gender presentation, gender identity, or sexual-orientation issues. Consequently, many spend far too much time conforming to gender stereotypes to fulfill a real-life test requirement, and far too little time defining a place in society for themselves. Although this situation has little impact on the efficacy of hormones and surgical procedures, it does mean that even far beyond Genital Reassignment Surgery some individuals will be facing exacerbated self-identification, presentation, and social-role issues that have affected them from the onset of gender-identity issues.

It is generally understood that the real-life test is considered a primary assessment tool. What is not readily recognized, however, is that the definition of what constitutes a real-life test may vary widely, depending on location, since each care provider or gender-identity clinic typically establishes its own hormone and surgical protocols. This fact frequently goes unrecognized by transgender consumers. Particularly vulnerable are those who feel such an overwhelming sense of gratitude and relief to at long last find a care provider sensitive to their needs that they will do just about anything to fulfill a care provider's real-life test protocol in order to reach their hormonal and surgical objectives.

Some care providers may strictly adhere to the HBIGDA Standards of Care; others have membership in this organization yet establish their own protocol, some university programs create protocols to facilitate research endeavors. Many of these unofficial standards and protocols are arbitrary and may discriminate against those who do not meet their requirements. This has been particularly true in the case of transgenderist individuals, who frequently seek hormone administration, aesthetic procedures, or gonad removal (castration), yet are not interested in Genital Reassignment Surgery, which is the end objective of many protocols. There are also other protocols that link hormone administration and aesthetic surgery (primarily, breast procedures) to a real-life test or to a desire for Genital Reassignment Surgery; these in some circumstances sabotage an individual's chances of successfully completing a real-life test.

Some (although clearly not all) individuals may have physical attributes so incongruent with their developing or establishing gender identity that a real-life test may be physically impossible. Such test attempts by individuals whose physical characteristics are markedly inconsistent with presentation are frequently met with ridicule, derision, and even physical violence. Minimally androgenizing hormones and surgical procedures should be available for the transgender individual intending to live in role part time. Those with an established goal of living in role on a full-time basis may be initially provided androgenizing hormones and minor, aesthetic surgical procedures, which later can be advanced into masculinizing or feminizing procedures, depending on the presentation desired.

There are those who call for the abolishment of real-life tests and appropriate protocols. Such is the case with what is generally called "hormones-on-demand" or "surgery-on-demand." To date, no known competent care provider has voiced support for this concept. Invariably linked with this concept, however, are several principles that should not be overlooked. Many transgender individuals and practicing Gender Specialists alike recognize that care providers are advised not to unnecessarily interfere in the lives of transgender people or set protocols that do not allow such individuals the same right of self-determination of gender identity routinely extended to nontransgender individuals. Nor should professionals erect unrealistic protocols as barriers to further treatment. Protocols that fall short of these essential principles amount to nothing more than discrimination and an abuse of consumer trust.

Most real-life tests are designed to achieve the following goals:

- Prevent inappropriate or unprepared individuals from undergoing hormone administration or surgical procedures.

- Provide surgeons, professionals, and insurance companies with protection against negative outcomes in malpractice suits initiated by dissatisfied or regretful postsurgical patients.
- Protect nontranssexual and unprepared individuals from undergoing hormone administration or surgical procedures and incurring physical, psychological, or social damage.

The Guidelines do not endorse the abolishment of the real-life test for transgender individuals seeking hormone administration or surgical procedures. Instead, the Guidelines present recommendations for hormone administration and aesthetic or Genital Reassignment Surgery that adhere as closely as possible to the principle of self-determination for all transgender individuals, while preserving real-life assessment functions that are recognized and usable by professionals, surgeons, and insurance providers.

Gender Specialist

The *Gender Specialist* may be a professional, paraprofessional, or peer-support care provider. The Gender Specialist is an active practitioner in psychotherapy, counseling, or education directly oriented toward gender-identity issues. It is recommended that care providers interested in establishing themselves as Gender Specialists undergo a minimum of two years of direct supervision or consultation with a practicing Senior Gender Specialist who is recognized as having advanced experience in providing consultation to peer practitioners.

Senior Gender Specialist

The *Senior Gender Specialist* is a care provider who has actively practiced as a Gender Specialist for five years. Senior Gender Specialists are deemed appropriate to provide assessment and evaluation letters, as recommended for Genital Reassignment Surgery. At their discretion, Senior Gender Specialists may also provide training, supervision, or consultation to Gender Specialists.

Care providers who hold advanced degrees in psychology, medicine, sexology, clinical social work, or other medical or mental health fields may become Senior Gender Specialists following two years of active practice while receiving consultation in a role as a Gender Specialist. Those holding advanced degrees in sexology may have completed coursework that included training in gender-identity issues and therefore already possess skills necessary for supporting transgender clients.

Principles of Gender-Specialty Practice

Providing support to transgender clients requires a specialized body of knowledge that extends beyond the traditional training offered to psychotherapists, psychiatrists, and other mental health professionals. In recognition of this and of consumers' interests, the Guidelines endorse care providers who have committed themselves to seeking gender-specialized education, supervision, and peer consultation.

Curriculum for Gender Specialists should include:

- Familiarity with suicide and crisis intervention.
- A basic ability to recognize mental health disorders requiring appropriate referral.
- An ability to promote consumer awareness of critical gender-oriented consumer needs.
- Appropriate intervention and educational skills relating to "safer sex" and sexually transmitted disease.
- An understanding of basic gender- and sexual-identity concerns.

Familiarity with these subjects may, in most circumstances, be gained through recognized coursework and certification programs in an academic setting.

Mainstream care provider organizations and regulatory agencies at the present do not recognize transgender consumer needs and issues, or Gender Specialists. Care providers who self-identity as Gender Specialists are therefore encouraged to maintain formal membership or affiliation with recognized specialty provider organizations familiar with gender-oriented medical, psychotherapy, and consumer education. Examples would include the American Educational Gender Information Service (AEGIS), the Harry Benjamin International Gender Dysphoria Association (HBIGDA), and the International Foundation for Gender Education (IFGE). These organizations serve a critical professional need in providing up-to-date information on gender issues to which Gender Specialists typically would not have access via traditional professional channels.

We urge Gender Specialists to be aware that many transgender men and women are unable to afford basic medical and mental health services. Furthermore, a disproportionately high number of these individuals are people of color, HIV-positive, or transgender youth who are also socially or medically underserved. Public mental health services are encouraged to recognize this problem. Bearing in mind that profiteering is unethical, Gender Specialists should consider providing services on a sliding scale or without charge to selected individuals. Optimally, practitioners undergoing the process of supervision might volunteer a portion of their time to assist those with legitimate need.

Gender Specialists are encouraged to maintain letters of recommendation and collaboration from their Gender Specialist supervisors, consultants, and peers, as well as up-to-date state licenses, evidence of continuing educational credits, and complete, accurate résumés. Consumers are advised to inquire about and check the references of care providers specializing in gender issues. Because licensure in a traditional health field is not enough to guarantee proficiency in gender issues, consumers are encouraged to inquire about a care provider's standing by contacting a local support organization—AEGIS, HBIGDA, or IFGE.

Transgender Populations

Care providers, in their endeavor to support transgender individuals and consumers in their self-identification goals, should understand the various types of
transgender individuals and their specialized needs. Care providers and consumers are advised that usage of labels is inherently risky, particularly because no
single reference can include all the needs of each individual. Identification as a
transgender individual or as belonging in any one transgender subpopulation
remains the responsibility solely of the person exploring his or her own gender-
identity issues. Moreover, hasty self-definition carries heavy risks: no one should
rush into surgery or other irreversible life changes without significant reflection
upon the consequences, particularly since individuals often do not fall entirely
into one category or another, but, rather, into a number of categories.

Irresponsible usage of labels may result in the following situations:

- Care providers who stop listening once they decide an individual falls
  within a subpopulation.
- Encouragement of an individual to conform to models that are inconsistent
  with that individual's needs or self-identity.
- Individuals who feel they may want or are ready for hormones or surgery,
  and aggressively pursue such, when in actuality they are only experiencing a
  few coming-out highs in relation to a new self-discovery of gender identification.
- Transgenderist or transsexual individuals who feel pressured to conform to
  stereotypes in order to please friends, partners, or care providers and thus
  receive support, hormones, or surgery that may not be right for them.

Transsexuals

Transsexuals are individuals who feel an overwhelming desire to permanently
fulfill their lives as members of the opposite gender. For such persons, an interest
in crossliving, sex hormones, and Genital Reassignment Surgery is most often
paramount. Transsexuals commonly experience the most acute effects of gender
dysphoria. This phenomenon generally commences during early childhood and
remains throughout an adult's lifetime. If suppressed, gender-identity issues may
be brought to the surface during intense periods of change or personal crisis.

Support initially includes assessing and addressing gender dysphoria and
parallel issues. At this time, the counseling focus should be on ruling out underlying personality or psychotic disorders. Ongoing counseling includes exploring
and restructuring internal coping mechanisms and references to self-identity.
Transition itself is a lengthy and difficult process, requiring in-depth exploration
of support, relationship, employment, and other survival issues. Following the
Guidelines includes educating, assessing, and referring individuals for hormone,
cosmetic, and surgical options.

Transvestites or Crossdressers

Transvestites or crossdressers are individuals who dress in clothing of the opposite gender for emotional satisfaction or erotic pleasure, or both. Transvestites wishing to permanently retain their biological sex express little or no desire for hormones or Genital Reassignment Surgery. Frequently, a recurring desire to crossdress provides an outlet for the individual to explore feelings and behaviors associated with the opposite gender. At times, a sexual fetish may be emphasized or an individual may wish to completely crossdress and discreetly pass as a member of the opposite gender for a limited time. These individuals are generally heterosexual, less frequently bisexual, gay, or lesbian. Traditionally, the majority of these individuals prefer to be known and referred to as *crossdressers* rather than *transvestites,* which is the more clinical term.

Supportive counseling provides the individual an opportunity to move beyond denial and to explore safe options for integrating and supporting crossdressing needs. Addressing social hostility and gender stereotypes helps reduce fears about being found out and thus jeopardizing relationships, employment, or social status. Building communication and relationship skills helps crossdressers introduce their needs to family and friends or attend "safe" private social activities, thus reducing isolation.

Transgenderists

Transgenderists are individuals who live in role part or full time as a member of the opposite gender. Sometimes their transgender identity is carried into the workplace; more often it is not. Emotionally, these persons need to maintain certain aspects relating to both their masculinity and femininity. Understanding this process can be difficult, particularly in situations where an individual's gender identity constantly fluctuates or where he or she is unaware that the transgenderist identity exists. Transgenderists are frequently interested in hormones and occasionally in cosmetic surgery and castration, but not Genital Reassignment Surgery. Because professional literature regarding transgenderists is sparse, the vast majority of these persons are unrecognized by care providers and have difficulty obtaining services or validation. Occasionally transgenderist individuals may self-identify with the label *bi-gender.* (See the Special Advisory, below.)

Androgynes

Androgynes or those with androgynous presentations, contrast with transgenderists by adopting characteristics of both genders or neither. Examples of individuals who self-identify as androgynes include those who present bi-gender mannerisms, those who intentionally wear androgynous or gender-neutral clothing, and those who do not wish to be identified as either male or female. An individual who self-identifies as an androgyne may wish to be identified as both male and female. Some individuals may self-identify as androgynes to fulfill identity needs; others may do so to challenge social stereotypes. (See Special Advisory, below.)

Special Advisory on Transgenderists and Androgynes

Neither transgenderist nor androgyne individuals should be required to conform to transvestite, transsexual, or other stereotypes or support models. In the past, such ill-suited advice was erroneously encouraged by misinformed professionals and consumers. For some, the end result was a misdirected focus on Genital Reassignment Surgery rather than integrating their actual gender-identity needs. Support for these individuals provides an opportunity to define their place within the gender spectrum, reduce isolation, and focus on options correlating with their unique needs.

> Neither transgenderist nor androgyne individuals should be required to conform to transvestite, transsexual, or other stereotypes or support models. The end result could be misdirected focus on Genital Reassignment Surgery rather than integrating their actual gender-identity needs.

Intersex or Hermaphrodite Individuals

Intersex or hermaphrodite individuals are those with medically established physical or hormonal attributes of both the male and female gender. Some, but not all, of these individuals self-identify as transgender. Though these conditions are relatively rare, they are well documented in the literature of general medicine and endocrinology. Gender Specialists may encounter these individuals and are advised to be familiar with their support needs.

Examples of intersex or hermaphrodite conditions include androgen insensitivity syndrome and congenital adrenal hyperplasia. When these conditions are detectable at birth, these individuals are almost always assigned a gender on the basis solely of physical appearance. Occasionally, these conditions do not appear until puberty or shortly thereafter. The practice of assigning gender in utero or at birth has been successful in some cases but questionable in others. Those cases that are successful do not draw much attention; however, unsuccessful cases may result in sex reassignment during puberty or later on in life. Tragically, some individuals are never able to find a sense of gender congruency after having been surgically altered without appropriate presurgical counseling or informed consent. This is particularly true in situations where parents made final surgical decisions without the child's understanding the full consequences of such procedures.

It is common for pubertal and adult medical treatment to include psychological referral for the individual and family. Physicians are advised to refer such cases to care providers familiar with these individuals' special needs and a full understanding of the various medical interventions available. Improper counseling or lack of informed consent regarding juveniles can result in serious long-term consequences. Individuals who are unable to adjust in an assigned gender role are often mistakenly classified by physicians as having a severe psychiatric disorder and thus unnecessarily victimized. Intersex or hermaphrodite individuals in particular should have the opportunity to self-determine gender identity.

We advise that postnatal and pre- and postpubertal intersex or hermaphrodite conditions not be determined by physical appearance alone, but include parental counseling and informed consent, hormonal and genetic evaluation, regular prepubertal medical follow-up, youth-oriented counseling, and informed consent of the young person. Intersex or hermaphrodite youth should not be subjected to testing or research beyond what is required for medical intervention, particularly since children cannot speak for themselves but must rely on a parent's informed consent. Gender Specialists are advised that ongoing support for these individuals may include (but is not limited to) concerns regarding exploitation and medical victimization; gender, sex, and self-identity development; isolation; and other transgender-related concerns. Individuals whose intersex or hermaphrodite condition is caused by congenital adrenal hyperplasia may have other birth defects, as well.

> Intersex or hermaphrodite youth should not be subjected to testing or research beyond what is required for medical intervention, particularly since children cannot speak for themselves but must rely on a parent's informed consent.

Drag Queens, Kings, and Performance Artists

Drag queens, kings, and performance artists are individuals who crossdress for entertainment, for sex-industry purposes, to challenge social stereotypes, or for personal satisfaction. These persons are stereotypically associated with gay and lesbian society. However, it should be noted that a small proportion of gays as well as lesbians identify as gay male or lesbian crossdressers and, as such, have needs paralleling the heterosexual crossdresser. These issues would include social support and problems with victimization, relationships, and identity integration.

Transgender Youth

Typically, transgender youth are persons under age twenty-one who self-identify as transgender or who have questions about their own gender identity. These young persons frequently need specialized professional and community resources, services, and protection. The Guidelines emphasize the fact that, as a result of family and social abandonment, many of these young people encounter victimization through homelessness, drug use, and prostitution. Transgender youth are a hidden and underserved population. More information about youth issues and the Guidelines for their care can be found in Chapter 8.

Medically Compromised Individuals

The Guidelines advise that medically compromised persons, including HIV-positive individuals, not be discriminated against or discouraged from seeking or denied equal access to medical and psychological support services on the basis of their medical status. Prior to the adoption in 1990 of the Americans with Disabilities Act, federal, state, and private institutions and practitioners routinely denied basic gender-oriented support services to these individuals. Assessment of each person's quality of life, his or her medical and psychological history, and his or her self-identity as a transgender individual should all be factored into service-provider decisions. A special focus on transgender HIV and AIDS issues can be found in Chapter 6.

Diabetes, prostate disease, high blood pressure, epilepsy, aging, alcoholism, and substance abuse are additional issues that may affect transgender individuals' lives as well as their access to support services. Future editions of *Transgender Care* will provide further information on these concerns, as it becomes available through professional and consumer channels.

Professionally and Scientifically Victimized Individuals

Transgender Care promotes awareness that transgender individuals have been victimized in the past and remain at risk of victimization by government and private academic and scientific institutions, gender programs, psychoanalysts and other therapists, behavioral scientists, and other professional persons and organizations. Without informed consent or advisement that realistic and psychologically healthy options do exist to fulfill transgender needs, transgender individuals have been inhumanely subjected to research methods using intimidation, electroconvulsive therapy (ECT or "electric shock"), sensory deprivation, psychoactive medications, and other noxious treatments. In the past, these studies, conducted under a faulty psychopathologic framework, were often used in an attempt to "cure" transgender-oriented behaviors. Gender Specialists now recognize that a transgender identity is a primary element of the transgender individual's self-identity and psychological make-up.

Academic or scientific research should be viewed as being without merit by professional and transgender communities if the individuals studied were solicited without full informed consent, under nonadvisement of other treatment-oriented alternatives, or under the use of coercion, sensory deprivation, psychoactive or other pharmacological medications, or behavioral-aversion techniques. It is recommended that professionals proposing to do research on transgender individuals do so within the framework of a review process that includes professional peers and transgender consumers.

It is recommended that all consumers inquire into the background of and request references for any organization or professional claiming to have developed successful "cures" or "treatments" for transgender behaviors or identity. Parents of youth should be particularly wary of detrimental approaches by professionals and verify that they are placing their child under the care of a recognized transgender program or Gender Specialist.

Transgender Care is intended to promote awareness that even at present there remain transgender individuals who have been victimized by these processes. Professionals and transgender communities need to address these issues and create a forum where victimized individuals' needs and grievances can be addressed.

Institutionalized and Incarcerated Individuals

One subpopulation of transgender individuals consists of those who are incarcerated in correctional facilities or are receiving long-term inpatient care at a hospital or mental-health facility. The Guidelines recognize the special needs of institutionalized individuals facing gender-related issues and advises that no facility should discriminate against them or deny them access to any service or care that is available to others.

Transgender Care also advises that government or private institutions and correctional facility administrations protect transgender individuals from others in the institutional population to prevent victimization (rape, beatings, and so forth) as a result of their gender-identity issues. Failure to protect these individuals may result in suicide or homicide. Victimization of transgender persons is also known to be carried out by institutional staff or encouraged by staff in nontransgender populations. Institutions are advised to provide inservice training of staff to prevent these situations.

The Guidelines advise that government or private institutions and correctional facilities provide hormone treatment to transgender individuals, as outlined in Chapter 3. Failure to provide hormones has been linked to an increased risk of self-mutilation (auto-castration), heightened clinical depression, behavioral difficulties, illegal drug use, and suicide attempts. These circumstances may place institutions and correctional facilities at liability, depending on state, provincial or federal laws. Hormone administration, in addition to support groups or psychotherapy or both, where needed, can dramatically reduce the potential risks that accompany gender-conflicted conditions or that occur in response to preestablished transgender identities, as might be the case for individuals who previously received hormones outside the institutional or correctional facility. The symptoms and behaviors accompanying both gender dysphoria and hormone withdrawal in previously established transgender individuals are frequently misperceived as manipulative gestures on their part, In fact, malingering and misrepresentation by transgender individuals are rare.

Socioeconomically Disadvantaged Individuals

Transgender Care is intended to promote recognition among care providers that social and economic marginalization frequently accompanies the transgender experience. Family, social, and community rejection, in addition to reduced educational and employment opportunities, create an environment in which transgender individuals are commonly subjected to discrimination, homelessness, un-employment, and poverty. Medical, mental health, and social services commonly fail to recognize or address the needs of transgender individuals.

Transgender Care notes that owing to socioeconomic hardship, many trans-gender individuals, particularly those within minority subpopulations, are tar-geted as desperate victims by unscrupulous care providers who offer hormones, silicone injections, aesthetic and gender-reassignment surgeries or other services without informed consent, appropriate medical administration, or follow-up. At times, individuals are coerced into trading sex for services. These practices are detrimental to both ethically practicing professionals and transgender individuals alike, and sometimes such practices lead to the death of the latter. Professionals and consumers should be wary of any individual posing as a Gender Specialist yet having no references or affiliation with appropriate gender-specializing orga-nizations.

Transgender Care notes that transgender individuals, particularly those going through transition processes, experience severe emotional, physical, and financial burdens. Legitimate Gender Specialists, care providers, and support organiza-tions know that it is unethical to charge transgender individuals for research services, to charge them for treatment that cannot benefit the individual, or to charge fees in excess of those normally charged to nontransgender persons for similar services.

Scientific, medical, and mental health professionals are strongly discouraged from portraying transgender individuals or transgender-associated experiences, feelings, or thoughts as pathologically diseased, mentally ill, deviant, or in any other manner that exacerbates marginalization of the transgender individual within social, medical, and mental health infrastructures. Information on up-to-date charting and insurance-claim processing using nonpathologic models may be may be found in the Psychiatric Diagnosis section of Chapter 2. Professionals and gender-specializing organizations are encouraged to adopt uniform language that is not deprecating to transgender men and women.

Mental Health

Chapter 2

Hundreds of thousands of people experience uncertainty or emotional distress regarding their gender identification. What should be a natural human process of self-examination and exploration is often treated with negative reactions by parents, family, friends and acquaintances, coworkers, and employers, as well as the public at large. These reactions are due to misinformation, social prejudice, or cultural taboos.

Individuals experiencing concerns about their gender identity may suffer social isolation, emotional anguish, distorted self-image, and even misdiagnosis by health professionals. A boy's feminine appearance or preference for behavior usually associated with girls—such as playing with dolls beyond the age of three years or so—will often create such anxiety for the parents that the child may be presented to school officials, religious leaders, the family physician, or very commonly to mental health professionals. Adults may be referred or self-present to similar authorities, who frequently lack knowledge or hold biases regarding any form of gender identification that appears to challenge social stereotypes.

As a consequence, harmful external forces may impact the gender-exploring individual through moral condemnation, refusal to communicate, physical or emotional violence, professional misdiagnosis, or inappropriate clinical care. Until recently, the focus for providing support to transgender individuals has followed several rigid pathways. Earliest forms of treatment revolved around research, compiling of statistics, theorizing about origins, and endlessly searching for nonexistent cures, while commonly failing to address actual transgender support needs. In time, it became evident that gender identity, much like sexual orientation, is not fixed to socially created stereotypes but is instead a dynamic process inclusive of a wide range of human needs, experiences, and behaviors.

This chapter contains important information that will assist transgender individuals and care providers in supporting every individual's right to self-determination regarding his or her own gender identity. Included is information that demystifies various support models, identifies models that are outdated, and provides information about current medical and psychotherapeutic charting and insurance claim measures that reflect the individual's rights.

Mental Health Services

Mental health services are based in the fields of psychiatry, psychology, clinical social work, and support counseling, fields that endeavor to improve the happiness and level of functioning of individuals seeking such treatment. Psychiatrists are doctors of medicine with specialty training in prescribing psychoactive medication as well as providing psychotherapy. Psychologists are not physicians, but specialists trained in psychotherapy and psychological testing. Clinical social workers are mental health professionals who have training in psychotherapy and case management. In addition, there are experienced support counselors who provide support counseling and community resource information. Persons who receive assistance from any mental health providers are variously called *patients, clients, consumers,* or *individuals* receiving health care. Forms of mental health treatment include psychiatric medication, residential rehabilitation, and psychotherapy or counseling designed to impact favorably upon a client's thoughts, feelings, or behavior.

Individual and Group Support Counseling

Transgender persons often find themselves isolated from family, friends, and co-workers because they have been marginalized by society. In addition, they often lack reliable role models. Valuable information and emotional support can be found in either individual or group support counseling with a gender-specializing support counselor. These forums allow the client maximum control in discussing his or her needs and may include the exploration of social, family, sexual-orientation, health, and relevant gender-oriented issues, all at costs far below that for traditional private psychotherapy. The approach is typically individualized to address present-day needs, with insightful advice and information given in a confidential setting. As with any support relationship, the individual may need to shop around to find a qualified support counselor who fits one's personality and needs. Such a counselor should possess the experience and information needed to address gender-identity issues and to provide education regarding medical treatment options.

Self-Help and Social Support Groups

Self-help support groups have evolved to fulfill important consumer mental health needs, especially since individual and group psychotherapy have become less available as a consequence of increased professional rates and diminished insurance coverage for these services. Support and social groups for transgender individuals can vary in setting, structure, and goals. Some are designed as drop-in places where individuals exploring gender concerns primarily receive coming-out support and referrals, while making important social connections. Other groups place an emphasis on providing a confidential atmosphere for cross-dressers, sometimes with similar interests or social status. Other groups focus on various political agendas. The majority of support groups combine these functions and welcome virtually any individual. There are also support groups for partners, spouses, and "significant others" of transgender individuals. Information about these groups can be obtained through local and national transgender support organizations.

One of the issues most frequently raised about self-help and social support groups concerns facilitation. Is the facilitator familiar with gender-identity issues, or is he or she a newly self-proclaimed expert, having just "come out of the closet"? Does the facilitator encountering individuals in the coming-out process have the capability to recognize an actual mental health disorder and its associated symptoms, and to subsequently make an appropriate referral? Individuals are advised to visit several support groups until they find one that best suits their needs and personality. If information and advice received in a support group does not feel right or make sense, one should ask questions or seek out the support of a recognized Gender Specialist. Additional support group pointers are included in Chapters 9 and 10.

In addition to seeking out contact with members in the organized transgender community, consumers are advised that a wealth of information about transgender issues exists in printed form. Much of this literature is written by transgender authors who often are both professionals and consumers. A useful resource listing found in the Appendix features organizations that distribute academic and consumer literature.

Individual and Group Psychotherapy

Psychotherapy is a clinical service conducted by licensed mental health professionals only after years of academic training and supervised clinical work with clients. Therapists may offer either individual (one-to-one) or group psychotherapy, or both. Individuals may wish to consider the cost, comfort level, and accessibility of each modality in making a treatment choice. In the course of psychotherapy, clients experience changes in behavior, attitudes, mood, relationships with others, insight, energy level, expectations of oneself, and many other aspects of functioning. Goals for the individual are jointly developed by the therapist and the client, and are modified as treatment progresses. Therapeutic change may take considerable time, though brief psychotherapy may change some responses to stress within as few as ten to twelve sessions.

Some common forms of individual and group psychotherapy include insight-oriented or psychodynamic therapy, cognitive-behavioral therapy, and self psychology; there are, however, many other psychological approaches. Because the field of psychotherapy is so varied, clients are encouraged to ask potential therapists what type of therapy they practice and how its theoretical dynamics are applied in supporting a transgender client's needs. Clients wishing to explore gender-identity issues with a new therapist or their current therapist are encouraged to inquire about the therapist's experience as a Gender Specialist. Many individuals discover well into the therapeutic process that the cause for their distress is related to gender-identity issues, yet they have developed an ongoing relationship with a therapist unfamiliar with these issues. In such cases, having two different therapists may be an option. As an alternative, the primary therapist can arrange for consultation regarding gender-identity issues with a Senior Gender Specialist.

Psychiatric Diagnosis

Until recently, the field of mental health remained rooted in treating transsexualism or any uncertainty about gender identity as a sexual perversion, immature developmental stage, psychotic state, or delusional distortion of self-image. This historical diagnostic labeling of all forms of transgender identification is gradually giving way to a depathologized view of transgender individuals. The latest (fourth) edition of the American Psychiatric Association's (APA) *Diagnostic and Statistical Manual of Mental Disorders* (*DSM*-IV), published in 1994, has moved closer to defining only the emotionally distressed subgroup of transgender individuals as exhibiting a bona fide mental disorder, "Gender Identity Disorder," while partially validating the fact that many transgender persons do not evidence gender-associated confusion or emotional distress.

■ ─────────────
Many transgender persons do not evidence gender-associated confusion or emotional distress.

As with the APA's now defunct "Ego Dystonic Homosexuality" classification, it is generally believed by most Gender Specialists and consumers that future editions of psychiatric diagnostic manuals will not attribute any psychopathologic diagnosis to transgender status per se, particularly as Gender Specialists and transgender consumers provide the APA and other professional organizations with more information on gender-identity issues. However, transgender individuals, like others in the general population, may continue to benefit from the professional treatment of mental disorders unrelated to transgenderism, and to derive psychological support from mental health care providers, if only for recovery from the traumas that external family and societal forces have inflicted upon them.

As professional organizations move toward the depathologization of gender-identity issues, it is important that professionals and consumers be aware that these changes (as well as the acceptance of them) are not likely to be uniform. Numerous medical and psychotherapy texts, diagnostic tools, and medical or psychotherapy research and treatment protocols are still likely to refer to transsexualism and associated gender issues as pathologic conditions or sexual perversions. Furthermore, the clinical files of transgender individuals previously in psychiatric treatment are likely to have pathologic references. We advise that these pathologizing references be removed from texts, diagnostic tools, research and treatment protocols, and client medical charts or clinical files. Inclusion of such material further stigmatizes transgender individuals.

Inclusion of deprecating material or references to transgender persons or needs is also unnecessary in filing insurance claims. Psychiatric and psychotherapy insurance claims may utilize any *DSM*-IV diagnostic category that reflects the true nature of the problem being addressed by the support process. These categories might be, for example, adjustment disorder with either anxious, depressed, or mixed features; generalized anxiety disorder; major depression; personality disorder; and so forth. More information about applying diagnostic criteria to the actual symptoms a transgender client presents can be found below in the "Key Mental Health Issues" section. Medical documentation for insurance claims processing with regard to Genital Reassignment Surgery or other surgical procedures should state that the procedure is indicated based upon medical necessity. Insurance claims should also include additional documentation citing cases where insurance companies have paid for these procedures.

At the heart of the issue of supporting transgender individuals is the premise that psychiatrists, psychotherapists, and mental health counselors diagnose and treat only that which is disordered and diseased. There is no reason why psychiatrists and other mental health professionals cannot be charged with the responsibility of recognizing gender-identity issues without the necessity of labeling them as disorders. Treatment and professional support by a psychiatrist or other mental health care provider should not stigmatize those seeking support, thus further contributing to clients' difficulties.

■ ───────

> There is no reason why psychiatrists and other mental health professionals cannot be charged with the responsibility of recognizing gender-identity issues without the necessity of labeling them as disorders.

Differential Diagnosis

Mental illness is common in all cultures; the incidence of such illnesses ranges from the high rates of mood disorders (e.g., a greater than 40-percent lifetime incidence of depression in the United States) to the much lower rates of schizophrenia (0.1 percent to 0.2 percent in United States). The *DSM*-IV serves as a statistically based classification system that is used internationally as a clinical guide for distinguishing the symptoms, duration, severity, causation, prevalence, and treatability of various mental disorders. Transgender persons have long been subjected to diagnostic labeling, either by well-meaning attempts to establish successful treatments, or intentionally biased efforts to marginalize or exploit transgender people.

Mental health providers who have acquired sufficient knowledge and understanding of gender issues have come to recognize that *transsexualism* is properly used only as a descriptive term for one subpopulation of the transgender community, which otherwise shares the same risk for mental disorders as the general population. Therefore, psychiatric diagnosis and treatment of transgender persons should not differ from that provided to nontransgender individuals suffering depression, phobias, personality disorders, and the like. Care providers unfamiliar with gender-identity issues who are involved in the assessment of transgender individuals for the exclusion of mental health disorders are advised to seek consultation with an experienced Gender Specialist.

■ ———————

> Care providers unfamiliar with gender-identity issues who are involved in the assessment of transgender individuals for the exclusion of mental health disorders are advised to seek consultation with an experienced Gender Specialist.

Care providers are advised that although some studies have established a higher-than-normal incidence of severe personality disorders, psychosis, and mental illness among transgender individuals, such studies are unreliable without controlled comparisons with transgender persons who do not require any form of mental health care. Moreover, such studies underestimate the impact of stressors associated with transphobic discrimination. These include sexual assault, harassment, and violence; abandonment by family, friends, and other support persons; loss of employment and unequal access to career opportunities; self-medication through substance abuse; legal harassment and other forms of gender-based discrimination.

Although we discourage the diagnosis of gender identity disorder as it is defined by the *DSM*-IV, we agree with the *DSM*-IV listing of the mental and biological disorders that should not be confused with the evaluation of gender-identity concerns. The following *DSM*-IV diagnoses are selected because some of their typical symptomatology may involve gender issues and they are likely to figure in psychiatric misdiagnoses of transgender individuals.

Transvestic Fetishism. Described as a separate disorder from gender-identity disorder in *DSM*-IV, transvestic fetishism is an inappropriately termed "diagnosis" that seeks to differentiate between those persons with a desire for crossdressing alone and those children or adults who identify with the gender opposite to their physical or biological appearance. Such a diagnosis inappropriately pathologizes gender- and sex-based behavior that transvestic persons typically enjoy without harm to themselves or others—very often while sustaining intimate personal relationships. In asserting that "this disorder has been described only in heterosexual males," *DSM*-IV fails to recognize that crossdressing is well known to occur among heterosexual and lesbian women, as well as among gay-male female impersonators or drag queens (see section on transgender populations in Chapter 1).

The motivations for crossdressing vary among individuals, and the continuing emphasis by the psychiatric community on the single purpose of erotic gratification may be an attempt to stigmatize persons whose nonconformist presentation and behavior is poorly understood by psychoanalytically oriented mental health professionals. The only justifiable use of the designation of transvestism, without the presumptive sexual association with fetishism, is descriptive. The transsexual's desire to change his or her physical gender is usually absent for transvestites. Both groups are predominantly heterosexual, but they include people of all sexual orientations, races, and other demographic variables. Transvestites tend to crossdress part time as an auxiliary persona, as opposed to the transsexual's full-time and singular personal identity.

Gender-Identity Disorder Not Otherwise Specified. Examples given in the *DSM*-IV are biological intersex conditions such as androgen-insensitivity syndrome and congenital adrenal hyperplasia, as well as anxiety manifested as stress-related crossdressing and preoccupation with castration without a desire to acquire the sex characteristics of the opposite gender. Notably, some individuals with biological intersex conditions do self-identify as transgender. Others prefer to associate their condition as a medical disorder.

Schizophrenia. Schizophrenia is a rare but chronic and severe mental illness with a biological predetermination. Schizophrenia is present in all cultures worldwide and affects one out of a thousand Americans. It is typified by unreal beliefs that defy any conceivable truth. A psychotic belief may include being a famous religious or political leader, fear of pursuit by unseen magical forces, or, rarely, an irrational conviction that one has become a person of the opposite physical gender. This crossgender identification is readily distinguished from a transgender identity by the presence of a key feature: the schizophrenic individual suddenly becomes a whole new, fantasized person; in contrast, a transsexual's awareness of possessing a discordant psychological identity from his or her physical sex emerges gradually, and his or her pursuit of changes in physical appearance so as to approximate the opposite physical gender as much as possible is rational. For example, a schizophrenic man may announce that he has become a woman overnight, having undergone physical transformation into the female gender without surgical or hormonal aid, and that he now possesses such impossible female attributes as pregnancy or menstruation.

Body Dysmorphic Disorder. Body dysmorphic disorder is a delusional condition in which the patient believes that her or his physical body is inexplicably altered, perhaps with features of the opposite gender, with no objective physical change or psychological gender identification to justify such a belief. For example, a woman may become anxiously preoccupied with a belief that her jaw is becoming masculinized—squarer and more elongated—such as to cause her to resemble a man. She does not desire to become male but remains convinced that a supernatural force is causing her physical transformation.

Malingering. Malingering is a condition of professed mental distress in order to achieve a specific, desirable benefit that usually is not immediately disclosed to the evaluating mental health provider. An example: someone may claim to be transgender for the purpose of gaining access to employment or housing opportunities restricted to the opposite gender, or may present with gender confusion in an effort to qualify for psychiatric disability benefits. It should be noted that cases of malingering that involve falsely presenting oneself as a transgender person are extremely rare. This is possibly due to the heavily negative social consequences and scrutiny that the adoption of a transgender identity would likely carry.

Differentiation between an individual who is genuinely transgender identified and one who is merely attempting to pass him or herself off as such is readily accomplished by taking into consideration the amount of consistency existing in an individual's own account of her or his gender-related needs, self-identification, history, and presentation. An individual's presentation cannot be the sole factor taken into account in the care provider's decision-making process because, although some individuals may be acutely aware that they have a transgender identity, the possibility exists that the individual may not as yet exhibit a fully defined physical gender presentation congruent with self-image because of physical or circumstantial reasons. Typically, malingering individuals are noted for being extremely insistent that their needs be met immediately, even when a care provider has not yet acquired sufficient decision-making information. By contrast, transgender individuals are more likely to accept that their needs are partially met while the care provider seeks additional information.

Borderline Personality Disorder. Borderline personality disorder is an often severe condition of poor adaptation to life in general. This condition is primarily associated with a regular pattern of extreme indecisiveness, emotional outbursts, self-injurious acts, unstable and intense personal relationships, and frantic efforts to avoid real or imagined abandonment. Additionally, the individual may have complications of major depression, substance abuse, and brief psychosis. Occasionally a borderline personality disorder may feature temporary, impulsive cross-dressing, persistent demands to be addressed as a member of the opposite gender without a congruent presentation (or no efforts at presenting as such), or an expressed hatred of the individual's own gender.

Each of these behaviors needs to be carefully examined so as to rule out the possibility that a transgender identity may indeed be present. It should be noted that transgender individuals, particularly those with the most acute symptoms of gender dysphoria, may attempt self-injurious acts (primarily, auto-castration) if they are unaware that support is available for their gender concerns. Generally, self-injurious acts such as attempts at auto-castration will disappear entirely once an individual is aware that support exists for gender-identity concerns. Individuals with extreme gender dysphoria may express hatred toward their biological sex attributes, including their genitalia, although this feature typically will subside with the discovery that support options are available and as the individual begins adjusting to a new gender role.

Borderline personality disorder should also be ruled out where transvestites with an actual transgender identity may crossdress impulsively when unable to satisfy their crossdressing needs owing to fear of discovery or social reprisal. Isolated incidents of strong emotional outbursts should not be confused with a borderline personality disorder, since transgender individuals may react with appropriate anger to recurrent social pressures or authoritarian decision-making processes that deny them an opportunity to fully explore or receive support for gender-identity needs. This would also include individuals who are repeatedly denied hormone administration or who are suffering the physical effects of hormone withdrawal.

Dissociative Identity Disorder. Commonly referred to as a "split personality," dissociative identity disorder was formerly called multiple personality disorder in previous *DSM* editions. Individuals diagnosed with this condition present with distinct personalities as parts of a divided self-identity. There are two or more alter personalities, often of different genders, ages, manners of speech and dress, with distinctly different behaviors such that one personality will not easily be mistaken for another. This condition is often caused by exposure to severe physical, sexual, or emotional trauma in childhood. By withdrawing into a childlike state of mind, or creating a new adult personality, the individual attempts to cope with a challenging threat. Self-harmful behaviors, angry outbursts, crying spells, and other symptomatic states may be a characteristic of different personalities, or "alters." Switches between personalities can occur rapidly, and are commonly frustrated by amnesia with regard to the existence of other personality presentations. Psychotherapy and medication for symptomatic relief are recommended treatments.

It is essential to distinguish alter personalities of opposite genders as they present in someone with multiple personalities from a singular and mature transgender identity shift. In the latter situation, the cross-gender identity is not marked by any significant personality change nor amnesia. The transition from one gender to another occurs across psychological and physical planes and is experienced as self-fulfilling and stress-relieving for the transgender individual, in contrast to the increased confusion and insecurity felt by the person with a dissociative condition.

Obsessive-Compulsive Disorder. Obsessive-compulsive disorder, or OCD, is a serious mental health problem affecting four million Americans. Adults and children with this condition are distressed by repetitive obsessive thoughts or fears that are often accompanied by ritualized behaviors in a futile attempt to ward off an intolerable anxiety state. The treatments of choice for OCD are behavioral therapy to recondition programmed thoughts and rituals, as well as antidepressant medications such as clomipramine, fluoxetine, fluvoxamine, or paroxetine. For persons with OCD, facilitation of the compulsive habits does nothing to diminish the individual's internal distress, whereas transgender persons are most often relieved by support and acceptance of crossgender dress, demeanor, further defining a sense of transgender self-identification.

Although commonly referred to as "compulsive" or "addictive," repetitive crossdressing either for validation of a transgender identity or for emotional gratification (as with transvestism) is not an unavoidable nor elaborate ritual requiring clinical intervention. An OCD condition should be ruled out when a transvestite's seemingly compulsive and addictive behavior is in actuality an anxious response to the individual's being unable to satisfy her or his crossdressing needs for fear of discovery, social reprisal, or an inability to sufficiently incorporate her or his transgender identity within present-day circumstances. It should be noted that crossdressing needs are of a preexisting nature, and when an individual's ability to express those needs is inhibited, he or she may build up to a point where the individual feels compelled to crossdress. Additionally, transvestites may experience some emotional release or escape after having encountered a stressful event or change of circumstance. These types of situations cannot in and of themselves be classified as a ritualized, compulsive behavior solely designed to avoid an anxious state.

Caution: Consumers are advised that having one or more feelings, ideas, behaviors, or experiences as described in this section, the DSM-*IV or other professional publications does not necessarily constitute having a mental disorder. Self-diagnosis is typically inaccurate and extremely dangerous. Individuals who are having sociocultural difficulties or psychological symptoms that they believe might be due to a mental disorder are strongly advised to seek consultation with a qualified mental health professional.*

Diagnostic labels are designed to assist mental health professionals to distinguish between the characteristics of different mental disorders, so as to be able to provide appropriate support and treatment to individuals who need it. Both transgender and nontransgender individuals dealing with a mental disorder are reminded that being diagnosed or "labeled" is a confidential matter between the client and a professional mental health care provider, and that such diagnostic labeling does not negate a person's human rights, legal protections, or the opportunity to self-determine sexual orientation, gender identity, or overall quality of life.

Psychoactive Medications

The careful evaluation of transgender persons who voluntarily seek support or mental health treatment usually results in treatment plans that do not involve medication. Medication is best reserved for serious mental illnesses such as schizophrenia, major depression, and panic disorder. When a diagnosis of a mental disorder is confirmed by a mental health professional, the severity and nature of psychological symptoms may indicate consultation with a psychiatrist and use of a psychoactive medication in a comprehensive mental health treatment program. An individual should seek to become informed about the choices among recommended treatment options in order to select the most suitable course of treatment.

Antipsychotic or Neuroleptic Medications. Used primarily for psychotic mental disorders such as schizophrenia, antipsychotic medications are powerful, highly toxic agents that are sometimes used in small doses for sedation of nonpsychotic emotional distress. Sometimes called major tranquilizers, traditional antipsychotic medications work to block the transmission of disturbing thoughts or to quell agitation. Because their side effects are common and potentially permanent, these agents should be used only under the close management of a psychiatrist and with full disclosure of treatment objectives, side-effect risks, and alternative treatments. Some examples of traditional antipsychotics are haloperidol, chlorpromazine, thioridazine, and thiothixene; however, some newer antipsychotics such as clozapine, olanzapine, and risperidone sometimes have reduced side effects or improved efficacy.

Antidepressants. A wide variety of medications work with brain chemistry to improve mood from states of sadness or anxiety. Sleeplessness can also be relieved, and the type of antidepressant prescribed by a physician or psychiatrist may be selected according to the desired amount of sedation at night versus the degree of stimulation. Most experiences of emotional distress concerning gender issues would not be prolonged or severe enough to require medication. However, the development of suicidal thoughts or prolonged deficiencies in self-care would suggest that a discussion of antidepressant medication with a psychiatrist is indicated. Although newer forms of antidepressants (such as fluoxetine, paroxetine, sertraline, fluvoxamine, venlafaxine, and nefazodone) have some unique qualities, traditional antidepressants such as doxepin, nortriptyline, and desipramine may be of equal benefit. With gradual improvement of depressive symptoms, use of antidepressants should be considered short-term, and they should rarely be prescribed for more than a year of successful symptom relief.

Antimanic or Counterimpulsive Agents. Used for the treatment of manic depression, also known as bipolar affective disorder, antimanic agents are medications that can be effective in relieving uncontrollable mood swings, anxiety spells, or outbursts of anger. These include lithium, carbamazepine, and valproic acid.

Sedatives and Antianxiety Agents. Benzodiazepine and Valium (diazepam) family of drugs are the sedatives most widely prescribed for anxiety. However, their use must be limited because of their addictiveness. Alternatives include milder sedatives such as chloral hydrate, hydroxyzine, buspirone, and diphenhydramine (Benadryl).

Crisis Intervention

At one time or another, nearly everyone, including those without mental illness, experiences a sense of hopelessness and an inability to change seemingly intolerable things in life. Although difficult, it is essential to allow oneself to acknowledge painful emotions and seek the support of health professionals or peer support groups, particularly when other efforts to deter suicidal thoughts have proven inadequate or when suicidal courses of action seem close at hand.

Suicidal ideas usually develop when an individual feels there is no support for his or her needs or after perceiving that only negative outcomes are possible from any known options. Such "tunnel vision" may further limit the person's ability to identify possible alternative forms of support. Many suicide attempts do not result in death, but they may cause serious physical or emotional injury. It is vital that therapists take any attempt seriously, discuss safeguards against repeated attempts with the individual, and redouble efforts toward resolution of the causative stressors. Self-injury may be an expression of suicidal tendency, or a desperate and often repetitive attempt to channel emotional distress into physical pain or a visible representation of distress.

Research in suicide prevention at the Los Angeles Suicide Prevention Center has identified seven basic factors that can be assessed to judge a person's "at-risk" potential for completing suicide. These are ranked in the order of importance and described in Table 2.1.

To the care provider who encounters a transgender person in crisis, particularly those providers unfamiliar with transgender identities and concurrent issues, the range of experiences and crisis situations may at first seem overwhelming, sensational, or even surreal. Once the care provider becomes familiar with gender-identity issues, he or she will recognize that these crises are likely to be initiated by an individual's lacking in the coping mechanisms needed to support gender and self-identity integration, not by an underlying psychopathology.

Professionals actively engaged in crisis and suicide intervention may encounter a highly confused individual who has temporarily impaired communication,

Table **2.1**
Risk Factors in Potentially Suicidal Individuals, in Rank Order

1. Current Plan	The degree of planning and the specificity of details in the person's plan for suicidal death; this includes time, place, and means
2. Stress	The stressors, as perceived by the person at risk, which they feel are precipitating the current suicidal situation
3. Prior Suicidal Behavior	The person-at-risk's history of previous suicidal gestures and attempts, including modeling by close family members
4. Symptoms	Distressing personal responses to stressors include: emotional (mood fluctuations, crying spells); intellectual (slowed, diffuse, or constricted thinking); behavioral (fatigue, withdrawal, agitation); biological (eating, sleep, sex habits); ongoing maladaptive coping mechanisms such as substance abuse
5. Resources	Physical and emotional systems which the person feels are helping, caring, or supportive, including: other persons (family, friends, care givers); groups and organizations to which the person belongs; economic assets
6. Age	Youth are more likely to attempt and complete suicide attempts, as typically they have fewer resources and are more reactionary than older adults, who may be more mature, stable
7. Gender	Males: more likely to attempt and complete suicide attempts, generally choose more violent forms of suicidal (guns, hanging), find themselves in more difficult social situations without anyone to confide in Women: more likely to use more passive suicidal attempts (overdose, self-mutilation) and contact others before doing so (calling hotlines)

Source: Adapted from handouts of suicide and crisis intervention workshops of the Department of Public Health, State of California.

relationship, and functioning skills. In many cases, negative stereotypes reinforce transgender individuals' fears, and so their conditions commonly reach crisis proportions before they seek help. Prior to this point, most transgender individuals will have searched endlessly for a "cure." Some attempt to compensate for their transgender needs through chemical or relationship dependencies. Others periodically attempt to purge themselves of crossgendered behaviors and materials, possibly through adopting a hypermasculine or hyperfeminine image or career, all in an attempt to escape their gender issues.

Parallel issues commonly accompany and mask gender-identity concerns. These include victimization, depression, isolation, and low self-esteem; self-mutilation or suicidal acts; concerns over sexual identity or HIV infection, or both; disturbances in marital and personal relationships; and difficulty with employment.

At the apex of the crisis are those situations in which individuals have expressed or appear to have intentions of harming themselves or others, or in which they are acting out in some manner that is contrary to their own or others' safety. In situations where the care provider is unable to "contract" a credible verbal or written agreement "to do no harm and to immediately contact crisis support services when those feelings arise again," the care provider has no recourse other than to follow through with standard crisis-intervention procedures, including authorized involuntary detention or victim notification.

> *Transgender Care* advises that because public-safety officials and mental health workers are likely to encounter transgender individuals, these professionals need to be apprised of specialized transgender issues and crisis needs. No matter how confused a transgender individual may appear to be, it is quite possible that she or he may be unaware of her or his own gender-identity issues and believe there is no place to turn for help regarding overwhelming feelings.

Perhaps the most severe transgender crisis is that of an attempted, or completed, auto-castration or genital mutilation. This occurrence is most common among transsexuals and transgenderists, although it has been acted out by cross-dressers as well. The stronger the transgender identity, the higher the possibility that this may be attempted by those who do not perceive the availability of support services or the existence of credible solutions to their circumstances. One random survey found that approximately 1 in 18 transgender individuals has entertained thoughts of carrying out self-mutilation or castration. Asking whether a transgender individual has had these thoughts is a key element in any crisis evaluation.

Individuals actively contemplating, as well as those who have attempted or actually completed, auto-castration or other self-mutilating acts are making a tortured cry for help. In circumstances where such thoughts are expressed, the care provider should seek out a credible verbal or written "no self-harm contract" with the individual, whereby she or he agrees not to carry through such intentions and to seek support if these thoughts should arise again. These individuals also need to be screened for suicidal ideation. They should be made to understand that, despite their hopelessness and self-destructive ideation, realistic options and support for their dilemma do exist. Much like the suicidal individual, many of those involved with self-injurious behavior or ideation are isolated and in a great deal of emotional pain. Moreover, they may actively question their own decision-making processes in areas extending beyond gender-identity issues.

An individual who has entertained auto-castration or thoughts of self-mutilation often feels a great deal of contrition and shame. Those who have followed through with such plans often fear ridicule as well as incarceration or institutionalization for having committed a self-destructive act. However, except under the condition of an obvious or expressed intention of escalating self-destructive behavior, incarceration or institutionalization is generally inappropriate and rarely occurs where information about gender-identity issues or a Gender Specialist is readily available to assist crisis care providers. Care providers need to be apprised that the ridicule individuals fear is highly possible. Those specialists called in to consult in emergencies should remain aware that nonempathetic and uninformed professionals quite commonly find these occurrences foreign, titillating, and sensational. For example, recently a chief of psychiatry of a major psychiatric center capitalized on such an incident in order to make his professional autobiography more sensational.

In circumstances where an individual has acted out auto-castration or other self-mutilation, a professional care team that includes medical and gender-specializing psychological support should be assembled as soon as possible. Treating physicians are advised to follow proper medical protocol in assessing and treating wounds or injuries and to consult with a Gender Specialist for postcare mental health support.

When an individual is provided short-term hospitalization as the result of a crisis, in most circumstances hormone administration is appropriate if she or he is already receiving it. Physicians are advised that preexisting depressive conditions may be aggravated by a lack of hormones in the postcastration individual or by excessive hormone dosages in precastration individuals. (See the Guidelines at the end of this chapter.)

The reader should bear in mind that suicidal individuals and others prone to self-injury are actually a small percentage of the total transgender population. Moreover, in most circumstances these individuals are not aware that they have gender-identity issues or that transgender resources exist.

San Francisco's Tenderloin district has a high population of transgender persons; a high proportion of these people are impoverished, ethnically diverse, and transitory. They survive as well as they can through a combination of low wages, Social Security, public assistance, or prostitution. It has been our experience that this microcosm exemplifies the hardships that are common to the transgender community at large. Care providers should be apprised that low-income transgender women and men are generally subject to a higher-than-average risk of physical or sexual abuse (including rape), HIV infection, malnutrition, homelessness, and substance abuse.

Transgender individuals who are homeless find themselves on the lowest rung of the social ladder, even among other homeless populations, and are at a much higher risk for victimization than their housed counterparts. This may be due in part to individuals' having an incongruous presentation as a result of their lack of access to gender-specific articles of clothing and self-care (e.g., make-up) or electrolysis. An incongruent presentation is also likely to result in housing placement difficulties and reduced access to other resources.

Some individuals are fortunate in building resources and are able to move beyond these hardships; however, the remainder frequently become trapped in cycles of despair. This social phenomenon is in no way limited to San Francisco's. They exist nationally, and the hardship evident in San Francisco is only intensified by the city's magnetism to transgender people as a mecca for liberalism and social acceptance. In contrast to other areas, San Francisco is both fortunate and unique in having a good network of medical, mental health, and social support services for transgender people. These services, however, are in no way guaranteed; funding is constantly being threatened by private and public budget cuts and political whims.

The city's oldest established resource is the Gender Identity Program located at the Center for Special Problems, a San Francisco Department of Public Health clinic. Since 1967 the program has provided psychotherapeutic, educational, and peer support services to low-income residents. A desperately needed new service has recently been added in the form of a transgender clinic held on Tuesdays at the Tom Waddell Medical Clinic. At this public medical clinic, transgender individuals who have low incomes or are homeless may receive checkups and primary medical care, hormones, and recommended blood monitoring, HIV screening and information, as well as counseling and social services referrals. Other similar resources include the Tenderloin Self-Help Center, which is a major resource for the disenfranchised who are seeking supportive resources, and the Tenderloin AIDS Resource Center, which provides support for those dealing with HIV or AIDS issues.

In addition, there are other agencies in the city that serve the special needs of transgender people of color. Most of these are HIV or AIDS related. The Asian AIDS project's transgender program provides HIV and AIDS prevention education through outreach and direct services case management targeted at Asian and Pacific Islander transgender populations. The Brothers Network offers HIV and AIDS as well as transgender support services targeted to African American transgender populations, and Proyecto Contra Sida Por Vida provides HIV and AIDS prevention education through outreach to Latino and Latina transgender individuals.

As a final comment on the programs and services provided within San Francisco, it should be stated that although these resources tend to be overcrowded, with waiting lists for services, they are better than nothing at all. Transgender Care considers these (and similar resources) as essential in helping the transgender individual avoid being caught up in the cycles of despair. Gender Specialists, public-health agencies, and the transgender community need to recognize the general lack of resources and to advocate the establishment of similar services wherever they may be needed.

Victimization

One common theme addressed by these programs is the high rate of victimization suffered by transgender individuals. Any professional supporting transgender needs will encounter such individuals and should be aware of the victimization models specific to transgender individuals. Victimization serves to undermine an individual's self-esteem in overt and covert forms. This process should not be confused with an individual's integration issues as a result of having a transgender identity.

The acts that victimize transgender individuals vary from subtle forms of harassment and discrimination to blatant verbal, physical, and sexual assault. The last may include violent beatings, rape, and even death. One example is the case of Brandon Teena, a Nebraskan FTM teenager who was gang-raped and beaten for having usurped male privilege, and then killed later by the same attackers. An example of a more common occurrence is that of a lower-income transgender woman in San Francisco's Tenderloin district who was followed home, sexually assaulted, savagely beaten to death, and left lying partially disrobed in an alley.

These individuals are among the few whose cases are documented; the majority of victimizations of transgender persons never become matters of record. This situation exists because transgender individuals have little societal support or access to legal recourse, particularly where they are disenfranchised. Finally, it should be noted that law enforcement agencies and personnel can be hostile toward transgender persons and are often the chief perpetrators of the same victimization and abuse they are designated by society to prevent. Gender Specialists, community leaders, and transgender individuals can all make a difference by calling on law-enforcement agencies to provide officers and other personnel with sensitivity training workshops and transgender-related educational materials.

Tragically, one of the most common, yet least talked about, forms of victimization in the transgender community is rape. Not only is sexual violence common against MTF transgender individuals, the fact that incidents are rarely prosecuted indicates how unimportant this crime is thought to be (when it happens to a transgender person) by the criminal justice system. Moreover, in addition to their indifference or discomfort addressing sexual concerns, Gender Specialists, community leaders, and transgender individuals rarely discuss rape. One characteristic that places MTF transgender individuals at a high risk of victimization is that they typically have not been conditioned to guard against misogynistic sexual violence from an early age. In contrast to individuals raised in a female role from early childhood, transgender women do not acquire this knowledge until later on in life, many times only after suffering a traumatic experience.

Sexual violence against MTF individuals is not solely based on a woman's being transgender. It clearly reaffirms that sexual violence is primarily a woman's problem. This can be recognized by the fact that the subject is so readily dismissed because it involves women being victimized by men for being women. Typically there is little if any press coverage when a transgender woman is the victim of violence (including domestic violence), even when the violence results in death.

The tragic case mentioned earlier, which involved Brandon Teena, helps reveal the status of women in today's society. The story of Teena's rape and murder attracted national media attention solely because of the prevailing opinion that such an FTM individual deserved the attack because "she" dared to assume the male role with all its attending privileges and status. Conversely, the prevailing opinion where MTF transgender women are concerned is that they deserve it because they "want" to be women. Currently two movies are in production regarding Brandon Teena; however, to the best of our knowledge no movies exist that document the high levels of sexual violence enacted against MTF individuals.

Regrettably, the tragedy of sexual violence becomes even more apparent when one notes that few individuals report having been raped for fear of compounding their victimization by risking insensitive treatment by law-enforcement officers. The victims see little hope of recourse when most local law enforcement does not consider preoperative transgender women to be female and thus not capable of being raped. This is particularly so when either local law or opinion does not consider male-on-male rape criminal. Individuals see little sense in seeking support from traditional rape crisis treatment centers that are unfamiliar with transgender issues and needs. Fortunately, in San Francisco organizations such as Community United Against Violence (CUAV) have included transgender women and men in their target populations. CUAV has both transgender staff and advisors, and we hope that other gay-lesbian-bisexual anti-violence and rape programs will become more informed of transgender persons' needs.

Care providers need be aware that rape is systematically endorsed in jails and prison systems, as guards and administrators either turn their heads or encourage this activity because keeping violent criminals in "relationships" tends to make populations more manageable. As a result, transgender individuals frequently become victimized by aggressive prisoners or are pushed into providing sexual services for one or more individuals. Rape under similar circumstances is also prevalent in institutionalized mental health populations.

Regrettably, governments and court systems have been slow in reviewing these circumstances, and typically when transgender individuals seek legal or human rights redress, the cases are turned away. For example, there is the case of Dee Farmer, an MTF transsexual inmate who sued the government because it acted with reckless indifference toward her well-being by putting her in with the general male population of a federal prison, where she was repeatedly beaten and raped.

In turning the case away, U.S. Supreme Court Justice David H. Souter issued the majority opinion that Ms. Farmer's rights were not violated nor did anyone act with reckless indifference toward her. It is important to point out that the court consistently referred to Ms. Farmer as "he" and "him," despite the fact she had undergone hormone therapy and was diagnosed as a transsexual.

We believe that Justice Souter's unconscionable opinion clearly illustrates the prevailing indifference toward transgender individuals. In this environment, Ms. Farmer's possession of a transgender identity became punishable alongside her criminal activity. Such opinions may seem solely applicable to the circumstances they are intended to address; regrettably, however, they also play a large role in shaping attitudes about transgender people outside institution walls.

If these situations and attitudes are to change, transgender individuals must vigilantly demand their human rights, and professionals who gain from working with these individuals must promote nonpathologizing support models for and descriptions of transgender people, inside as well as outside governmental institutions.

Key Mental Health Issues

For practical purposes, when completing psychologic and psychiatric diagnosis of transgender men and women, it is important for the clinician to understand correctly which issues these persons most commonly face. Having a transgender identity is not in and of itself pathologic, but care providers and consumers should also understand that persons with gender issues may be vulnerable to a variety of mental health disorders. We have found that in both community clinic and private practice settings transgender persons are not much different than others who experience major life changes, relationship difficulties, chronic medical disorders, or significant discrimination on the basis of a minority background.

We as authors recognize that not all persons agree that having a transgender identity is not in and of itself mentally disordered. These people are welcome to their opinions, although we do invite them to note that nearly all the mental health literature that stigmatizes transgender persons is based on the premise that people are ill if they do not conform to society's notions of how a person should be and act. Additionally, some transgender individuals may believe that they are mentally disordered after experiencing life-long internal shame and external opposition to their having a transgender identity.

Finally, some transgender persons fear that if they do not embrace the illness model, they will not receive hormonal and surgical interventions. We encourage care providers and consumers to develop treatment models that support the individual's right to self-determination yet address any true mental disorders an individual may be experiencing. Consumers may do this by encouraging care providers to view hormone administration and surgical interventions as treatments for medical conditions using a quality-of-life model. Care providers may do similarly by applying diagnostic criteria to the actual symptoms a client presents.

Care providers can also spend time understanding the issues and trends that are associated with transgender persons. For example, we have observed that transgender persons frequently abandon traditional psychotherapy after a couple sessions or after receiving a hormone recommendation letter. After doing so, these individuals often rely on group or peer support services when they need additional counseling regarding gender identity issues.

This tendency indicates several dynamics. First, it reflects that after adopting a consistent gender identity and resolving related interpersonal issues, some individuals have no other mental health disorders needing treatment. They make the sensible choice not to invest their time receiving help where none is needed. However, after abandoning therapy, some persons may have unresolved issues even after having adopted a consistent gender identity. Group and peer support facilitators need to be aware of this and be prepared to refer individuals to professional assistance when they present difficulties that extend beyond a group or peer focus.

Care providers and consumers should understand that transgender persons frequently receive erroneous mental health information or may feel resistant to seeking help for any difficulties they are experiencing. Some may avoid seeking mental health services because they fear care providers will interfere with their privacy or attempt to discuss gender issues when doing so simply is not necessary. We encourage care providers to develop a rapport with transgender men and women, learn their needs, and respectfully raise concerns about their mental health. Also, whenever possible, care providers should provide transgender consumers with easy-to-understand information about mental health disorders.

The most common mental health issues transgender persons experience are depression as well as adjustment, anxiety, personality, and posttraumatic stress disorders. Like the general population, transgender men and women may also experience schizophrenic, psychotic, and other mental health disorders. Many mental health issues can be addressed in a psychotherapeutic setting. However, more severe disorders may call for the use of psychoactive medication, which can provide short-term relief of symptoms so that an individual can begin building coping mechanisms to deal with his or her difficulties.

Persons who wish to read more about these mental health disorders or locate diagnostic criterion may do so by consulting the latest edition of the American Psychiatric Association's *Diagnostic and Statistical Manual of Mental Disorders,* or any recognized psychiatric or psychological textbook, although readers are reminded that outdated literature frequently is deprecating toward transgender persons. Consumers may also find self-help books on mental health disorders useful; these can be found at most large bookstores.

Adjustment Disorders

An individual having significant difficulty adjusting after a divorce, losing a job, or adapting to other distressing circumstances may exhibit symptoms of one of several adjustment disorders. These disorders may have associated features of depression, anxiety, disturbed conduct, or a mixture of these features. This diagnosis is flexible and may be applied to single, repeated, or chronic stressors or events.

An example: An FTM individual who is comfortable living as a male may develop anxiety about finding a new employment position ever since he encountered transphobic discrimination in his last place of employment. His feeling anxious is seriously inhibiting his ability to come to terms with the past and move on to seek new employment He feels angry, depressed, and concerned that because of his transgender status, his former employer may not provide him a good employment reference. He also worries that in the future he may face discrimination, and this interferes with his ability to seek work.

Anxiety Disorders

When a person's symptoms of fear, panic, phobias, obsessions, and compulsions interfere with daily living and productive relationships, a person may then have one of several anxiety disorders. Such disorders may have associated features of depression, shame, and low self-esteem. Anxiety disorder diagnoses are flexible, and may be applied to a single, repeat stressors or events.

An example: In San Francisco, where a significant number of transgender persons live, an MTF individual may feel comfortable living as a woman and socializing with her friends. However, even though she has never been harassed and most people are accepting of her, she feels afraid to ride the bus alone. She is afraid that people will harass her on the bus and therefore takes a bus only when accompanied by a friend. Furthermore, when safe at home, she feels anxious to the point of having panic attacks at the mere thought of riding the bus.

Post-Traumatic Stress Disorder

Post-traumatic stress disorder is a specific type of anxiety disorder that is experienced by persons who feel anxious as a result of emotionally reexperiencing a traumatic event; such as being assaulted, raped, robbed, or otherwise violated. This disorder typically has associated features of depression, anxiousness, flashbacks, or disturbing dreams following a single or repeated series of traumatic events.

An example: An FTM individual who is in the coming-out process has been verbally harassed by neighbors over the past several months. One evening as he was entering his apartment building's elevator, several men jumped in after him. They physically attacked him, called him a "faggot," and left him lying in pain. When he showed up at his therapist's office a day later, bruised and disheveled, he stated that he had encountered some difficulties but was "over it." Soon after the event he began to report nightmares, flashbacks, and heightened reactivity to any events that suggested the original assault.

Depression

Depression is the leading mental health disorder faced by both transgender and nontransgender persons, and therefore is discussed in more detail than the other diagnoses. Unless an individual's depression has progressed to crisis proportions, in many circumstances he or she will not seek help for this debilitating disorder, which robs people of time, energy, and the joy of living. This is tragic, because depression is one of the best understood mental illnesses, with recognizable symptoms and effective interventions.

Depression is a mood disorder characterized by extended feelings of sadness, loss, restlessness, discouragement, hopelessness, self-doubt, and guilt. These feelings are often accompanied by noticeable changes in a depressed individual's regular sleeping, eating, and sexual habits. They are also likely to have changes in self-perception, think negative thoughts on an ongoing basis, have difficulty making decisions; sometimes, they contemplate self-destructive acts. Their emotions typically swing sharply between feeling angry, sad, melancholic, and moody. Depression is not about having one or several isolated bad or low-energy days; it is about having an emotionally poor quality of life, day after day, with no hope of relief in sight.

> Depression is not about having one or several isolated bad days or low-energy days; it is about having an emotionally poor quality of life, day after day, with no hope of relief in sight.

The state of mind that characterizes depression indicates why people do not seek treatment. The more severe the depression, the more limited an individual's ability to think realistically or recognize options that might improve her or his quality of life. Simply stated, most depressed persons routinely discount treatment options until everything else has failed. This type of clouded judgment also frequently slows the resolution of gender issues. Depressed transgender persons frequently feel compelled to move ahead in their transition without seeking adequate support. Also, in order to gain acceptance and reduce emotional turmoil, they may disclose their transgender issues without having taken into account potential consequences or the effect upon others.

Transgender persons frequently avoid treatment for depression because it is widely believed that in order for treatment to be effective, both gender-identity and depression issues must be addressed at the same time. This is not always the case. In some situations it is possible to provide symptom relief without having to immediately deal with gender-identity issues. Individuals may seek support for their depression, stressing that they are not interested in discussing gender-identity issues until they feel safe doing so, if it should it become necessary. Those who feel that disclosing their gender issues may prove compromising or be met with negativity may choose not to. Rather, they can make use of the break from emotional anguish that is available through traditional depressive-symptom relief to seek gender-specialized assistance with their crossdressing or gender-identity issues.

Having two care providers, one who dispenses depression treatment and the other who offers gender-specialized support, is useful in many circumstances. This is particularly so when a transgender person does not yet have a sufficient level of communication skills and knowledge about gender-identity issues to disclose them to a helping professional unfamiliar with such issues.

Transgender hormone administration also may play a causal role in depression. Because hormones are powerful chemicals, an increase or decrease in dosage can bring on changes in mood. Transgender persons and their physicians need to recognize that routine laboratory testing of blood-based hormone levels helps ensure that dosages are effective, yet not so high as to create debilitating mood swings or dangerous medical complications. Gradual changes in hormone dosages are a sensible precaution, providing an opportunity for the individual to make both the physical and emotional adjustment. Moreover, individuals who are initiating hormone administration frequently are poorly prepared for the emotional changes that go with it. These persons are encouraged to adjust their thinking and seek support for their needs, much as women do during menopause. This is particularly so for transgender women who choose to cycle their hormones so as to mimic the biological rhythms genetic women experience.

Care providers need to be aware that a lack of access to hormones also produces high rates of depression, emotional mood swings, and occasionally suicidal feelings. This is particularly so when public institutions, and medical or mental health providers, deny transgender persons access to hormones because it is against policy or care provider staff are unfamiliar with gender-identity issues. Transgender persons should not be denied access to hormones or be cut off from existing prescriptions solely because a care provider is not interested in or unfamiliar with transgender support. Transgender hormone administration is a routine medical procedure, and transgender persons are no less entitled to informed medical care than other patients.

Transgender persons can suffer depression caused by situations or disorders that are in no way related to gender issues. Transgender persons need to recognize this and should research their treatment options before things reach a crisis. It is senseless for individuals to suffer from depression when successful treatment options exist. In many circumstances, even severe and long-term depression can be halted with early intervention.

Sexual Orientation

The matter of sexual orientation represents an ongoing concern for transgender individuals and those providing specialized support care, partly because the terms *sex, sexual orientation,* and *gender identity* are interchanged erroneously. It is imperative that those professing competency in gender-identity issues fully understand these terms and how they are appropriately used.

Sexual orientation refers to the gender identity of those to whom an individual is erotically attracted, that is, to the same sex, the opposite sex, or both. Dr. JoAnn Roberts, in her book *Coping with Crossdressing* (King of Prussia, PA: Creative Design Services, 1992), points out that *sex* or *biological sex* is what enables individuals to fulfill a sexual role in intimacy and love-making. Biological sex also plays the central role in an individual's procreation potential. *Gender identity* refers to an individual's identification with maleness and femaleness, as well as how these feelings (and their subsequent needs) are internalized and possibly presented to others.

Individuals may not always present their gender-identity needs outwardly or, for that matter, disclose their sexual orientation casually. For example, a transgender individual in the process of coming out is engaged in what can best be described as an exploration of his or her gender-identity needs and may begin to present them outwardly only when she or he has reached sufficient awareness of those needs and feels comfortable sharing them with others. This coming-out process is in many ways similar to the coming-out process individuals may go through when discovering or redefining their sexual orientation. It is of vital importance to recognize that both sexual orientation and gender identity involve full spectrums of individual needs and presentations. This means that individuals are not limited by inflexible stereotypes, but instead have many avenues from which to create a sense of self-identity and express individual needs, as well as to create a vehicle for intimacy and eroticism.

Commonly, when an individual begins exploring his or her gender-identity issues, or begins crossdressing, these activities are misinterpreted as that of an individual uncertain about his or her sexual orientation. This is why so many transgender individuals do not seek support, for fear of homophobic persecution. Examples of this would include the heterosexual male crossdresser who confuses his crossdressing with homosexual behavior, as well as the pretransition transsexual who feels that his or her transgender feelings mean that he or she is gay or lesbian. These types of issues add more weight to the argument that anyone supporting transgender individuals or providing education about gender-identity issues must fully comprehend these dynamics and be able to explain them to others.

Transgender individuals (as well as their nontransgender counterparts) may explore and develop a spectrum of sexual orientations ranging from attraction to members of the opposite sex to attraction to those of the same sex. One difference between transgender and nontransgender individuals' sexual orientation is that for the latter, it is more likely to stabilize near puberty. Some transgender individuals may not have benefited from this process and may feel (though not necessarily always express) uncertainty concerning their sexual orientation at or about the time that they are exploring gender-identity issues. Whether the individual's sexual orientation actually changes permanently is an open question and varies from individual to individual. Thus, he or she should be encouraged to explore these issues without preconceived expectations. Some will find their exploration reaffirms previous erotic experiences; others may experience this as a time of change. In doing so, they develop new interests and desires that complement their new identity.

Supporting transgender individuals with concerns about their own sexual orientation can often best be understood when the support process is viewed in two stages. The first stage involves providing educational information regarding gender identity and sexual orientation. This provides the individual with the basic tools needed to be able to differentiate between these basic characteristics and their associated behaviors. Although this informational stage may not provide resolution of the individual's concerns, many at this stage find short-term relief as the puzzle pieces begin falling into place and they gain a clearer understanding of their feelings and behaviors.

The experienced care provider will also assure the individual that many others have been successfully supported through this confusing and difficult process. At this initial stage of concern regarding sexual orientation, transgender individuals and care providers alike may be uncertain as to which issue to explore first when uncertainty exists also about the individual's gender identification. Typically, it is best to focus on the subject that currently most affects the individual's day-to-day circumstances, although others may benefit from exploration of both concerns simultaneously. Frequently, individuals with simultaneous concerns regarding gender identity and sexual orientation will find resolution for the latter shortly after fully grasping and relating to newly acquired information on gender-identity issues. It should be stated, however, that some transsexual individuals' sexual orientation may change after Genital Reassignment Surgery. This is particularly likely for those individuals who avoided sexual experiences while living in role presurgically.

Once information is gathered, several clues may emerge that help in identifying which sexual orientation a person may have after gender identity has stabilized. Consistency in actual experiences is one such clue, particularly as an individual repeats pleasant experiences. Fantasy also plays some role in this determination process; however, in some circumstances fantasy may just be that, fantasy. For the person involved in this self-discovery process, this can be a time rich in exploration and fantasizing or fraught with guilt and concern. Much depends not only on the attitudes and past experiences of the individual but also upon society and relationships as well as her or his support relationships. Care providers must be cautioned against pushing an individual into adopting one sexual orientation over another simply to please others (including care providers), who may have their own ideas about what may be best for the transgender individual. In the past, numerous transgender individuals have felt pressured to adopt a particular presentation with the hope that this might improve their access to hormones or surgery. Such situations are particularly tragic in that they undermine any real chance for the individual to receive pertinent support for her or his actual sexual orientation. Individuals in all circumstances need to be allowed the opportunity to develop independently their own gender identities and sexual orientations.

If determining one's own sexual orientation at the same time one is resolving gender issues isn't confusing enough, one last issue, briefly covered here, also must be dealt with, not only at this time but extending to transition and beyond as well. From closet to grave, transgender individuals are forced to confront professional and societal situations in which their transgender status is misperceived as being synonymous with specific sexual orientation. This situation becomes all the more difficult when people persist in misidentifying transgender individuals out of ignorance or prejudice. It is essential to recognize that not all misconceptions are inherently evil or malicious. Large segments of society simply know very little about gender identity and sexual orientation because these are not issues they have had to deal with firsthand.

One group directly affected by transgender issues are spouses, partners, and significant others. When initially introduced to their partner's transgender status, they often question their own sexual orientation, at the same time expressing the same concerns with respect to their partner. To illustrate, the wife of a pretransitional MTF transgender individual may question if she has a latent lesbian orientation because her husband is now interested in feminine pursuits and she is willing to go along in this dynamic to preserve the relationship. Conversely, the male partner of an FTM individual may have similar questions about having a latent gay orientation or transgender identity.

In most cases, it is unlikely that the partner would be either. In other cases, for example, a wife who remained in a relationship with a post-transitional MTF individual may find she had a latent bisexual or lesbian orientation that came to surface only as a result of role play or through her partner's transition. Many partners remain in relationships for reasons extending beyond sexual role fulfillment. They may wish to maintain the present relationship for its financial benefits, companionship, and intimacy. Others may have children and decide to remain in the relationship for that reason. Partners of transgender individuals who find themselves addressing sexual-orientation issues are encouraged to seek support from a knowledgeable counselor, therapist, support group, or social organization.

Sexual Orientation Profiles

References to sexual orientation can initially be confusing to professionals and consumers alike. As a general rule, an individual's sexual orientation is not based on biological (birth) gender, but is a reflection of her or his self-identification. If you need to know but are unsure of someone's sexual orientation, simply ask the individual how he or she prefers to be identified. Following are classical sexual orientations as well as others with which the reader may be unfamiliar.

Pre- and Postoperative Transsexuals, Transgenderists, and Androgynes

These are individuals who self-identify as a member of the opposite gender on a part-time basis or who live in role full time.

Where there is a(n)	individuals self-identify as
opposite-sex attraction . . .	heterosexual transgender man or woman.
same-sex attraction . . .	lesbian transgender woman or gay transgender man.
both-sex attraction . . .	bisexual transgender man or woman.

Crossdressers or Transvestites, and Some Transgenderists

Crossdressers and transvestites who self-identify as members of their primary biological sex crossdress for the purpose of exploring their opposite-gender persona. This may include a mixture of social, fantasy, and sexual explorations.

Where there is a(n)	individuals self-identify as
opposite-sex attraction . . .	heterosexual, crossdresser man or woman.
same-sex attraction . . .	gay or lesbian crossdresser man or woman.
both-sex attraction . . .	bisexual, crossdresser man or woman.

Asexual Individuals

Asexual individuals have no erotic attraction for others. In some circumstances, asexuality may be an integral element of a person's self-identification. At other times, asexuality may be a temporary aspect of an individual's self-identification that precedes her or his exploration of a gender transition. After the individual has explored and self-defined his or her gender identity, he or she may then move on to explore sexual-orientation issues.

Transgender Attractions

Although they fall outside classical sexual-orientation parameters, transgender individuals who are attracted to others like themselves should not be overlooked. In some circumstances, transgender individuals seek out other transgender individuals for companionship and sexual interaction because they feel unable to attract or maintain sexual interaction with nontransgender individuals. Others, including those who may initially feel that they are transgender, may have deeply rooted fantasies revolving around other transgender individuals that are an integral element of their sexual orientation.

Pansexual Attractions

The term *pansexual attractions* is a liberating and newly coined reference to individuals who are primarily attracted to all individuals and all sexes.

Transvestic Fetishists

Transvestic fetishists are those who crossdress solely for sexual arousal. Many are quite removed from the publicly open transgender community, and although the behavior is widespread, socialization between fetishists is uncommon, except perhaps in closed fetishist circles and groups. Usually these individuals are self-identified as gay, straight, or bisexual males or females, with the label applied to their primary sexual orientation, not to transitional behaviors.

Role Play

Throughout society, many individuals of all sexual orientations, including transgender people, find meaningful sexual expression through a wide variety of role-playing activities. Unfortunately, role playing is often portrayed as deviant or "sick" behavior, when in fact it is an excellent opportunity for sexual expression and release as well as personal growth, when conducted within safe boundaries. Role-playing activities may include (but are not limited) to dominant-submissive (sadism and masochism) experiences, reliving childhood fantasies by playing a baby, dressing as a uniformed maid or officer, and the like.

Disclosure Concerns

Perhaps the most significant mental health and social support issue faced by transgender individuals revolves around the disclosure of one's transgender status and needs to others. Because disclosure plays such an important role, it should be no surprise that nearly every transgender publication prints disclosure-oriented advice, as well as materials reflecting the concerns individuals have before (or after) disclosing within social and family relationships. Coming out and disclosing one's needs does not come without consequences, including potential losses. Regrettably, many individuals disclose in situations where there is no apparent advantage, when they lack preparation for the event, or before they have acquired adequate disclosure skills. Loss of supportive relationships can be a tragedy. It is not difficult to understand why people view the prospect of disclosure with great anxiety or fear, even though the desire to express their self-identity and needs eventually surfaces in some form. Transgender issues never simply go away.

One of the most difficult disclosure situations can occur when an individual is in the midst of a crisis situation: she or he might be suicidal, facing institutionalization, or immobilized with fear of the consequences of disclosure. In such circumstances, the individual should be discouraged from disclosing her or his transgender status unless doing so is absolutely necessary. With that exception and wherever possible, disclosure should be delayed until after the individual is no longer in acute crisis and has an experienced gender-specialized support network in place. Prior to disclosing to others randomly, it is suggested that individuals possess a basic comprehension of the difficulties they are facing, an ability to communicate their needs, and the awareness that, with time and effort on their part, these needs can be addressed. If during (or after) a crisis, an individual is unable to set aside disclosure needs, it is strongly advised he or she seek consultation from an empathic person familiar with the disclosure process who can provide either direct guidance or third-party mediation.

A key component of most crisis situations is a deep feeling of isolation. Some individuals may view their transgender feelings and behaviors as so removed from that which is socially acceptable, they are unaware that support exists at all. Others, although recognizing their needs as gender-identity issues, may be unaware that gender-specialized support is available in their location. In many rural locations such support is in fact not available. Most major cities, however, have available some form of transgender resources, although even these may be extremely difficult to locate. In circumstances such as these, transgender individuals should be reassured by care providers that they are not alone and that support is available or can be located.

Disclosure under less-than-ideal circumstances is not limited to individuals in crisis. For example, some individuals may become overzealous about coming out as a result of discovering their own transgender identity. Or they may believe that doing so will correct others' perception of their behavior as odd. Still others, in reaching out for support, will occasionally be pushed into disclosure situations by overzealous members of a support or social group or by people with personal or activist agendas.

In many circumstances, being forced or even choosing to disclose without being fully prepared for what disclosure involves can have devastating consequences. Individuals who are emotionally unready to encounter negative responses or even indifference may overreact when met with unanticipated responses. Overreacting may further heighten alienation and rejection by others. At times, an individual may feel rejected or discriminated against, despite the fact that the confidante may have supportive feelings but is uncertain how to express them. Unfortunately, many individuals who encounter (or create) less-than-optimum disclosure situations may suffer severe blows to their self-esteem or have their emotional or mental stability called into question by others. The majority of such situations can be avoided by use of discretion: disclosure should be based on the others' need to know or be done selectively to gain support until adequate communication skills are acquired.

Themes revolving around disclosure issues vary from individual to individual, as well as from one transgender subpopulation to another. Generally speaking, the more comfortable one is with his or her transgender issues, the easier disclosure will become. However, sometimes disclosure skills can grow rusty from lack of use. For example, postoperative transsexuals who find themselves deeply integrated into the fabric of mainstream society may awaken one day to realize that they have drifted away from gender-specialized support systems or have grown unaccustomed to disclosing their transgender status to others. Though many transgender individuals might envy someone in such a situation (particularly because it would indicate that an individual has "passed" for a nontransgender individual), few of these envious individuals recognize that once transgender issues resurface, those who have assimilated into society may find themselves with no place to turn for help for fear of being found out.

Fear of discovery and isolation exist in a variety of forms throughout transgender populations. For example, closeted heterosexual crossdressers invest a great deal of energy in hiding their crossdressing behaviors and transgender identities. They do so by building up the illusion of a secure life, during which times they bury their crossdressing desires so successfully that even their family may not know. Remarkably, many crossdressers are so successful at keeping their secret hidden that children and close friends may never know that the individual is a crossdresser. Most knowledgeable Gender Specialists are quick to recognize that this secretive process is burdensome and isolating. As a result, these illusory periods of security are in fact times when crossdressers are most likely to engage in self-destructive or addictive behaviors with the hope of alleviating crossdressing needs or masking the pain of isolation.

With little or no support for their transgender identity and with such an illusory dynamic in place, it is not uncommon for crossdressers to find themselves dealing with crossdressing needs at the same time that major life changes or crises occur. For example, many closeted crossdressers find themselves powerfully drawn to crossdressing in response to a change of employment, a death in the family, or even the birth of a child. To compound the issue, in most such situations the individual is also likely to lack accurate gender-specialized information and thereby find himself or herself unable to reach out for support and fearful of being found out. From the individual's point of view, being found out poses numerous dire consequences—loss of a spouse, employment, friends, and so forth. Those who hide their transgender identity and crossdressing needs sometimes come to find that they might have been better off by being honest with themselves and seeking support in the first place. Even if the support is just one empathic person, or contact with other crossdressers through a computer bulletin board service, at least the individual has found an outlet for discussing needs and feelings during stressful periods.

Those who intend to crossdress within a social context or live in role part or full time require special savvy and communication skills. In the face of prevailing social values and fixed gender stereotypes, these individuals can in many (but not all) cases face rejection, abandonment, harassment, or discrimination. Transgenderists and transsexuals are strongly advised to seek support during their initial coming-out contacts. These individuals have an ongoing need to refine their self-presentation and disclosure skills, to resolve situational anxiety resulting from negative disclosure contacts, and—of primary importance for those carrying transgender issues into the workplace—have support around workplace disclosure. Further information about workplace disclosure can be found in the scenarios in Chapter 10.

One disclosure issue that may not be readily apparent is the added concerns individuals may have as a result of being in a subpopulation of the larger transgender community. Such individuals may fear additional rejection from others as a result of their particular status and needs. Examples would include transgenderists and androgynes who do not fully discuss their needs in front of transsexuals or crossdressers; individuals with HIV who fear persecution or ostracization; gay, lesbian, bisexual, and in some cases heterosexual individuals who may be reticent to talk about their orientation or share intimate thoughts for fear of alienation from others.

Basic Disclosure Tools

The following principles for disclosure are simply those that guide any process of sharing with others. They can be applied in various communication endeavors and need not be limited solely to a coming-out process.

Reflect upon the Consequences

The late therapist Roger Peo recommended asking the fundamental question "Will this improve my relationship with this person?" More often than not, disclosure is not necessary in nonintimate situations and should not be undertaken unless one feels that it will add quality to the relationship. Individuals newly discovering their transgender status may feel much relief at having reached an understanding with their feelings. However, they should be wary of telling every single person they meet. Most nonintimate acquaintances such as coworkers or neighbors do not have a need to know about the individual's transgender status.

Contemplate How Disclosure Will Affect Others

Disclosure will in all likelihood introduce dynamics that affect other individuals, particularly those in intimate and family relationships. A spouse or significant other will worry about how the issue affects children, other family members, and employment, as well as about the amount of money and time that will be spent on crossdressing and other transgender activities. Even more serious questions face the partners of those who believe themselves to be transgenderists or transsexuals. In addition, all face concerns and questions about hormones, Genital Reassignment Surgery, and, above all else, the potential loss of the person they married or with whom they have a deep commitment.

Prepare for Communicating

Preparing for disclosure is much like preparing for a business meeting; it can be helpful to assemble a list of items to discuss and to organize thoughts about these items. A well-prepared description of the individual's own position can help ease everyone's tension and fears. Individuals uncertain as to whether disclosure is right for them are strongly encouraged to solicit support from an objective, empathic individual experienced in disclosure firsthand, or a Gender Specialist. Doing the preceding will help prevent situations where an individual would come across as too dramatic or in crisis, and incapable of asking for help when dealing with serious issues.

Make an Appointment

No one likes being shocked. Setting aside a special time and space for disclosure will help reinforce the importance of one's own needs and at the same time will show respect for the other person's feelings and needs.

Validate the Relationship

Reaffirming the relationship, its positive strengths and one's caring for the other person, can be an important starting point. This is a good time to seek out a confidentiality agreement, if one seems necessary.

Relieve Stress by Revealing

The person who approaches disclosure feeling nervous and afraid may find that admitting these feelings to the other person may help elicit empathy and concern. It also may help relieve these feelings just to acknowledge the difficulty of this process. Expressing such feelings is good, but one should remember that overemotional or uncontrolled outbursts may draw unnecessary attention to the situation and alienate the other person.

Share the Facts

Staying with the basics usually is the best route to follow. One should, first, give a brief background about one's feelings and experiences, then state what is presently going on and describe one's needs simply. Giving too much information at one time may be confusing or offputting to the other person. Information should not forced on another person. If he or she seems uninterested, it may simply be just that he or she is uncertain how to react; such a reaction is not necessarily a sign of rejection.

Affirm and Respect the Other Person

Disclosure may not result in the acceptance hoped for, but others have not only the right to their own feelings, beliefs, and needs, but the right to express them. Recognizing this can only serve to strengthen one's interpersonal and communication skills. If differences seem to be headed toward an impasse, third-party mediation may be helpful. Some individuals will be wholeheartedly supportive, others will prefer to distance themselves, and some will become hostile and resentful. Most initial responses will fall somewhere in the middle, neither totally supportive nor totally critical.

Seal the Communication

No matter what the outcome, one should state appreciation for the other person's willingness to listen. Appreciation of the relationship should be reaffirmed, and communication sealed with an intimate gesture, if appropriate.

Reflect Inward

Disclosure to others is difficult. Any act of disclosure should be followed by reflection upon the courage it took. Any mistakes that were made should not be dwelt upon. Doing one's best is what is important. If damage control is needed, the advice or assistance of a third person should be sought.

Disclosure to Children

Disclosure to children calls for special consideration. Although increasing numbers of transgender individuals are choosing to share their crossdressing and transgender experiences with their children, generally, disclosure to children should be based on a child's need to know. This would include individuals who crossdress actively or intend to live in role.

During disclosure, young children may be able to process only small amounts of information at a time. The first conversation should not be a long, drawn-out one, and subsequently children should be invited to reinitiate conversation on the subject, as their interest dictates.

If the adult crossdresses regularly or lives in role, children may fear (and realistically so) rejection and harassment from peers. Children should be told that crossdressing or transgender needs (and associated issues) are the individual's alone, not the child's. Children who encounter rejection or harassment from peers need to be taught how to respond to this situation, and to seek the help of a third party as needed.

Above all else, children need to be reminded that they are loved.

Recommended Guidelines for the Residential Placement and Support of Transgender Individuals in Social Service, Mental Health, and Correctional Settings

> *Caution: A full understanding of these guidelines is not possible without reading the material in the preceding sections of this chapter. For additional information, see the section on institutionalized and incarcerated individuals in Chapter 1.*

1. Transgender identity and gender-identity issues are not mentally disordered, diseased, or pathologic. Thousands of transgender individuals lead well-adjusted lives as productive and law-abiding participants in society.

2. Transgender individuals are not known to have a higher incidence of mental health disorders than the general population, although stereotypes, social isolation, and prejudice are known to exacerbate circumstantial difficulties in the lives of transgender people.

3. Because transgender identity and gender-identity issues are not pathologic conditions, the presence of a transgender identity or fulfilment of transgender needs (such as a desire to crossdress, live in role, pursue and undergo hormone administration or aesthetic or Genital Reassignment Surgery) is not a reason to institutionalize, incarcerate, or detain transgender individuals in mental health, correctional, or similar residential facilities.

4. Those making decision about residential placement within mental health, social service, and correctional settings are advised to take into account an individual's current gender presentation and her or his actual placement request, as well as the individual's gender-related history. Placement decisions should also take into account the needs of other populations served at the receiving facility, although any decisions made should not prove discriminatory to any population.

5. Where uncertainty exists with regard to residential placement and support services or where care providers are unfamiliar with gender-identity issues, a Gender Specialist should be consulted for assistance in the negotiation and evaluation of placement decisions, as well as for staff and peer-sensitivity training.

6. Residential or correctional staff are advised that hormone administration should not be denied transgender individuals when they have a verifiable history of hormone usage, or when they fall within the criteria established in the Guidelines for Hormone Administration (see Chapter 3). Staff and physicians are reminded that in Recommendation 1b of the Guidelines for Hormone Administration, exceptions to the three-month assessment period may be considered by the evaluating Gender Specialist or prescribing physician if a well-established transgender identity exists and when other aspects of the Guidelines for Hormone Administration are observed.

7. Residential staff and correctional officers are advised to refer to transgender individuals in a manner respectful of each individual's stated preference for gender presentation and name and pronoun usage requests. They should also direct peers to respect the gender self-identification of transgender residents.

8. Residential staff and correctional officers are advised that some transgender individuals may be unable to voice their gender-identity needs after suffering a crisis situation. Therefore, residential staff and correctional officers are advised to consult a professional Gender Specialist whenever they are aware that an individual is transgender-identified but unable to speak on her or his own behalf.

9. Residential staff and correctional officers are advised that, in order to maintain their gender identification, transgender persons need gender-specific clothing, cosmetics, and toiletry supplies. MTF individuals typically need shaving razors, cosmetics (lipstick, blush, foundation, mascara), brassieres, female clothing, and the like. FTM individuals typically need binding material (large ace bandages), prostheses, and small shoes. Supplies for transgender persons may need to be "exception" or "catalog" ordered if not included on standard residential or inmate supply order forms. Shoes in small sizes and clothing in large sizes may also need to be catalog ordered.

10. Transgender individuals, in their interactions with mental health and social service providers, are advised that many staff and correctional officers may be unfamiliar with transgender identification and needs. With this understanding, transgender individuals are advised to express placement requests and support needs and to be prepared to explain their needs in calm, consistent, easy-to-understand language. If a care provider or correctional officer seems unfamiliar with gender issues and the needs of the transgender individual are not being met, the transgender person is advised to request to speak with a supervisor, or to ask that the agency consult with a Gender Specialist regarding transgender needs.

Transgender Hormone Administration

Chapter 3

Many psychotherapy and support models exist to address the various psychological, social, and interpersonal needs of transgender individuals. Hormone administration is offered to transsexuals, some transgenderists, and androgynes who wish to bring the body in line with an intended masculine, feminine, or androgynous presentation. Hormones are an essential element in any real-life test (see the definitions section of Chapter 1) for individuals considering Genital Reassignment Surgery, and they play a role in helping the transgender individual experience the physical and emotional changes that come with living in role.

Estrogens, progesterones, antiandrogens, and testosterone are natural or synthetic agents whose use is regulated by and may be legitimately obtained only through a physician. Hormones typically are prescribed for a variety of other health needs, including the treatment of enlarged prostate, pubertal and adult hormone regulation, postmenopausal estrogen regulation, and birth control. The use of hormones by the transgender client is intended to provide a sense of psychological and emotional fulfillment and to enhance the physical secondary sex characteristics of the desired gender. Depending on the individual patient's medical condition, medication side effects, and genetic predisposition, hormone administration can effectively produce intended psychological and physical outcomes.

Principles of Hormone Administration

Some physicians prefer to administer hormones with the written consent of the patient. The introduction of a written consent is somewhat unusual, given the fact that such contracts are not traditionally used with routine pharmacological treatment. They do, however, provide quick, easy reference for transgender consumers' understanding of hormone administration and its potential benefits and side effects. In no case should hormones be administered frivolously or without adequate consumer-accessible information and advisement.

The biologic dynamics of hormone administration are fairly easy for physicians and consumers to understand. Human sex hormones such as estrogens and testosterone are both secreted by all individuals. They are secreted in different amounts, however, depending on the person's biological gender. Normally, estrogens and testosterone exert their effect on target tissues when they bind to specific estrogen or androgen receptors in these tissues. This process results in the development and maintenance of secondary sex characteristics, reproductive function, and sex organ viability.

Men and women have different ratios of sex hormones as well as a concentration of receptors specific to their biological sex. Hormone administration in transgender clients targets these receptors and promotes the development and maintenance of the secondary sexual characteristics of the opposite sex. The amount of physical change varies from one individual to another. No two individuals will see the same type or degree of body change from the same dosage of the same medication. This is because the genetic (hereditary) make-up and physical metabolism of each individual differ. Most or all physical development brought on by hormone administration will gradually regress at individual rates after hormone therapy ceases.

Because hormones are strong chemical agents, their use does not come without risks and responsibilities. Much as the developmental action of hormones is specific to each individual, so too are the side effects, which can vary depending on age, metabolism, and previous and present health conditions, among other factors. A responsible hormone-administration program includes an ongoing working relationship between the individual and prescribing physician. Transgender individuals need to communicate changes in health, keep regular medical appointments, and have hormone levels in the blood and blood pressure monitored regularly.

In this era of medical specialists, many general practitioners unfamiliar with gender-identity issues are left feeling uncertain how to provide hormone administration to the transgender individual or if it is provided for under insurance coverage. As a result, general practitioners frequently choose to refer the individual to an endocrinologist or more commonly to tell the individual that they are unable to provide this type of support. As a consequence, transgender individuals, feeling they have no alternatives available, may resort to self-medication or seek out unscrupulous medical providers. These negative outcomes are realistically preventable through increased collaboration between informed consumers, experienced Gender Specialists, and competent physicians.

The decision to initiate a regimen of hormone treatment should be balanced between the physician and patient so as to ensure informed consent and professional responsibility by the physician, yet still enable self-determination by the transgender individual. A model hormone administration consent form is provided in Figure 3.1. In other words, the physician's role should principally be in

Background

This consent form is designed to provide accurate and up-to-date information on hormone administration for male-to-female (MTF) and female-to-male (FTM) transgender individuals. Transgender clients as medical consumers need to fully understand the therapeutic benefits as well as adverse or undesirable side effects. In all cases the information provided here should accompany consultation with a physician familiar with your individual medical history.

MTF Hormone Administration

MTF hormone administration is commonly provided orally (pills), by injection (shot), or by transdermal (on the skin) patch. Therapeutic benefits include feminization, breast development, softer skin, fat redistribution, potential weight gain, male hormonal suppression, and the development of other female secondary sex characteristics. Hormone administration will not affect preexisting baldness, facial hair growth, or raise voice pitch. Hormone administration may reduce penis erections and/or impair reproductive functioning.

For the majority of MTF transgender individuals, hormone administration is safe. However, some individuals are at high risk of developing certain serious diseases that can be life-threatening or may cause temporary or permanent disability or death. The risks associated with hormone administration increase significantly if you smoke; have high blood pressure, diabetes, or high cholesterol; or have a history of blood-clotting disorders, heart attack, stroke, angina pectoris, cancer of the breast or sex organs, jaundice, or malignant or benign liver tumors. In addition, users of Anandron or Androcur (cyproterone acetate, a synthetic steroid available in the United States only through foreign sources) may have visual difficulty adapting to darkness. All hormones may temporarily cause or aggravate depression, moodiness, or even euphoria until the body adapts to chemical changes, which takes anywhere from several weeks to months.

Estrogen Agents: Premarin (conjugated estrogen), Estrace (estradiol), Delestrogen Estraderm Transdermal System (estradiol valerate), Estinyl (ethinyl estradiol), TACE (chlorotrianisene), Ogen (estropipate), and Estragyn 5, Estrone AQ, and Kestrone 5 (estrone), and others.

Progesterone Agents: Provera (medroxyprogesterone), generic hydroxyprogesterone caproate, Ovral (norgestrel and ethinyl estradiol), and others.

Antiandrogen Agents: Anandron, Androcur (cyproterone acetate), Aldactone (spironolactone), Eulexin (flutamide), and others.

FTM Hormone Administration

FTM hormone administration is provided either by biweekly or monthly intramuscular injection or by transdermal patches that are applied nightly and regularly rotated on the upper arms, thighs, back, or abdomen. Typically, individuals

Figure **3.1** *Sample Hormone Administration Consent Form*

are trained in proper sanitation, self-injection, and needle disposal techniques by their physician. Therapeutic benefits include masculinization, body and facial hair growth, deepening of voice pitch, increased muscle mass, and the development of other male secondary sex characteristics. Side effects include facial acne, male-pattern balding, and reduced or interrupted reproductive functioning and menstruation.

For the majority of FTM transgender individuals, hormone administration is safe. However, some individuals are at high risk of developing certain serious diseases that can be life-threatening and may cause temporary or permanent disability or death. The risks associated with hormone administration increase significantly if you smoke; have high blood pressure, diabetes, or high cholesterol; or have a history of blood clotting disorders, heart attack, stroke, angina pectoris, jaundice, or malignant or benign liver tumors.

Testosterone Agents: Delatestryl (testosterone enanthate), DEPO-Testosterone (methyltestosterone), Virilon (testosterone cypionate), Androderm (transdermal testosterone patch).

Follow-up Care

Responsible hormone administration requires regular medical check-ups. These include tests for blood pressure, hormone levels, and liver functioning. Your primary physician should be informed immediately if hormone administration is creating any undesirable or adverse effects.

Consent

Signing this form acknowledges my request for transgender hormone administration. I have read this form in its entirety and have brought any questions to the attention of my physician. I agree to participate in physical examinations and blood tests as requested by my physician(s), and agree to bring to his/her attention any undesirable or adverse effects. If I intend to remain with a current partner, significant other, or spouse, I have disclosed my intentions to initiate hormone administration and have revealed its goals and potential side effects, to that individual.

_____   _____
Client Signature & Date   Physician Signature & Date

Figure **3.1** (*Continued*)

providing information as to potential risks and side effects of hormone administration while preserving the patient's right to pursue physical gender transformation as an outward representation of gender identity. Generally, in regard to insurance coverage, most hormone prescriptions are covered when billing and medical charting does not include unnecessary references to the individual's transgender status, particularly since hormones are routinely prescribed for various medical conditions, such as hormone imbalances and birth control.

Routine laboratory screening of all clients requesting sex hormone administration is advisable. Such screening is necessary to detect previously unknown risk factors, such as elevated blood cholesterol levels or liver dysfunction, which require referral for further medical evaluation. Regular postadministration hormone-level testing is recommended every three months during the first year to determine whether there are sufficient hormone levels in the bloodstream to reach and affect secondary sex–characteristic target tissues. The clinical goal of hormone administration is to adjust the blood levels of hormones so that for MTF individuals, they fall within the high-normal range for the estrogen level of reproductive-age nontransgender women, and for FTM individuals, they fall within the high range for testosterone level as used therapeutically in the treatment of some cancers. This is true for preoperative (gonads intact) and postoperative (gonads absent) individuals; however the hormone dosage differs.

> The clinical goal of hormone administration is to adjust the blood levels of hormones so that for MTF individuals, they fall within the high-normal range for estrogen level of reproductive-age nontransgender women, and for FTM individuals, they fall within the high range for testosterone level as used therapeutically in the treatment of some cancers.

Other useful screening tools include an HIV antibody screening as well as a urine drug screen, which is useful in identifying coexistent conditions that might pose additional risk. These preventive procedures are helpful in avoiding the development of major side effects, especially among those who are poor or medically underserved and who therefore may be at risk of higher incidence of illness. While useful on a medical basis, these tests should be given to the patient only on an optional basis or at the patient's request, as mandatory HIV antibody and drug screening does little more than potentially drive needy patients away from crucial medical intervention. Both tests should be accompanied by pretest counseling, including "safe[r] sex" information where HIV issues are concerned. Physicians and their staff are reminded that the results of these tests (particularly HIV) are confidential and in some locations protected by law. Confidentiality measures are also required by many physicians' liability insurance policies. In some areas, patient charting requires additional confidentiality measures where HIV test results are concerned. In areas where confidentiality is not protected by law, care providers are advised that disregarding patient confidentiality is likely to endanger the individual's psychological, medical, social, family, and employment circumstances.

Hormone administration, as in the case with any medical intervention, is designed with specific outcomes in mind. It is imperative that physicians and consumers communicate so that hormone administration may be tailored as closely as possible to the individual's actual needs. Typically, those who desire to live in role full time will request regimens that produce "more" feminizing or masculinizing effects. Transgenderists, or those who live in role part time (or less), typically will request prescriptions producing moderate androgenizing effects.

It is important for both physicians and clients to understand that more hormones do not necessarily mean better results. In fact, the opposite is often the case. In MTF individuals, excess estrogen highly increases the risk of blood clots without improving feminization; it also exacerbates depression. In FTM individuals excess testosterone is primarily converted into estrogen, which can exacerbate breast cancer as well as produce violent so-called "roid rages" detrimental to the individual's psychological and social well-being.

> It is important for both physicians and clients to understand that more hormones do not necessarily mean better results.

The use of lower hormone levels not only helps safeguard against these risks but also aids the physician and client in evaluating the response to hormone administration. Most clients are very eager to see the physical development of cross-gender secondary sex characteristics. Among some transgender women, breast size is often the primary focus as a perceived measure of femininity. In some instances, the estrogen level will be supratherapeutic (e.g., 400 pg/mL or greater), and no further increase in prescribed estrogen is warranted. Additional time may be required for further physical development.

Realistic expectations for physical development in response to sex hormones are important. Because so many of our physical characteristics are determined by our genetic or biological characteristics, transgender persons may make an approximate comparison of likely results with biological relatives of the gender to which the transgender person seeks to assimilate. In other words, a transgender woman dissatisfied with her breast development should first have a serum estrogen level checked; if maximally therapeutic serum estrogen levels have been reached, she may look to female relatives to get a sense of whether her breast size falls within or short of the range of breast sizes typically found among other women in the family who share her genetic predisposition.

Transgender individuals who are initiating hormone administration are strongly advised to disclose this important step to their partner, spouse, or significant other, particularly in situations where both individuals intend to maintain an existing relationship where intimacy, sharing, and trust are essential factors. Failing to disclose under such circumstances is patently dishonest and illustrates that the individual is not ready to take this important step. A thorough knowledge of the goals and potential side effects of hormone administration is needed by the significant other so that she or he may assess how this change will affect her or him, as well as the transgender partner. Disclosure of an individual's intention to initiate hormone administration requires forethought and a review of communication skills. (See the principles of disclosure outlined in Chapter 2.) Transgender individuals who have difficulty disclosing or feel the need for additional help communicating this important step to a significant other may do so through a third person (such as the individual's Gender Specialist or prescribing physician) who is capable of relaying hormone administration's goals and potential side effects.

> *Caution: The prescription dosages and combinations contained in this section are for physicians' information only. Effective and safe transgender hormone administration can be provided only by a licensed physician (M.D. or D.O.), with individual treatment plans based on routine laboratory testing of hormone levels and knowledge of the patient's health history and predisposing physical characteristics. Physicians are advised to seek additional prescription usage and contraindication information on each product by consulting the most recent* Physician's Desk Reference *(PDR) or the manufacturer.*

Hormone Regimens: Biological Male to Transgender Female (MTF)

Conjugated Estrogen, or Premarin

Description. Conjugated estrogen, or Premarin, is the primary agent used in MTF hormone administration. This product is derived from the urine of pregnant mares. Generic or synthetic conjugated estrogens may not be consistent in dosage; therefore, they are not a suitable replacement for Premarin, and in many circumstances they are not approved for insurance coverage (Medicare or Medi-Cal). The expected physical changes from Premarin usage are increased breast size, decreased testicular and prostate size, increased fat tissue under the skin, shifting of fat tissue to the hip area, reduced coarseness of body hair, and initial weight gain from increased water retention. Total body weight may not always change. The pitch of the voice or length of the penis will not change. Baldness will not be reversed.

The additional use of a progestational drug (progesterone and progestins) with estrogen may have an increased effect upon the physical changes produced by estrogen, especially upon breast development.

Individuals can expect moderate breast growth within two years of consistent hormone usage. However, it should be noted that breast growth is most commonly comparable to that of other genetic family members. Biological clocks in individuals often differ on the basis of racial background, and these differences also may affect growth. Maximal testicular decrease is usually achieved within one year consistent usage.

In patients over age 40 who have not had gonad removal, there is an increasing trend to replace Premarin with the new transdermal estradiol product Estraderm (50–100 mg applied to the skin twice weekly). The objective of patch usage is to minimize threat of phlebitis (blood clotting) in patients of advancing age and to make estrogen available to persons unable to use Premarin. Note: Although the transdermal estradiol product may reduce risks of phlebitis and thromboembolism (increased blood clots in legs, lungs, eyes, and brains), other contraindications remain the same as those listed for Premarin.

We recommend that, when MTF transgender hormone administration with persons who have not had gonad removal is initiated, Premarin be prescribed in the initial range of 1.25–2.5 mg daily. We have found that, even though many transgender clients have taken much higher estrogen dosages in the past or more potent forms of estrogen such as injectable estradiol, lower dosages of Premarin are generally sufficient for maximizing serum estrogen levels and physical changes while minimizing side effects. (See Table 3.1 for an example of the effect of estrogen.) Serum levels occasionally remain low, and a dosage up to 5.0 mg daily can be safely and effectively prescribed.

In patients having gonad removal (orchidectomy or Genital Reassignment Surgery) or other major surgery, hormone administration should be discontinued two weeks prior to surgery and not resumed for three weeks after surgery, to prevent thrombosis or blood clots within major arteries. Three weeks after gonad removal, Premarin may be reintroduced at 1.25 mg daily and adjusted to the lowest possible dosage on the basis of blood laboratory values for post menopausal women. Individuals castrated before fully developing new secondary sex characteristics, such as auto-castration patients, may benefit from slightly higher dosages of Premarin in addition to either a progesterone, an antiandrogen, or both.

Patients who three to six months after initiating Premarin have not had gonad removal, depending on predisposing physical characteristics, may find it beneficial to have an accompanying medication introduced to maximize breast

Table **3.1**

The Effect of Estrogen Administration on Serum Hormone Levels in One Transgender Woman

Premarin Dosage (mg/day)	Date of Test	Testosterone (ng/dL)	Estrogen (pg/mL)
1.25	3/8/95	12	420
2.5	8/3/95	10	520
3.75	5/4/96	—	1300

For further information see, Table 3.2.

> In patients having gonad removal (orchidectomy or Genital Reassignment
> Surgery) or other major surgery, hormone administration should be discon-
> tinued two weeks prior to surgery and not resumed for three weeks after sur-
> gery, to prevent thrombosis or blood clots within major arteries.

development, minimize hair follicle production, or both. There are a variety of
hormone combinations available to achieve these goals, and although many physicians prescribe either or both a progesterone and an antiandrogen, we cannot
recommend any one particular combination as more effective than others. Generally, each combination has predictable associated results, and we advise physicians
to match the associated result with the patient's predisposing physical characteristics and stated goals. Routinely prescribed combinations and associated results are
as follows: Progesterone combined with Premarin has an increased effect upon
physical changes produced by estrogen, particularly upon breast development; anti-
androgens combined with Premarin block testosterone efficacy on target tissues,
enhance estrogen efficacy, and most prevent hair follicle production.

Another routinely used combination is Premarin with birth control medications, specifically those containing norgestrel and ethinyl estradiol (Ovral). Norgestrel is a progesterone agent that increases estrogen effectiveness and breast
development; however, it does not prevent hair-follicle production. Ovral, the
single available brand of norgestrel and ethinyl estradiol, is easy to prescribe and
readily accessible to consumers. Premarin and Ovral are also a combination of
choice for transgender women who ask to cycle hormone administration so as to
mimic the natural biological rhythm of genetic females. With cycling, Premarin
administration is continuous while Ovral is cycled—twenty-one days on and
seven days off. Physicians may advise their clients that although there are no
contraindications against cycling, doing so within the first year of hormone administration may slow the development of new secondary sex characteristics.
Additionally, these persons should be prepared for the emotional changes associated with any change in hormone levels.

Although extremely rare, some persons claim to have a dermatologic allergic
reaction to Premarin. Although Premarin primarily contains estrone, it may also
contain impurities and horse estrogens not found in humans. Premarin may be
replaced with Ogen (estropipate) or Estrace (estradiol), which are synthesized in
a plant base. Additionally, spironolactone is less likely to cause rashes. Alternative
estrogen therapies also include the following: oral synthetic ethinyl estradiol (Estinyl: dosage 0.1–0.5 mg/day), intramuscular estradiol valerate (Delestrogen:
15–80 mg/month), estradiol undecanoate (200–800 mg/month), estradiol cypionate (Depo-Estradiol: 1–5 mg/week), or estradiol benzoate (0.5–1.5 mg two
or three times per week).

Side Effects. Complications for transgender women with biological risk factors
or for those who have had excessive estrogen therapy include the sequelae of

thromboembolism (blood clots in the legs, lungs, eyes, brain—as in strokes—or other organs); a tenfold increased risk of breast cancer; liver disease; heart disease, including myocardial infarction; high blood pressure; sterility; and mood changes (e.g., irritability, depression, or euphoria); decreased sexual desire without affecting sexual arousal. Smoking increases the risk of blood clots with estrogen therapy, particularly after age 40.

Progesterones

Description. Progesterone is largely responsible for the physiological changes associated with menstrual cycles in biological females. Progesterone is also frequently prescribed as a supplement to estrogen therapy for transgender women. Provera is the trade name for the most widely used synthetic form, medroxyprogesterone. Provera is most commonly administered orally at 2.5–10 mg/day. Micronized natural progesterone, available through compounding pharmacies, is administered 100–400 mg/twice per day. Micronized natural progesterone may also be given in the form of vaginal or rectal suppositories, and the dosages are the same as for oral progesterone. (Micronized natural progesterone may also be independently tested in blood levels: 4–25 ng/mL, the same ranges as during ovulation). Progesterone is also available in hydroxyprogesterone caproate, given by injection at 250 mg per month. Combinations of these with Premarin are routine approaches toward effectively suppressing testosterone and maximizing breast size. Norgestrel .5 mg with ethinyl estradiol .05 mg, a birth control agent, is also routinely used as a replacement for Provera.

Side Effects. Complications for transgender women with biological risk factors or with a history of excessive progesterone usage include thromboembolism (blood clots) in the legs, lungs, eyes, brain—as in strokes—or other organs; a tenfold increased risk of breast cancer; liver disease; heart disease, including myocardial infarction; high blood pressure; sterility; mood changes (e.g., irritability, depression, or euphoria); and decreased sexual desire without affecting sexual arousal.

Spironolactone

Description. Spironolactone is a commonly prescribed antiandrogen that decreases testosterone levels by limiting its synthesis and by blocking its effects upon target tissues. Estrogen levels are increased, The dosages of spironolactone range from 200 to 600 mg/day. Serum levels of testosterone are reduced to within the average range found among biological females (20–80 ng/dL). Also a treatment for hirsutism in biological females, spironolactone reduces male-pattern hair growth and penile erections, while increasing breast development.

Side Effects. Side effects include weakness, fatigue, decreased appetite, weight gain, headache, and excessive thirst or urination.

Flutamide

Description. The only form of flutamide available in the United States is sold under the trade name Eulexin; it is prescribed in dosages of 750 mg/day (250 mg/three times daily, orally). It is not as effective as cyproterone acetate, but it has been widely used for prostate disease with excellent results. Like other anti-androgens, it can markedly reduce body hair and allow lower estrogen dosages.

Side Effects. The side effects of flutamide include hot flashes, loss of libido, diarrhea, nausea, and other mild gastrointestinal disturbances.

Cyproterone acetate

Description. Cyproterone acetate is a synthetic steroid most often sold under the trade names Anandron and Androcur. These medications contain the same active chemical ingredients but were originally marketed for separate medical purposes by different manufacturers. Cyproterone acetate directly reduces testosterone levels and effects, especially when accompanying orchidectomy and electrolysis of facial hair. Prescribed at 50–100 mg/day, these medications decrease hair on the limbs and trunk of the body, with little effect upon facial hair. Preexisting masculine hair growth such as beard growth and baldness are only slightly reduced. Cyproterone acetate allows for more effective estrogen administration with smaller dosages. This agent is considered a standard regimen for hormone administration in European countries, Canada, Mexico, Australia, and New Zealand. Cyproterone acetate is not available in the United States except through foreign sources. U.S. residents obtaining pharmaceuticals from foreign sources are advised not to self-medicate and to work with their physicians to obtain maximum hormone benefits with optimum regular follow-up care.

> Cyproterone acetate is not available in the United States except through foreign sources. U.S. residents obtaining pharmaceuticals from foreign sources are advised not to self-medicate and to work with their physicians to obtain maximum hormone benefits with optimum regular follow-up care.

Side Effects. Some persons on cyproterone acetate therapies may experience difficulty visually adapting to darkness. The manufacturers' inserts list other side effects.

Hormone Regimens: Biological Female to Transgender Male (FTM)

Injectable Testosterone

Transgender men usually have quite effective development of male sex characteristics of facial hair, increased muscle mass, male-pattern pubic hair growth, and thickening of skin with injections of testosterone cypionate or testosterone enanthate (200 mg twice monthly). Testosterone cypionate is more commonly prescribed, as it is most effective in producing masculine characteristics. Oral testosterone agents are not used in FTM hormone administration because they do not produce intended effects as a result of being overprocessed in the liver. The testosterone dosages included herein are for use by FTM individuals who have not had removal of estrogen-producing organs, and should faciliate the common goal of cessation of menses within three months. FTM individuals who have had surgical removal of estrogen-producing organs require lower dosages of testosterone. Dosages for FTM patients who have had castration should be adjusted to produce testosterone serum levels of 225–900 ng/dL.

Self-Injection

Like those with diabetes mellitus, FTM transgender individuals occasionally self administer injections under a physician's prescription and instructions. Self-administration is not advised during the first three months of initial hormone administration because of the necessity for the physician to monitor effects. Typically, after individual dosage requirements are assessed, physicians provide a three- to six-month supply of hormones and a needle prescription. Minimally, long-term medical follow-up should take place biannually, follow-up should be more frequent if the individual's health status requires it.

Most physicians prescribe single-usage needles. However, to save money some individuals "clean" and re-use needles. To prevent transmission of the HIV virus and other viruses transported by body fluids, individuals re-using needles should clean them with chlorine bleach. Chlorine bleach must completely fill both the syringe and the needle for at least 30 seconds to ensure effectiveness against HIV infection. This procedure should be repeated three times, rinsing with water between each bleaching and at the end of the cleansing process. This recommendation is the most up-to-date from the Institute for Community Health Outreach (ICHO) in San Francisco, California.

Transdermal Testosterone

Transdermal patches can provide successful hormone administration in place of intramuscular injection. Applied preferably before bedtime, two patches provide 5 mg of testosterone daily. Patches may be worn on the upper arms, thighs, backs, or abdomen, and they stay intact during most activities, including showering. Individuals who regularly replace and use patches will find that their consistent delivery system eliminates the peaks and troughs associated with intramuscular injection. Additionally, users will find that when transdermal patches are paired with regular blood testing of hormone levels, mood swings are eliminated. Otherwise, contraindications and side effects remain the same as those associated with intramuscular injection.

Side Effects

The major risks associated with excessive doses of testosterone are increased cholesterol and higher lipid levels; heart disease, including myocardial infarction; mood changes (irritability or depression); male-pattern baldness; acne; and cessation of menses within three months of continual usage. Smoking increases the risk of coronary heart disease in FTM individuals using testosterone.

Mood changes, sometimes called "roid rages," typically occur in the initial stages of testosterone administration, primarily because of body chemical adjustment. These mood changes can be experienced as feelings of irritability, intense anger, or depression. Symptoms can also be exacerbated by preexisting clinical depression. Unbearable or uncontrolled moodiness may be relieved by lowering agent dosage. Symptoms lasting six months or longer, after initial hormone administration, may require a psychodynamic approach, that is, instruction in anger management.

Acne predominantly occurs with testosterone cypionate administration. Major outbreaks are more likely to occur during the initial stages of hormone administration, subsequently dissipating as the individual's system becomes accustomed to the hormone regimen. Over the long term, some individuals have an outbreak of acne within a few days after a dose; less frequently, others may have an outbreak a few days before a dose is due. Most outbreaks occur in the chest and back areas; fewer individuals experience outbreaks on the face or neck. Acne may be best managed with twice-daily cleansing. Severe eruptions and infections (acne vulgaris) may be treated with physician prescribed topical therapy (benzoyl peroxide, tretinoin and topical antibiotics), or systemic antibiotics (tetracycline, doxycycline, erythromycin, or other antibiotics), or both topical and systemic medications. Antiandrogen therapy in FTM transgender individuals would be counterproductive.

Natural Hormones and Compounding Laboratories

In recent years there has been a growing trend among consumers, particularly transgender women, of seeking natural hormone products, ranging from newly developed lubricants to natural estrogens. Physicians can often individualize prescription formulas to address a wide variety of cosmetic and medical needs.

Micronized natural estrogen or progesterone may be used as a replacement for synthetic hormones. In cases where male-pattern balding is at beginning stages, various topical applications can be compounded and may prove successful (e.g., minoxidil 2%–4%, Retin-A (tretinoin) 0.05%, spironolactone 2%, estradiol 0.05% diluted to 60mL/topical base, applied twice daily). The preceding is one such formula (unstudied), and physicians are advised to develop formulas that are individualized to match patient symptoms. Individuals on maximum hormone regimens will not receive additional benefit from topical hormone compounds. However, persons initiating transition or who are not interested in the full feminizing effects of hormone administration would benefit from the usage of the hormones contained in topical compounds. This latter group of individuals would include pretransitional transsexuals, FTM transsexuals, transgenderists, and crossdressers.

Consumers are encouraged to discuss the benefits of using formulary prescriptions with their physicians and are reminded that insurance coverage may not be applicable for compounded prescriptions. A local formulary pharmacy may be located by calling the International Academy of Compounding Pharmacists (800-927-4227). Natural estrogen products are available through a variety of merchants, including Bajamar (800-255-8025) or the Women's International Pharmacy (800-279-5708).

Clinical Laboratory Values

Regular blood testing is an integral part of hormone administration. Before hormone administration begins, blood tests should be done so as to provide a baseline for later reference with regard to hormonal effects on blood chemistry. The data in Table 3.2 reflect normal values in biological females and males. The normal values are based upon average cumulative results for all adult persons tested by SmithKline Beecham Clinical Laboratories (800-332-7525). Physicians are advised that values vary widely among laboratories, and the results of any individual blood test must be interpreted by the physician who orders the test.

For precastration MTF individuals, the female values should be referenced. Optimally, therapeutic estrogen levels in these MTF individuals will fall within the 400–800 pg/mL range, and testosterone will fall between the high female and low male ranges. In postcastration MTF individuals, estrogen values may fall in subtherapeutic ranges from 40 to 400 pg/mL, and testosterone will fall between 25 and 95 pg/mL as standard for biological females. In pre- and postcastration MTF individuals, estradiol may fall within 10–400 pg/mL. (See Table 3.3.)

For FTM individuals whose gonads remain intact, the male values should be referenced. Testosterone levels in these FTM individuals should fall within the 225–900 ng/dL range, and estrogen should fall under 400 pg/mL. In FTM

Table **3.2**

Normal Blood Chemistry Values in Biological Femals and Males

Test	All Adults	Female Only	Male Only	Units
Estrogen		40–400	<40	pg/mL
Estrogen	(Therapeutic)	400–800		pg/mL
Testosterone		25–95	225–900	ng/dL
Prolactin		3–30	2–18	ng/mL
LH		0.8–57	2.5–6	mIU/mL
FSH		08–21	0.9–15	mIU/mL
Estradiol		10–400	<50	pg/mL
Prolactin		3–30	2–18	ng/mL
Glucose	70–125	Fasting		mg/dL
Urea Nitrogen	7–25			mg/dL
Creatinine	0.7–1.4			mg/dL
Sodium	135–146			mEq/L
Potassium	3.5–5.3			mEq/L
Chloride	95–108			mEq/L
Magnesium	1.2–2.0			mEq/L
Calcium	8.5–10.3			mg/dL
Phosphorous	2.5–4.5			mg/dL
Protein	6.0–8.5			g/dL
Albumin	2.2–4.2			g/dL
Bilirubin	0–1.3			mg/dL
Alkaline Phosphatase	20–125			U/L
Lactate Dehydrogenase	0–270			U/L
GGT	0–65			U/L
ALT (SGPT)	0–48			U/L
AST (SGOT)	0–42			U/L
Uric Acid		2.5–7.5	4.0–8.5	mg/dL
Iron	25–70			μg/dL
Triglycerides	<200			mg/dL
Cholesterol	<200			mg/dL
White Cells	3.8–10.8			thous/μL
Red Cells		3.9–5.2	4.4–5.8	mill/μL
Hemoglobin		12.0–15.6	13.8–17.2	g/dL
Hematocrit		35–46	41–50	%
Platelets	130–400			thous/μL

Table **3.3**

Reference Ranges

Testosterone	25–95 ng/dL for biological females
Testosterone Therapy	225–900 ng/dL for transgender males (FTM)
Estrogen	40–450 pg/mL for biological females
Estrogen Therapy	400–800 pg/mL for transgender women (MTF)

individuals whose gonads have been removed, testosterone may fall between 225 and 900 ng/dL, and estrogen may be less than 40 pg/mL. (See Table 3.3)

Recommended Guidelines for Hormone Administration

Caution: A full understanding of these guidelines is not possible without reading the material in the preceding sections of this chapter. They contain relevant pharmacological, medical, psychological, and insurance information. Depending on individual patient medical condition, drug side effects, and predisposing physical characteristics, hormone administration can effectively produce intended psychological and physical outcomes.

■ _____

The Guidelines acknowledge that until recently, nontranssexual transgender populations seeking hormone administration have been ignored by professional standards. We recommend hormone administration as appropriate to all transgender populations. No individual should be denied hormones solely on the basis of self-definition of gender identity.

Any FTM or MTF transgender individual may be referred in writing by a Gender Specialist to any physician with a recommendation for hormone administration under the following guidelines:

1. The recommendation letter maintains that the individual wishing to initiate hormone administration has maintained a counseling or support relationship with a recognized Gender Specialist for a minimum of three months.

1a. The counseling or support relationship is left under a broad interpretation wherein the support specialist and client mutually agree on how time should be used. Although full disclosure regarding the effects and contraindications of hormone administration fall under the responsibility of the prescribing physician, Gender Specialists will provide an assessment of the individual's level of knowledge concerning hormone usage and desired outcome.

1b. Exceptions to the three-month assessment period may be considered by the evaluating Gender Specialist or the prescribing physician if a well-established transgender identity exists and other aspects of the Recommended Guidelines for Hormone Administration are observed.

2. Transgender individuals appropriate for hormone administration include those who have in the preceding three months consistently expressed interest in the permanent physical changes brought on by hormones, to bring body in line with an intended masculine, feminine, or androgynous appearance. In the transsexual individual, early hormone administration reduces social stigmatization and enhances the possibility of a successful presentation.

2a. The referral maintains that the transgender individual has the capacity to clearly understand anticipated physical, emotional, and social changes, as well as any drawbacks associated with hormone administration.

2b. The individual is not currently suffering from self-abuse, suicidal behaviors, psychotic thought patterns, or severe psychological symptoms. Gender Specialists uncertain as to whether these conditions exist are recommended to seek professional mental health consultation.

3. The prescribing physician is advised to take steps to ensure that the individual will follow prescribed dosages, keep regular medical appointments, and allow recommended laboratory tests and physical exams.

3a. Physicians may at times encounter individuals who desperately resort to black-market hormones or the use of others' prescriptions for a variety of reasons, such as the lack of emotional support, advisory information, or financial ability. Additionally, some persons may be impaired by alcoholism, substance abuse, or inadequate decision-making skills. These latter individuals are often unable (or unwilling) to maintain recommended levels of medical follow-up. The physician may therefore initiate short-term prescribing contracts utilizing lower dosage regimens until the individual has demonstrated a capacity for responsible self-care.

3b. Physicians are advised to remain abreast of the mental health and support concerns of their patients through active consultation with a qualified Gender Specialist. They should also may maintain up-to-date references, where supporting transgender individuals is concerned, through continued contact with professional transgender support and educational organizations.

3c. Physicians are advised that including a transsexualism diagnosis in medical charting may compromise an individual's workplace stability. This is particularly so if the person has not come out in the workplace and is currently establishing transition goals. Physicians may utilize a diagnosis of hormone imbalance or other applicable diagnosis to prevent placing their patient in a compromising situation.

4. Routine liver-function tests should be made, and cholesterol levels, blood pressure, heart rates, and weight gain should be closely monitored. A preadministration baseline hormone level screening should be done, with subsequent three-month follow-up after hormone administration is initiated. Long-term hormone-level monitoring should occur every six to twelve months as determined by individual health needs.

5. To date, there are no known physical side effects in the cessation of hormone administration in MTF individuals. Although feminization will gradually reverse, complete reversal of breast-tissue growth and reintroduction of virility may not be possible without surgical or hormonal intervention. In FTM individuals there have been several isolated cases of internal bleeding associated with abrupt testosterone cessation. Physicians and FTM individuals are advised to monitor testosterone cessation, providing for gradual reduction should bleeding occur. Masculinization is difficult to reverse; it requires voice therapy, electrolysis, and breast augmentation.

6. Transgender individuals intending to remain with a permanent partner, significant other, or spouse are advised to disclose their intentions of initiating hormone administration, as well as its goals and potential side effects, to that partner.

7. With the exception of physician-prescribed estrogen creams used to increase lubrication and vaginal cellular wall thickness, nonmedical estrogen creams as well as herbal hormones are not efficacious substitutes for traditional hormone administration. At most, these products may enhance hormones that are already present in the human body. Transgender individuals are advised to be wary of merchants offering products with claims of producing rapid feminization or masculinization.

8. Transgender men and women who are institutionalized or incarcerated are advised that many institutional policies provide for hormone administration, counseling, and group support. However, frequently institutional administrators and physicians circumvent these policies and may refuse to provide transgender persons access to medical and psychological care. In these circumstances, individuals are advised to document their requests and institutional responses, file appeals or grievances per institutional policy, and contact legal assistance and institutional rights organizations.

9. Pharmaceutical regulation and prescription drug availability frequently varies between countries and locations. If a prescription drug is not legally available or cannot be compounded, physicians are advised to consult the *Physician's Desk Reference* (*PDR*) or other professional reference in order to determine what suitable replacements exist.

Transgender Aesthetic Surgery

Chapter 4

Aesthetic surgery, as we use the term, refers to cosmetic surgical procedures that do not involve the genitals. Motivation for seeking these procedures is as varied as the individuals who seek them, but for most, an underlying wish to bring body in line with a desired gender presentation is paramount. Results can vary, depending on the surgeon's skills, patient's physical health and age, the quality of postoperative medical treatment, and patient self-care. Most procedures approximate desired outcomes, but consumers are advised to frame their expectations cautiously, as no amount of plastic surgery can fully reproduce naturally acquired attributes.

Principles of Transgender Aesthetic Surgery

As with any surgical procedure, the effects are usually permanent, or at least long-lasting, and as such, will have social, psychological, and physical consequences. *Transgender Care* discourages individuals from seeking any procedure without first having acquired a full understanding of the procedure and secured reliable references for the practicing surgeon. The decision to undergo a cosmetic or surgical procedure should not be made lightly. It should be an important part of self-integration and reflection processes.

Transgender individuals who intend to remain with a partner, significant other, or spouse are strongly advised to disclose their intention to undergo an aesthetic surgical procedure to that individual, as failure to do so may severely damage trust values in that relationship. In addition, a significant other will often play an important role in an individual's postoperative recuperation process. Thus, knowledge about the goals and complication risks associated with the procedure should be made available to them.

It should be noted that nontransgender individuals are not required to fulfill any mental health recommendation process to obtain aesthetic surgical procedures, and in some cases such procedures may be covered by insurance. Although some procedures are carried out as emergency medical interventions, such as in the case of injury by accident or fire, the majority of these procedures are sought by consumers purely for personal cosmetic reasons.

Transgender Care advocates that it is unnecessary to require mental health recommendations of transgender consumers when such endorsements are not sought from nontransgender individuals. Rather, it is strongly advised that transgender consumers both self-initiate a waiting period and talk with more than one surgeon, after deciding a procedure is right for them. Consumers should also speak with a few individuals who have undergone the anticipated procedure. If uncertain as to how long a waiting period is appropriate, individuals should consult with either a surgeon or Gender Specialist for further information.

It should be noted that *Transgender Care* represents the first time that breast augmentation for MTF individuals and mastectomy or chest reconstruction for FTM individuals have been clearly defined as *aesthetic* surgical procedures. These procedures do not affect reproductive capacity, are not as surgically invasive as genital reassignment, and are cosmetically reversible. Furthermore, an individual's use of these procedures in many circumstances may reduce social stigmatization and enhance the possibility of a successful presentation. Unlike genitalia, rarely displayed publicly, the presence or absence of breasts plays a large role in a woman's or a man's gender presentation.

Depending on where transgender consumers receive support services, they are likely to encounter different real-life test protocols (see Chapter 1) as they initiate a search for breast or other surgical procedures. This is because each gender program, clinic, and private practitioner establishes a referral protocol on the basis of staff psychotherapeutic or medical training, staff knowledge of gender issues, and perhaps a research protocol. Although some care providers may have up-to-date knowledge on support issues and available procedures, others may be utilizing a protocol that is not inclusive of all transgender populations or their needs. Additionally, many out-of-date protocols may still link breast or chest procedures with an individual's intention to seek Genital Reassignment Surgery. We advise against such linkage, as it has proven exclusionary to transgenderist populations and does not properly take presentation issues into account. The Guidelines take into consideration these issues, while at the same time preserving consumer and medical precautions.

Consumer Preparedness

Aesthetic or cosmetic surgical procedures are designed to help enhance an individual's physical presentation by minimizing the physical characteristics of gender that the individual does not want, and by enhancing those gender characteristics the individual desires. Consideration of any aesthetic surgical procedure frequently introduces a host of questions between the surgeon and surgical candidate: Will the surgery result in the desired presentation? What motivations lie behind the individual's wish for surgery? Could the individual's desire to have multiple procedures be a sign of a compulsion?

These all are legitimate questions, and each should be discussed between surgeon and candidate. Surgery can, in most circumstances, approximate a desired presentation, although no one should expect miracles. Bringing body in line with a desired gender presentation seems to be a reasonable motivation for aesthetic surgery; however, the surgical candidate should not view the surgery as an immediate remedy for existing social, relationship, or presentation difficulties. One cannot broadly judge how many surgeries are too many, although surgical candidates should be apprised that since each surgery is an invasive procedure having its own recovery time, numerous procedures in one location increases complication rates while lowering chances of proper healing.

In the past, being a well-informed medical consumer has not been emphasized as a priority for transgender individuals, and all too frequently consumer education is overlooked by care providers in giving referrals for aesthetic and other surgical procedures. Considerable emphasis has typically been placed on care providers' "assessing" a transgender individual's appropriateness for a masculinizing or feminizing aesthetic surgical procedure despite the fact that non-transgender individuals rarely undergo such grueling scrutiny when requesting similar cosmetic surgeries to bring their bodies in line with their desired physical presentations.

Breast augmentation mammoplasty in MTF transgender individuals and mastectomy or chest reconstruction in FTM transgender individuals have generated the most controversy. In all too many instances, nontransgender women can walk into a cosmetic surgeon's office, hand over a credit card, and with few questions, receive breast implants. Ironically, those transgender women who were unaware of or chose to ignore professional opinions simply searched until they found a surgeon willing to perform the procedure. In contrast, numerous transgender individuals have endured great difficulty, with physical discomfort and gender dysphoria, by following care providers' advice and forgoing such procedures for long periods of time while living in role.

Every controversy has its own tragedy, and so too does this one. More than a few individuals have been erroneously advised by care providers that breast augmentation was impermissible unless done in conjunction with Genital Reassignment Surgery. Frequently such misguidance was accompanied by pressure toward one particularly overpriced surgeon while failing to advise the individual about alternative surgeons, procedures, or prices. One person spent seven years under the influence of such a professional, who even went so far as to discourage her from meeting other transgender individuals. Situations such as these become likely when transgender individuals mistake self-promoting colonizers of a particular medical process for trustworthy professionals. Readers interested in consumer awareness will find additional information in the section on consumer preparedness in Chapter 5.

Types of Procedures

Male to Female

Breast Augmentation. Breast augmentation is a surgical procedure whose objective is to simulate or enhance natural breasts. Silicone envelopes containing saline (salt water) are placed either behind the breast gland or behind the pectoralis major muscle of the chest. The approach can either be inframammary (below the breast), periareolar (near the nipple), or axillary (through the armpit area). There has been some controversy regarding the use of silicone gel implants, and they have been taken off the market by the U.S. Food and Drug Administration as a result of concerns that silicone may leak and collect in areas affecting major organ function. Saline breast implants have shown no such side effects.

Possible side effects include loss of physical sensation around the breast and nipple areas, as well as coolness of the skin. Implants can also rupture and cause whatever material is within the envelope to leak into local tissues. In these cases, the implants are removed and replaced. It is strongly suggested that the transgender individual first determine if hormone administration would provide sufficient breast development before seeking breast augmentation surgery. Generally speaking, however, breast augmentation is a safe procedure that may be done alone or in conjunction with other procedures, such as Genital Reassignment Surgery.

Silicone Injections. Needle-injection gelatinous silicone has been declared illegal in the United States and in most countries with similar food and drug precautions. Silicone migrates and deposits throughout the body, dangerously affecting major organ function. This procedure is most commonly offered by incompetent and unscrupulous doctors and other practitioners who prey off the transgender community, especially sex-industry workers. Gelatinous silicone injected by needles should not be confused with the semi-rigid silicone type of prosthesis surgically implanted for facial enhancement, FTM genital construction, and other procedures. Semi-rigid prostheses are commonly used and legal in most places. See the section on alternate procedures, below.

Tracheal Shave. Tracheal shave is a surgical procedure that reduces prominence of tracheal cartilage, also known as the "Adam's apple." Although a seemingly simple procedure, it is somewhat delicate because the vocal cords are tethered directly behind this structure. Change in voice pitch and hoarseness may occur postsurgically, although neither is usually permanent. Permanent damage can result after a tracheal shave if there has been prior damage to the voice box; otherwise, no other contraindications are known to exist for this procedure.

Voice Augmentation. Voice augmentation is a surgical procedure used to tighten vocal cords in MTF transgender individuals to bring the voice into a higher range. This procedure is considered experimental and is not widely performed. Voice augmentation is indicated only after an individual has made a dedicated effort at adjusting her speech in collaboration with a speech pathologist. The procedure, with its inherent risks, should not be considered a substitute for skills that can be learned through individual effort and training. Additionally, individuals who smoke are usually not allowed to undergo the procedure.

Out of eight individuals we contacted with who have undergone the procedure, two have reported good results and began speaking immediately. The remaining individuals reported undesirable complications, including loss of voice well beyond postoperative recovery time, undesirable tones, unexpected pitch and huskiness, and shortened duration of conversations. One individual we spoke with found herself unable to speak more than a few hours per day. Another stated that within six months of surgery, her voice became an octave lower than it had been prior to the procedure.

False Rib Removal. Widely performed in Europe, surgical removal of the false rib is a procedure typically not available in the United States. The procedure allows for an individual to have a smaller waistline; however, it cannot replace the benefits of regular exercise and a healthy, low-fat diet. Side effects include potential damage to lower chest wall rigidity, impairment of lower lung inflatability, as well as contraindications typically associated with general surgery.

Female to Male Bilateral Mastectomy or Chest Reconstruction

Bilateral mastectomy is a common surgical procedure wherein the breasts are permanently removed and the nipple complex is repositioned to give the appearance of a masculine chest. Scarring is typically minimal, although the postsurgical patient should be prepared for a one-month recovery period during which arm usage is initially discouraged to protect the surgical site against rupture of the sutures or other serious damage.

The Guidelines suggest a six-month waiting period before referral is made for a bilateral mastectomy or chest reconstruction procedure. Many FTM individuals may have been living in role for a significant amount of time prior to seeking the procedure; however, this is not always the case. Consumers and professionals are encouraged to consider referrals on a case-by-case basis. Physicians, Gender Specialists, and FTM individuals are advised that long-term preoperative breast binding for presentation purposes can result in damage to the chest and cause breathing difficulties.

Alternate Procedures for Both Populations

Alternate procedures primarily sought out by MTF individuals are numerous and include rhinoplasty (nose augmentation), face lifts, acid peels, chin reductions, forehead lifts, and brow shaves. FTM individuals who develop severe acne scarring may find professional dermatologic treatment of this condition beneficial. Because this surgical specialty field is constantly expanding, these procedures are too numerous to discuss in detail. For a brief overview of MTF facial reconstructive procedures and plastic surgery information, please see the detailed essay by Dr. Douglas Ousterhout (Chapter 17).

Recommended Guidelines for Aesthetic Surgery

The Guidelines acknowledge that nontranssexual transgender populations seeking aesthetic surgical procedures have been ignored by previous professional standards. We additionally acknowledge that for some individuals, fulfilling a real-life test would be virtually impossible without some type of prior surgical intervention. Consequently, we recommend aesthetic surgery as appropriate to all transgender populations, since no individual should be denied surgical intervention solely on the basis of self-definition of gender identity. Gender Specialists, physicians, and other care providers are cautioned to strongly advise consumers to undertake a six-month waiting period prior to aesthetic surgery, once a consistent decision to have a procedure has been made. Care providers and surgeons are further advised that in some circumstances a real-life test may be physically impossible prior to surgical intervention.

> *Caution: A full understanding of these Guidelines is not possible without reading the preceding sections of this chapter. They contain relevant medical, psychological, insurance, and historical information, as well as vital consumer educational information. Readers are reminded that aesthetic surgical procedures can effectively produce the intended physical and psychological outcomes with a balanced consideration of the patient's surgical preparedness, variable risks associated with all surgical procedures, and recognized medical and consumer recommendations.*

1. Any transgender individual may be referred in writing by a Gender Specialist or an individual's primary physician under the following guidelines:

1a. The referral maintains that the individual has consistently for at least six months expressed within the counseling, support, or medical relationship her or his interest in the permanent physical changes brought about by the surgical procedure.

1b. The referral maintains that the transgender individual has the capacity to clearly understand and accept responsibility for the physical, emotional, and social changes, as well as any contraindications, associated with the procedure.

2. Competent surgeons are advised to screen patients for preexisting health conditions that might hinder surgical outcomes, as well as to practice accepted surgical procedures. This includes following universal blood and body fluid precautions to reduce the possibility of blood-transmitted diseases.

3. Surgical approaches to HIV-related and other immunosuppressive conditions are covered in the guidelines at the end of Chapter 6.

4. MTF consumers considering aesthetic surgical procedures that enhance secondary sex characteristics such as breast augmentation are strongly advised to first undergo hormone administration, allowing an opportunity for adequate therapeutic results to develop, before undergoing a physically invasive surgical procedure. Maximum breast growth varies from individual to individual, depending on predisposing physical characteristics, and is typically achieved within one or two years of uninterrupted hormone administration.

5. Both MTF and FTM consumers are strongly advised where at all possible to undertake a minimum six-month, full-time real-life test prior to undergoing any aesthetic surgical procedure. It is essential that aesthetic surgery directly correlate with having experienced both six months of hormone administration and living in role part or full time. This experience serves to confirm that the goal of surgery is to bring a person's physical body in line with actual gender identity. Although sometimes procedures are wholly or partially cosmetically reversible, the consequences of undergoing aesthetic surgery do include serious physical, emotional, social, and financial implications.

6. Breast-binding, particularly in large-breasted FTM individuals, may result in permanent dermatologic scarring. This factor should be considered by physicians and FTM individuals during a mastectomy or chest reconstruction presurgical interview.

7. Consumers considering a cosmetic or surgical procedure are advised to fully research a proposed surgeon's credentials, affiliations, and references.

Genital Reassignment Surgery and Gonad Removal (Castration)

Chapter 5

Genital-reassignment procedures include gonad removal and genital removal as well as reconstructive procedures such as orchidectomy, penectomy, genito-vaginoplasty, or labiaplasty for the MTF individual; or hysterectomy, oophorectomy, salpingectomy, vaginectomy, genito-phalloplasty for the FTM individual. For purposes of clarity, the term *Genital Reassignment Surgery* (GRS) refers to preexisting gonad and genital removal as well as to neo-genital surgical construction. *Gonad-removal surgery* (castration) refers to the removal of reproductive glands only.

The Guidelines specifically use *Genital Reassignment Surgery* instead of *Sex Reassignment Surgery,* or *SRS*. The old terminology is outdated and stereotypical. A transgender person's "sex" is not reassigned completely by a surgeon. Transition is also accomplished with the aid of hormone administration, aesthetic surgeries, and living in role part or full time as a member of the opposite gender. The words *genital reassignment* more accurately portray the goals as well as the outcome of surgical procedures designed to remove gonads or reassign and reconstruct a transgender person's genitals in order to bring the physical body in line with outward gender presentation. Legally, particularly within the United States, a transgender man or woman may have his or her sex reassigned on paper (identification) by the physician who provides hormone administration. These individuals' legal sex is changed without actually having had a genital-reassignment procedure.

By conservative estimates, since the late 1970s approximately 10,000 Genital Reassignment Surgeries have been successfully performed worldwide. This figure includes approximately 4,500 surgeries performed on U.S. residents; 2,500 in western Europe and North Africa; 1,500 in the United Kingdom (in England and Australia the procedure is provided to citizens under national health coverage); and 1,000 in the Southeast Asian and Pacific Rim countries. These estimates are based on interviews with surgeons and consumers in those locations.

Gonad-removal surgery (castration), particularly among MTF transgender individuals, is estimated to exceed 10,000 worldwide. This figure is based on an estimate that for every Genital Reassignment Surgery performed, approximately one castration is performed on a transgender individual, who may or may not undergo GRS at a later time. Castration is primarily sought out by those who foresee a long-term inability to undergo GRS because of financial or health barriers. In some situations, castration may have benefits beyond meeting psychological and physical needs, entering the world of the spiritual. For instance, in India castration is routinely performed by group leaders for those undergoing initiation into a life-long spiritual caste of Hijra individuals.

Principles of Genital Reassignment Surgery

Clearly, both Genital Reassignment Surgery and castration are medical procedures that assist the individual in bringing the physical body in line with self-identification of gender and social presentation, and both can effectively produce the intended psychological and physical outcomes. As with many surgical procedures that have gained significance over the past decade, Genital Reassignment Surgery and gonad removal are no longer considered experimental.

As Gender Specialists have come to recognize a transgender individual's self-definition of gender identity as a healthy process, we believe that surgeons and insurance providers must view Genital Reassignment Surgery and gonad removal as established, essential procedures benefiting the medical and psychological well-being of many transgender persons when provided under recognized guidelines. To date, numerous reconstructive surgeons have provided these procedures to the life-long benefit of their patients. In some circumstances, insurance providers have covered costs when insurance claims adjusters have been made aware of up-to-date information and guidelines.

While surgeons constantly refine surgical techniques so as to provide higher post-surgical patient satisfaction with Genital Reassignment Surgery, standards defining a surgical candidate's appropriateness for GRS remained in question because they did not include all transgender populations. Furthermore, while the majority of surgeons, psychotherapists, and gender organizations seek to protect unstable individuals from permanent mishap, others frequently question why surgery-on-demand is not available, or why crossliving requirements exist at all. These controversies have heightened as more transgender individuals surface and seek gender-integrating procedures.

Some professionals and consumers feel that educational information and guidelines should remain hidden and inaccessible to consumers, while others share the authors' belief that guidelines should be openly established and should reflect both professional expertise and transgender consumer experiences and rights. Authored, reviewed, and promoted by a team of professionals and consumers, the Guidelines presented herein promote professional and transgender consumer education and interaction, as well as the highest quality of psychological, social, and medical services.

Requirements for a real-life test or the establishment of a permanent cross-gender identity prior to genital-reassignment procedures vary anywhere from one to four years, depending on the source of the recommendation. Because genital-reassignment procedures serve as a *confirmation* of a stable gender identity, the Guidelines promote an individual's referral for Genital Reassignment Surgery primarily as gender confirmation based on that individual's consistency and permanence while living in role. Lack of adequate crossliving experience and transient notions of not liking one's genitals are an insufficient basis for referral for Genital Reassignment Surgery.

The full transgender spectrum includes transsexuals, transvestites, transgenderists, and androgynes. Approximately 1% to 3% of these individuals actually undergo Genital Reassignment Surgery. Higher numbers have undergone gonad-removal surgery. Transsexuals who permanently live in role undergo both procedures in the highest proportions. Genital Reassignment Surgery is most common, but gonad removal is more commonly sought by those unable to afford Genital Reassignment Surgery as a result of long-term health, personal, or financial barriers. Transgenderists and androgynes who permanently identify as such and crosslive full time are occasionally interested in gonad removal surgery. This group is generally not interested in full Genital Reassignment Surgery. Transvestites or crossdressers are generally not interested in either procedure.

The most common concern addressed by established professionals as well as consumers within the transgender community focuses on individuals who prematurely seek out Genital Reassignment Surgery. Lost on these unwary individuals is the long-established necessity of fulfilling a real-life test, during which time a permanent, full-time crossgendered identity can be fully established and explored. These crossgendered life experiences provide background and preparedness for the permanent consequences of Genital Reassignment Surgery or gonad removal.

Despite strong community-based warnings and established professional standards, individuals are still detrimentally and prematurely seeking out surgeries. The Guidelines address this issue by providing particular focus on surgical preparedness. Generally, a presurgical transgender consumer will wait an average of two to seven years before undergoing surgery because of the high emotional, physical, cosmetic, and financial costs of actually establishing a new identity, as well as the high cost of financing surgery. Financially independent and other resourceful individuals may be able to obtain surgery more quickly, but this does not typically reduce the high emotional and physical stressors of such procedures.

Transgender Care is the first resource to highlight the necessity of emphasizing the postsurgical care needs of individuals who have undergone Genital Reassignment Surgery. Most individuals consider physician and hospital attention when planning surgery, but few go beyond this. We advise consumers not only to question surgeons regarding the level of postsurgical care to be provided, but also to ask postoperative individuals about their experience with postsurgical care. Regrettably, some individuals who fail to address these issues find themselves postsurgically in a position in which surgeons fail to return emergency calls or to leave standing emergency orders for hospital staff.

Because Genital Reassignment Surgery is a major surgical procedure, and one that typically involves traveling long distances, the Guidelines strongly advise individuals who have undergone the procedure away from home to have a gynecological or physical examination by a local physician no later than two weeks after hospital discharge. This is because medical complications are more likely to develop within the first week of hospital discharge. Individuals may not recognize that complications have developed, particularly since it may be difficult to distinguish between normal postsurgical discomfort and pain resulting from a serious complication. Even though postsurgical gynecological or physical examination by someone other than the surgeon does require an additional financial responsibility for the individual, it is crucial that individuals recognize the importance of this preventive measure as a safeguard against complications that might otherwise remain undetected and subsequently require more serious and costly medical intervention.

Additionally, *Transgender Care* suggests that the responsibility of a Gender Specialist to an individual undergoing genital reassignment does not end with presurgical counseling, evaluation, and providing a letter of recommendation. Most competent Gender Specialists recognize that providing postsurgical follow-up is also essential. In the past, however, some care providers have been known to provide a letter of recommendation and then give no consideration whatsoever to the postsurgical well-being of clients. A postoperative mental health check-in provides an opportunity for the individual to talk about his or her recent experience, as well as to find out about additional resources and options should difficulties arise in the future.

For Gender Specialists, maintaining contact also provides additional information regarding surgeons, surgical outcomes, and postoperative inpatient and outpatient care. A postoperative mental health check-in is advised within the first month after Genital Reassignment Surgery. Some Gender Specialists will include this visit as a condition of the individual's receiving a letter recommending surgery. Providing this visit as a courtesy creates additional incentive for the postoperative individual to seek assistance with any difficulties they may be having as a result of surgery.

Surgeons are also encouraged to take an interest in the individual's postoperative well-being by confirming that a surgical candidate has made arrangements for postoperative medical and mental health support. Surgeons may regard this as a tool to establish that the individual is concerned about self-care and will likely follow through with postoperative care instructions. Genital reassignment can be a highly emotional process for the transgender individual. Accordingly, it is advisable that surgeons provide the primary Gender Specialist with a follow-up letter discussing the postoperative individual's condition and surgical outcome, thus advising the Gender Specialist of any special care requirements which the client may require.

See Chapter 19 for more about genital-reassignment procedures, from the point of view of a surgeon.

Types of Procedures

Male to Female

Orchidectomy. Orchidectomy, or castration, is the removal of the testicles, either independently or in conjunction with full vaginoplasty. This is a one-step procedure, preserving scrotal skin for future labiaplasty work. Cosmetic results: minimal change. Costs: $500–$3,000 US.

Vaginoplasty. Vaginoplasty consists of the surgical creation of a neo-vagina by the use of penile tissues, lower intestinal section, enervated skin-graft tissue from patient, or a combination of all. Testicles are removed during this procedure. A neo-clitoris is created from original penile enervated areas. This is a one- or two-step procedure. Cosmetic results: Vary, from poor to excellent. Costs: $7,000–$30,000 US.

Labiaplasty. Labiaplasty is a final-stage operation to provide labial revisions. It is typically included with vaginoplasty; however, better results are usual when it is done as a follow-up procedure. Cosmetic results: Vary, from poor to excellent Costs: Vary.

Revisions. Revisions include repair of recto-vaginal fistula, postoperative removal of bulbospongiosus and ischiocavernosus muscles, and neo-urethral revision. Costs: Revision work may be included in the cost of the original procedure; for independent procedures, costs vary.

Female to Male

Hysterectomy. Hysterectomy is the removal of the uterus. A hysterectomy that includes oophorectomy and salpingectomy is often called a "radical" or "complete" hysterectomy. Cosmetic results: vary depending on whether procedure is done through the vagina or an abdominal incision. We recommend intravaginal removal of internal organs as a viable surgical alternative because the approach is less invasive. Costs: Vary widely.

Oophorectomy. Oophorectomy is the removal of both ovaries. Costs: typically, an addition to the cost of a hysterectomy.

Salpingectomy. Salpingectomy is the removal of the fallopian tubes. Costs: typically, an addition to the cost of a hysterectomy.

Phalloplasty. Phalloplasty is the creation of a neo-phallus by utilization of enervated graft tissues from the patient's body, typically from a flap of abdominal tissue or muscle and skin from the forearm. The procedure may include the use of testicular prosthesis implants. It may be done in one- or two-step procedures, with various drawbacks and results. Cosmetic results: extremely poor to moderately appealing; appears artificial yet larger than metoidioplasty. Costs: $40,000–$130,000 US.

Metoidioplasty or Metadoioplasty. Metoidioplasty is an advanced single or, more commonly, multistep microsurgical technique that is combined with testosterone administration. It involves freeing the clitoris from the hood, cutting and repositioning clitoral suspensory ligaments, and administering hormones to produce a natural-looking microphallus. A scrotum is created through multistep labial revision and the use of testicular prosthesis implants. Cosmetic results: fair to excellent, although always appearing smaller than the microphallus of phalloplasty. Costs: $5,000–$15,000 US.

Revisions. Revisions typically are numerous in phalloplasty and metoidioplasty, particularly in regard to the urethral extension (urinary tract) if provided with either procedure. Costs: may be included in the fee for the original procedure; for independent procedures, cost vary.

Consumer Preparedness

> This section is addressed to those who are preparing to have Genital Reassignment Surgery, but it also makes appropriate reading for individuals considering any aesthetic or gender confirmation surgical procedure.

Some experienced Gender Specialists and postreassignment transgender consumers have suggested that a real-life test of one year is too short and that individuals should wait longer before seeking out Genital Reassignment Surgery. The consensus behind this suggestion is that far too many transgender individuals do not adequately research a proposed procedure, nor do they interview a sufficient number of surgeons or individuals who have had the procedure. Furthermore, they are often inadequately informed with regard to what presurgical preparations are essential or what postoperative care entails. Subsequently, they undergo surgery inadequately prepared and discover this is so when it is too late. Additionally, transgender men and women frequently fail to recognize their role as consumers. Although we agree these concerns are important and call for discussion, we do not believe an increased period for real-life tests is going to make transgender individuals better prepared or more informed. Better preparation comes as a result of increasing consumer, care provider, and community information about the benefits and risks of surgery.

Gender Specialists and other care providers are frequently on the front line, providing consumers information about surgeons, presurgical preparedness, and potential surgical outcomes. However, because their primary role is in providing psychological and other gender-specialized support, as well as evaluation recommendations, care providers should not be viewed as the consumer's sole resource when making preparations for Genital Reassignment Surgery. Since professional gender support is provided chiefly by licensed therapists, the support and referral process is more likely to be viewed as a psychological support function. Consequently, transgender individuals may not always be viewed as consumers or encouraged to be such. Additionally, although Gender Specialists may in some cases practice the most up-to-date model of transgender support, this does not always mean that they are aware of the most up-to-date surgical procedures. As a final note, consumers need to be aware that many Gender Specialists develop associations with a particular surgeon and thus are more likely to endorse his or her "product" over another surgeon's, or fail to provide information or referrals to other surgeons. Additionally, those Gender Specialists working within a national health service program or university-associated gender clinic may be unable to provide referrals outside their care provider network or program as a result of legal or institutional policy.

Surgeons naturally take a major role in assisting the surgical candidate with the presurgical preparation process. However, not all surgeons can be depended upon to fully support a consumer's search process. There are many ethical genital-reassignment surgeons who would never oppose an individual's wish to obtain a second opinion, but in the absence of such a request, most would probably encourage an individual to use their surgical services and would be highly unlikely to encourage him or her to go elsewhere. Surgeons are likely to feel that their procedure is the best or most advanced and that he or she has the most experience. Surgeons working in collaboration with only one referring therapist or gender program (including university-associated gender clinics and national health service providers) are the least likely to support a consumer-driven process.

Educational support by the surgeon also varies as to the amount and quality of preoperative and postoperative information that is provided to the consumer. Some surgeons are extremely attentive to details, providing pamphlets describing the procedure in detail and addressing the individual's every conceivable need, both before and after hospital discharge. Some are able to provide the names of others who have successfully undergone their procedure and who have given their permission for sharing their confidential medical information. Other surgeons are considerably less effective in supporting prospective patients. They may provide less detailed information or refuse to provide contact information for individuals who have used their services. Others may be adept themselves but have poor support staff. Consumers are advised that a surgeon's or staff's unwillingness to communicate may indicate a lack of surgical competence or postoperative support. It is important to note that most cases involving negligence by a surgeon or staff are hallmarked by poor communications, a hushed or controlling atmosphere, or a condescending or patronizing attitude.

> Surgery should never be undertaken in an information vacuum or with a lack of respect for a patient's pre- and postsurgical needs.

It is imperative that transgender consumers recognize that they cannot be fully dependent on Gender Specialists, surgeons, or other care providers for all information regarding a surgical procedure. As consumers, individuals interested in a surgical procedure need to fully educate themselves about a procedure and thus demystify it: speak with surgeons, uncover information about pre- and postoperative care, and locate knowledge about the self-preparation process.

The relationship of transgender individuals, Gender Specialists, and genital-reassignment surgeons is an unusual one in that a potential for a serious abuse of power exists. Isolated, lacking transgender consumer information, or desperate for support, those in need of hormonal and genital-reassignment surgical procedures are often the last to recognize their status as a consumer. Individuals may frequently feel an overwhelming gratefulness and obligation to satisfy any requirement set by professionals, no matter how unusual. This dynamic sets the stage for professional negligence and abuse. It has happened in the past and unfortunately continues today. The Guidelines seek to eliminate such abuse by making transgender consumers more aware of their options.

Examples of such an abuse of power include:

- Individuals' being told that breast-augmentation mammoplasty is required (or available only) at the time of Genital Reassignment Surgery.
- Individuals' being told not to contact other transgender individuals because such contact may interrupt the individual's therapeutic process or that other transgender individuals tend to be of questionable character.
- Individuals' not being informed of the availability of transgender consumer and educational resources, or being told that no such support systems exist.
- Individuals' being informed that changing therapists or interrupting therapy would require starting over on a real-life test.

- Individuals' being told by a Gender Specialist that evaluation recommendations are provided only to one surgeon or, conversely, that a surgeon accepts recommendations from one Gender Specialist only.
- Individuals' being told that genital-reassignment procedures are experimental and that the individual is "lucky" to have found an understanding Gender Specialist able to provide a surgical recommendation.
- Individuals' being told that they will be denied surgery unless they prove their "womanliness" to the surgeon via sexual favors.

These examples are drawn from the recent experiences of transgender individuals. All took place in settings where long-established gender-specializing professionals practice in the United States. All these individuals became aware that they had been manipulated only after the fact, which made it difficult to pursue any legal or consumer protective action. Tragically, these individuals are psychologically or physically marked for life. The experiences they recount reveal powerful reasons for mistrust in the professional-consumer relationship, even though such practices are not common. What remains, however, is the fact that transgender consumers have far too frequently not researched their options. This highlights the question, How can transgender consumers be better informed and prepared?

View Genital Reassignment Surgery as a Life-Long Investment

The approximate cost of surgery for MTF individuals varies, from $7,000 to $50,000. FTM individuals may pay as much as $100,000, depending on the complexity of the procedure. This is a considerable amount of money for any individual. Much as one would not purchase a new or used car without shopping around, so it should be with Genital Reassignment Surgery. As in the case with any profession, there are excellent, good, fair, and poor surgeons (and surgical outcomes). The consumer should remember that the surgeon is providing and selling a product and service to the consumer—not the other way around. The high price of surgery makes this a very competitive industry.

The individual should talk to at least three surgeons before making a commitment to undergo Genital Reassignment Surgery. Even when the consumer has already chosen a surgeon, talking with other surgeons can provide additional information that may have been overlooked or forgotten in conversations with the first surgeon or office staff. Individuals who are citizens of countries where a national health service covers the procedure may find the consumer process different. For instance, in Great Britain only two facilities provide the procedure. As a result, national health service consumers are advised to be certain that surgeons are using up-to-date techniques, such as surgical creation of a clitoris in MTF procedures. A "free" procedure under a public plan may not be as desirable as an updated, state-of-the-art procedure offered in another country.

No one should undergo a surgical procedure on the basis of information provided by one person. Consumers should ask the surgeon for referrals to at least three individuals who have undergone their surgical procedure within the last several years and who have been in recovery at least six months (to avoid speaking with an individual who is still in the throes of a postsurgical bliss, having at long last achieved his or her goal). Additionally, consumers should make certain that the individuals they speak to have undergone all steps in a procedure if the surgeon operates in stages. They should ask if surgical revision was required postoperatively, and about their experience with postsurgical outcome and postsurgical care, as well as the surgeon's and hospital or hospice's care team attitude. They should also ask to see or ask them to describe the appearance of their neo-vagina or neo-phallus. An individual who has been in recovery for at least six months should also be able to give an estimate of the amount of sensitivity that has returned during the healing process. Three such estimates, though subjective, should enable one to assess a surgeon's expertise.

In speaking with individuals who have had surgery with a particular surgeon, the consumer should recognize these individuals' willingness to share about a very personal event. One should thank them, and keep the personal information they provide private. Additionally, the consumer should be aware that surgeons routinely provide contacts with former patients' permission because this is a consumer-driven medical market. Therefore, the consumer who wishes that her or his privacy be kept confidential by a physician should ask what the surgeon's contact referral and confidentiality policies are.

Consumers should ask any other questions that are of concern. It is especially important to ask surgeons if they provide follow-up surgical procedures and what those costs are. Finally, consumers should make contact with transgender community organizations such as AEGIS or IFGE for current information on surgeons, surgeries, and outcomes. (See the listing of resources in the Appendix.)

Research Insurance or National Health Service Coverage

In western Europe, Great Britain, and Australia, Genital Reassignment Surgery is likely to be covered totally or in part by a citizen's national health insurance. Individuals are advised to check their country's national health insurance policy or protocol to determine how to go about getting approval. When dealing with national health insurance, the consumer should expect long lines and a great deal of red tape.

In the United States getting insurance company coverage for genital-reassignment procedures is considerably more difficult, although not impossible. Private and employer-provided health coverage has paid for Genital Reassignment Surgeries where no exclusionary policies existed and where medical need for the procedure was demonstrated. Even though this established procedure is performed worldwide, U.S. insurance companies typically classify the procedure as experimental, and on that basis turn down coverage in most cases. These decisions can be overturned when an individual is willing to undertake a long documentation and research process. (See Chapter 16 for more detailed advice.) Also, in the United States Genital Reassignment Surgery is typically not covered under national Medicare, Veterans', or state welfare benefits. However, some procedures have been covered under these benefit programs where physicians have found available loopholes in coverage.

When planning for surgery, the individual should examine available insurance benefits to see if Genital Reassignment Surgery is specifically excluded. If it is not, it may be possible to force the insurance company to cover the procedure. When interviewing potential surgeons, ask each surgeon how willing he or she is to assist in the pursuit of a partial or full claim for the procedure.

Anticipate Pain and Discomfort

During and after surgery, including the time after leaving the hospital, pain control is a crucial factor in the experience. Pain-control strategies used during and following surgery may include intravenous agents, epidural analgesia, or intraspinal anesthetics or narcotics. These options and their costs should be discussed with the surgeon and anesthesiologist.

Pain and discomfort during the postoperative recovery period at home varies from individual to individual. A good anesthetic approach, however, can make postoperative recovery reasonably tolerable. Those contemplating surgery should ask the surgeons interviewed about pain control. They should also ask individuals who have had the procedure under a particular surgeon's care about pain control. Most individuals who have gone to good surgeons and have received good postoperative care report only moderate amounts of pain. Individuals who experience a great deal of pain are likely to have received poor postsurgical care while in the hospital.

Anticipate Other Costs

Some procedures may require that genito-electrolysis be performed prior to surgery in order to prevent hair growth inside the neo-vagina. Transgender women are advised to seek consultation with others who have had surgery and with surgeons in order to determine if genito-electrolysis is appropriate. Postoperatively, Genital Reassignment Surgery also may require follow-up or revision surgery, particularly in cases of vagino-stenosis, or strictures. Not all surgical techniques afford maximum cosmetic benefit. Does the surgeon provide follow-up and revision surgeries at no or reduced cost? If one is unable to return to the genital reassignment surgeon, is there a plastic surgeon nearby willing to do this work? Is revision surgery affordable if that need should arise?

Some surgeons do a procedure in two stages, for example, first a genito-vaginoplasty, then later a labiaplasty. Does a surgeon's fee cover both procedures? What about hospital costs and anesthesia?

Some of the more expensive procedures also come with better hospital care and amenities. Overall, most individuals are required to do some personal shopping prior to leaving home for surgery. Most surgeons will ask that you bring your own personal care items, such as ace bandages, elastic girdles, sanitary pads, clean pajamas and robe, solution of betadine vaginal douches, lubricant, and the like.

Many transgender individuals undergo genital reassignment using every last penny saved. Although understandable, this is to be discouraged. Surgery, like most situations in life, may create unexpected changes and needs. The individual traveling away from home to receive surgery should be certain that he or she can afford to make alternate travel arrangements, should the need arise. One individual who failed to plan ahead ended up riding cross-country by bus, as she was unable to afford the cost of an airline ticket after changing her departure date. Anyone traveling long distances should allow extra time for recuperating in a hotel or motel for several days before returning home. This will also provide additional opportunities to be in touch with the surgeon.

View Surgery as a Major Event

If possible, the individual undergoing surgery should arrange for a travel-care companion. Loved ones and family frequently feel useless during transition processes; this is an excellent opportunity for them to show their support when it is needed most.

Because genital reassignment is a major surgical procedure, complication risks exist. A durable power of attorney form provides the means to authorize a travel companion or family member to make medical (or other) important decisions on the surgical patient's behalf, should he or she be unable to do so. A completed and notarized copy of this form, in addition to any written instructions the patient may have, should be given to the surgeon during the presurgical interview appointment. Additionally, prospective surgical candidates are advised to have an updated will completed.

The surgical candidate should plan three to four weeks off from work for surgery and postsurgical recovery. Many individuals have scheduled surgery during a two-week vacation, only to later find upon returning home that they need to take off additional time for self-care. Recovering from surgery takes time.

Some surgeons prepare excellent presurgical information packets, but others do not. In talking with others who have had the procedure, the individual should keep notes listing surgical and travel-oriented needs, which can useful as financial preparations are being made.

View First-Month Recovery as Critical

Follow-up care by a gynecologist, urologist, internist, or general practitioner within two to three weeks after hospital release is a new principle established in the Guidelines. Individuals far too frequently undergo Genital Reassignment Surgery without appropriate follow-up medical care. From a medical perspective, if anything major is going to go wrong, it will generally occur within the first month of recovery. Having the surgical site examined will ensure that it is healing properly. Although the healing process may cause some discomfort, some individuals incorrectly assume that what is actually abnormal pain or discharge is expected. Even if everything "feels" all right, the postoperative patient should protect this life-long investment with timely follow-up care.

Focus on Pre- and Postoperative Emotional Well-Being

The operative candidate should focus on his or her emotional needs as well. Is the individual entering the surgical experience tired, worried, or without a positive frame of mind? Is the prospect of going into the hospital and having major surgery frightening? Are panic attacks a problem? Any such issues should be discussed with someone who can be trusted. One should not be afraid to be human. Surgery is an intimidating prospect for most rational individuals. The Gender Specialist providing counseling support or evaluations should welcome the individual's need to focus on emotional well-being before, as well as after, surgery. Checking in with the primary Gender Specialist, or with the individual who provided the most current recommendation letter (if there is no regular care provider) can provide an opportunity to talk about the experience, discuss available options, and explore any difficulties. For instance, individuals occasionally may have difficulty scheduling crucial medical appointments or having prescriptions filled in a timely manner. The Gender Specialist may be able to help.

Surgery is a stressful event. The candidate for surgery needs to respect his or her emotional well-being by sleeping well, eating healthy, and reducing stressful activities as surgery nears. Taking one or even several days off from work prior to surgery is necessary from a psychological perspective. Having several days' distance between work and going to surgery provides an individual with ample time for preparation, relaxation, and self-reflection.

Backing Out or Rescheduling at the Last Minute Is Okay!

Genital-reassignment surgeons traditionally require a hefty, nonrefundable deposit to secure a surgery date. This is designed primarily to deter unprepared or frivolous individuals from scheduling surgery without following through. Unfortunately, such policies fail to address the question of whether such a financial deterrent may possibly force some individuals to go through the surgical process when in fact at the last minute they feel as if backing out or rescheduling may be more appropriate.

Financial disincentives notwithstanding, many individuals cannot possibly imagine backing out after coming so close to fulfilling their intention to have Genital Reassignment Surgery. Saying "no" or "later," however, sometimes works out for the best. As an example, the principal author of this text provided a presurgical evaluation for an attractive transgender woman who was advised during her evaluation to wait and reschedule. Having crosslived well for more than fifteen years with an attractive presentation, she blended perfectly into non-transgender society. Alas, in preparing for surgery, she had depended on the advice in a ten-year-old magazine article. She was not aware of any other surgeons. She had not spoken to anyone who had Genital Reassignment Surgery, nor anticipated follow-up needs, including a gynecological exam. She expected to be up and running around, back to normal within two weeks, thus being able to return to her employment position, which required high levels of physical energy.

Her plight is an example of what can occur when an individual, after living in role for so many years, has isolated herself within mainstream society. She (like many) was simply not ready to have *any* type of major surgery. On advice, she canceled her surgery date and spent time shopping for a surgeon. She spoke with others who had had the procedure and planned to take more time off from work. At the time of this publication's final editing, she had undergone Genital Reassignment Surgery, which was performed by a very capable surgeon who was recommended by other consumers. She has reported that the postoperative care provided by the hospital was excellent, as was the result of her first gynecological exam. During her postsurgical mental health check-in, she radiated wellness and has now returned to work.

Deciding to cancel or reschedule is not the end of the road. For some, it is the beginning of a journey toward finding a better surgeon, or a more opportune time. For others, it is a time to wait until genital reassignment has been established as the right step. The individual who has second thoughts should not be ashamed to seek support and talk about it with someone he or she trusts. No amount of peer pressure should undermine the search for what is best. Remember, Genital Reassignment Surgery is irreversible.

Examine Unexpected Consequences

Genital Reassignment Surgery is an enormous step. Undergoing it, however, may result in some surprising and unexpected consequences. For instance, in the United States and many other countries, an insurance company's policy may contain an exclusionary clause that invalidates health or life insurance when an individual undergoes genital reassignment. This may be avoided in some circumstances by providing the company with a declaration of intent, court statement, or documentation that asserts that the procedure is medically necessary. In some areas, retaining driving licenses, passports, and other forms of identification may also present difficulties. It is best that an individual wait and get all these matters sorted out beforehand, rather than finding that life has fallen in pieces because he or she rushed headlong into an irreversible situation.

Recommended Guidelines for Genital Reassignment Surgery

Caution: A full understanding of these guidelines is not possible without reading the material in the preceding sections of this chapter. They contain relevant medical, psychological, insurance, and historical information, as well as vital educational information for the consumer. Readers are reminded that both Genital Reassignment Surgery and gonad removal (castration) can effectively produce intended psychological and physical outcomes with a balanced consideration of the patient's surgical preparedness, variable risks associated with all surgical procedures, and recognized medical and consumer recommendations.

Any transgender individual may be accepted as an appropriate candidate for gonad removal or Genital Reassignment Surgery when he or she can present to the surgeon two letters of recommendation, a primary recommendation letter and a supporting evaluation letter, as described in Recommendations 1 and 2:

1. A primary recommendation letter is provided by the individual's primary care provider, who may be either a Gender Specialist or Senior Gender Specialist with whom the individual has maintained a support or counseling relationship for a minimum of three months. The primary care provider and client shall establish goals oriented toward meeting the client's needs. Evaluations may include verification of material and information presented by the client, such as payroll receipts, legal records of change of status, or visual verification of electrolysis completion. However, because there are transgender men and women who work while living in role, without others' awareness of this fact, evaluations should not unnecessarily interfere with a client's workplace privacy.

1a. This letter should reflect the Gender Specialist's awareness that the individual has consistently lived in the new gender role full time for one complete year, in addition to having continuously expressed an intent to undergo a genital-reassignment surgical procedure. Living in role full time equates to twenty-four hours a day, seven days a week, continuously.

1b. The letter should state that the individual has the capacity to clearly understand the potential physical, emotional, and social changes and drawbacks associated with the surgical procedure. It should also state that the individual presently, and for the preceding three months, has not been suffering from any self-abuse, suicidal behavior, psychotic thought patterns, or other severe psychological symptoms.

1c. The letter should state that in the opinion of the Gender Specialist, the requested genital-reassignment procedure will enhance the individual's overall quality of life and facilitate confirmation of transgender identity needs.

2. A supporting evaluation letter is provided solely by a Senior Gender Specialist who, having seen the individual for a minimum of three sessions, states the following:

2a. An agreement with the overall observations, findings, and recommendations presented in the primary recommendation letter.

2b. An independent assessment of the individual's current psychological state as being appropriate for surgical candidacy.

2c. An independent assessment of the individual's presentation as being congruent with the individual's expressed self-image and the procedure's intended surgical outcome.

2d. An assessment of the individual's having adequately investigated the requested procedure and its alternatives, as well as having initiated preparation for pre- and postoperative needs, including practical considerations of, and the potential for, surgical complications.

2e. A statement providing the evaluating Senior Gender Specialist's opinion that the individual's undergoing the requested genital-reassignment procedure will enhance overall quality of life and facilitate confirmation of transgender identity needs.

3. Surgeons should establish that the individual is in a stable medical condition with no acute or chronic illness that might complicate surgical outcome.

3a. This would include a letter summarizing the candidate's medical status provided by a primary care physician, preferably dated within six months prior to surgery.

3b. Surgeons need to establish that surgical candidates have scheduled an appointment for medical follow-up with a primary-care physician, gynecologist, or urologist within two weeks of hospital discharge. Because the majority of transgender patients come from distant locations, surgeons are advised to provide the patient and the patient's primary physician with instructions and consultation on how to diagnose, treat, and refer for postsurgical gynecological and urological complications. This should include a written description of the anatomical procedures performed, particularly since they differ widely among surgeons.

3c. Surgeons need to establish that surgical candidates have scheduled an appointment for a postsurgical mental health check-in with one of the recommending Gender Specialists, within one month of hospital discharge. As a courtesy, surgeons are advised to provide the primary Gender Specialist or therapist with a postsurgical follow-up letter describing surgical outcome and any special care instructions. (A sample of the postsurgical follow-up letter may be found in Chapter 9.)

4. Hormone administration should be discontinued three weeks prior to major surgery and not resumed for two weeks after surgery to prevent thrombosis or blood clots in major arteries.

5. Surgical approaches to HIV-related and other immunosuppressive conditions can be found in the Guidelines at the end of Chapter 6.

6. Surgical considerations for transgender youth can be found in the Guidelines at the end of Chapter 8. Young consumers considering Genital Reassignment Surgery are advised to fully research, or obtain adult assistance in researching, a prospective surgeon's credentials, affiliations, and references.

7. Transgender individuals intending to remain with a partner, significant other, or spouse are advised to inform that individual of their intention to undergo a genital-reassignment procedure, as well as of the procedure's surgical goal and possible complications. In some circumstances genital reassignment may invalidate a legal marriage. Genital reassignment may also provide an opportunity for legal marriage to an individual of the opposite sex. Individuals are advised to check their local state, provincial, or commonwealth laws regarding legal changes in marital status.

8. Care providers are advised that no person shall be denied recommendations for genital reassignment on the basis of sexual orientation or because that individual derives pleasure from genital masturbation while living in role prior to surgery. In the past, gay FTM and lesbian MTF persons have been denied surgery because care providers felt that these individuals did not conform to society's standards. These practices are wrong and discriminatory. Furthermore, masturbation is a natural, healthy human function. If an individual is capable of separating this function from feelings of overall gender incongruency, maintaining physical sensitivity and emotional desire may benefit postoperative recovery of sexual function.

9. Some countries in Central and South America, eastern Europe, the Middle East, and other locations legally forbid residents to change their identification or live in role as members of the opposite gender prior to Genital Reassignment Surgery. Persons who do so may be subject to incarceration, torture, and death. Therefore, without serious appraisal of these situations, it would be inadvisable for transgender persons actually residing in those countries to attempt living in role prior to Genital Reassignment Surgery. Care providers may encounter foreign-resident transgender persons who, in the face of insurmountable odds, are seeking surgery yet have not lived in role full time. Several options are available in these situations: First, a person may temporarily move or become a student in a more hospitable country in order to live in role full time prior to surgery. Second, care providers who usually require or provide letters of recommendation of or to individuals who have been unable to completely live in role full time

should make exceptions on a case-by-case basis, and attempt to follow the
Guidelines for Genital Reassignment Surgery as closely as possible in all other
regards. Third, while making every effort to verify a surgeon's skills and cred-
ibility, individuals in these situations may seek surgery prior to living in role full
time from a surgeon who will accept this situation and not require letters of
recommendation.

HIV and AIDS

Chapter 6

We believe that discrimination against people with AIDS seeking medical care is a pervasive problem in this country. Medical practitioners are not at risk of contracting AIDS if they take the proper precautions.

—John Wodatch
Civil Rights Division
U.S. Department of Justice

When many people think of AIDS, their minds turn to gay and bisexual males, intravenous drug users, San Francisco, New York, Haiti, and perhaps Africa. What these individuals and places have in common is that they fit stereotypical media portrayals and financial allocations involving the AIDS epidemic. What does not come to mind, typically, is the reality that everyone is at risk of contracting the HIV virus, including transgender individuals. Sadly, transgender individuals along with other marginalized populations are rarely reported upon by the media; they are ignored unless someone of importance dies.

Providing support for HIV-positive individuals in addition to promoting HIV education among gender-specializing professionals and the transgender community generates a host of issues. Are transgender individuals having unsafe sex as a result of internalized transphobia, or an omnipotent feeling that "this can't happen to me"? Yes, certainly! Are transgender individuals a high-risk group for contracting the HIV virus? Absolutely. Some areas report infection rates as high as 70 percent among transgender populations. Are HIV and AIDS support services sensitive to transgender women and men available, particularly for people of color and other marginalized communities? Unfortunately, in most cases throughout the United States, the answer is no.

Transgender Support Services and AIDS

To gain insight, we can reflect upon the state of transgender support services in San Francisco. Until several years ago, no transgender-sensitive HIV and AIDS support services existed whatsoever, despite the fact that during the preceding decade San Franciscans had become increasingly aware of the AIDS epidemic. Fortunately, HIV and AIDS support services are growing in San Francisco today. The staff at the Department of Public Health's Tom Wadell Medical Clinic noted a high incidence of HIV seropositivity and behavioral risks among their transgender clients. Accordingly, the Transgender Tuesdays program was instituted; this is a specialized medical clinic to provide for the total health-care needs of transgender individuals that has been successfully operated for more than three years. Additionally, Ryan White Care Fund federal grants and city funding provided for the start-up of the Tenderloin AIDS Resource Center (TARC). The AIDS Case Management and Gender Identity programs of the Center for Special Problems jointly address social service and emotional-support needs for HIV-positive transgender persons. All three agencies have specialized support for the HIV-positive transgender individual, and the latter also provides support for those dealing with substance-abuse issues.

There are other agencies in San Francisco that focus on HIV and AIDS concerns among people of color. The Asian AIDS Project's Transgender Program provides HIV and AIDS prevention education through outreach and case management; it serves Asian and Pacific Islander transgender persons. The Brothers Network offers HIV and AIDS services and gender-support services for African American transgender persons. Proyecto Contra Sido Por Vida provides HIV and AIDS prevention education through outreach to Latino and Latina transgender persons.

Even though transgender support services specific to HIV and AIDS issues are developing in San Francisco, transgender-specialized services may not exist at all in most other places. The response of local and national transgender organizations has been depressing, particularly since most organizations have failed to publicize HIV-related safe-sex materials or even discuss HIV concerns. In what may be viewed as a negligent and self-destructive mentality, a large proportion of individuals and organizations appear to be more interested in exploring fantasy and prioritizing social functions. As a result, HIV disease silently ravages onward.

Fortunately, two transgender resources, both using the acronym AEGIS, have been developed to confront the AIDS epidemic. The first is the AIDS Education General Information System. Founded in 1985, this computer bulletin-board resource is operated by Sister Mary Elizabeth, and it manages the nation's largest public- access database of HIV or AIDS-related information. Featured in the May 1994 issue of the gay magazine *10 Percent,* this relatively little-known resource provides information on clinical trials and mental- and medical-health concerns, has dial-out services that connect to the National Institutes of Health, U.S. Public Health Service, and other government health agencies. Many of these same agencies rely heavily on AEGIS for information sharing.

The second AEGIS is the nationally recognized and transgender-oriented American Educational Gender Information Service. It also provides professional and consumer-oriented transgender educational information and resources. The Executive Director, Dallas Denny, M.A., has developed a "public advisory" campaign to confront the AIDS epidemic. These public advisory notices can be found in transgender publications worldwide. In addition to promoting AIDS education information, AEGIS promotes advisory information on a wide variety of other medical, mental health, and consumer issues.

Gender Specialists and others who provide HIV and AIDS support will find that the use of educational materials on prevention and building community awareness are effective tools in assisting transgender individuals, as with any population at high risk for HIV infections. Care providers serving transgender persons and other high-risk populations need to have a basic understanding of what HIV disease is, and a recognition of the dynamics that place people at high risk for the HIV virus.

Transgender individuals may take part in high-risk behaviors for a variety of reasons. Although heterosexual male crossdressers may deny interest in same-sex sexual activity, being in role frequently may include actual exploration of sexual fantasies. Some MTF transsexual women specifically avoid sex before and after Genital Reassignment Surgery because it is confusing or might raise uncomfortable questions regarding sexual orientation. After surgery, however, most individuals view themselves as newly liberated sexual beings. While sexual reawakening in and of itself is healthy, acting out risky behaviors is not.

Other variables that play a role in transgender individuals' engaging in unsafe sexual behavior include diminished educational or functioning skills and being under the influence of alcohol or drugs. Sex workers also place themselves at risk, particularly since some of their clients pay more for or demand unprotected sex. Therefore, sex workers, in addition to using protection, need to be regularly tested for the HIV virus and other sexually transmitted diseases. Most major cities provide this service through public health services at little or no cost.

Gender Specialists need to be aware that the AIDS epidemic has created a large cross-section of individuals who are (or choose to be) *misinformed* about the nature of the HIV virus. There are numerous individuals who have irrational fears of contact with HIV-positive persons or of catching AIDS through casual contact. Occasionally, individuals who are single may take this fear one step further by identifying it as a reason to avoid pursuing or maintaining meaningful relationships. Rather than confront the actual reasons for an inability or unwillingness to pursue meaningful relationships, the individual attributes HIV or AIDS as the cause of all his or her social isolation and loneliness.

Gender Specialists are advised that if an individual expresses interest in pursuing a sexual fantasy, the individual needs to be provided with "safe sex" and other preventive information even when the care provider doubts the individual's intent to actually pursue the interest. No care provider can accurately predict when an individual will develop the means to explore sexual activity. It is hoped that some day ethical guidelines will exist that require care providers to forewarn high-risk individuals and make contracts with them about safe practices. Unfortunately, some care providers fail to warn an individual even after he or she has indicated possible intentions of pursuing a sexual encounter. Failure to provide preventive education or to discuss AIDS issues happens when care providers feel uncomfortable discussing sexual issues. Care providers with these concerns are advised to bring them up in professional consultation with peers.

> Failure to provide preventive education or to discuss AIDS issues happens when care providers feel uncomfortable discussing sexual issues. Care providers with these concerns are advised to bring them up in professional consultation with peers.

Gender Specialists and other care providers, whether they work with individuals or groups, are on the front lines of inquiry regarding individuals' sexual issues or risky behaviors. Both individual care providers and agencies are advised to make educational materials about HIV prevention and preventive devices available to all, or at least to be prepared to tell clients where such items may be obtained. Preventive devices include (but are not limited to) latex or polyurethane (male or female) condoms, dental dams, water-based lubricants, and small bottles of chlorine bleach. Agencies are particularly advised to make preventive devices available at low cost or for free. Preventive devices often can be supplied to care providers at reduced costs or for free by major AIDS organizations or public health agencies.

There is no dispute that higher rates of HIV infection exist among institutionalized and incarcerated populations. All correctional facilities and hospitals (including mental health facilities) are advised to have preventive devices and educational materials available. Most administrations frown upon the general distribution of preventive devices and educational materials. Many correctional settings in the United States and Europe have side-stepped general distribution by making preventive devices and educational materials available anonymously through the counseling or medical programs of the facility. The cost of distributing these devices and materials can usually be included in a facility's budget and offset by public-health funding.

Regrettably, not all institutions or governments have given HIV prevention high priority, and additional advocacy is clearly needed. Where possible, legislation should be introduced requiring that HIV preventive devices and educational materials be made available to institutionalized populations. In many locations moral and religious politics are still key factors that interfere with prevention efforts. This is tragic, because elsewhere HIV prevention is understood to be a social and medical necessity, especially among institutionalized populations who eventually may be released into the general public.

Basic HIV and AIDS Information

AIDS stands for *acquired immune deficiency syndrome* and is caused by the *human immunodeficiency virus* (HIV). AIDS itself is an impairment of the body's ability to fight disease, leaving an individual susceptible to illness that a healthy immune system would easily protect against. Individuals with an active case of AIDS are susceptible to diseases known as "opportunistic infections," which can come from the environment, lie dormant within the body, or be transmitted from non-HIV-infected individuals. An individual with AIDS is at far greater risk of contracting diseases from a non-HIV-infected individual than vice versa.

The HIV virus that causes AIDS is primarily carried by and transmitted through exposure to blood, semen, and, to a lesser extent, vaginal secretions. Aside from sexual abstinence, the best way to avoid becoming HIV infected is to have protected or "safer" sex using a latex or polyurethane condom or dental dam. Individuals who share needles for intravenous drug use can best avoid HIV infection by thoroughly cleansing needles between uses with chlorine bleach followed by clean water. Chlorine bleach must completely fill (and remain inside) the syringe and needle for at least thirty seconds to ensure effective killing of the HIV virus. This procedure should be repeated three times, rinsing well with water between each filling of bleach and at the end of the cleansing process. This recommendation is the most up-to-date bleach disinfection procedure from the Institute for Community Health Outreach (ICHO) in San Francisco, California.

HIV viral transmission through saliva or tears is a rarity. With the exception of bites or the introduction of saliva directly into open cuts or wounds, few cases exist where saliva was the source of transmission. As an added precaution, individuals may wish to avoid deep, "French" kissing and should definitely avoid fluid exchanges around areas with open wounds or sores.

■ ——————

| AIDS cannot be spread by casual contact.

One cannot catch AIDS through holding, hugging, nonpenetrating kisses, massages, or any other activity where body fluids are not exchanged. Love, compassion, support, and communication are encouraged in interaction with an individual who has contracted the HIV virus or has an AIDS condition. An individual's HIV status is a personal and confidential matter that should not be disclosed to others without the individual's permission.

All individuals who even once have had unprotected sex (exposure to blood, semen, or vaginal secretions), shared needles, or possibly received a blood trans-fusion within the past ten years should be tested for the HIV virus. This is a blood test for the presence of antibodies to the HIV virus, but a positive test for HIV does not mean a diagnosis of AIDS unless other signs of immune system dysfunction are diagnosed by a physician. Individuals uncertain of prior contacts or who feel that they may possibly have encountered the HIV virus should also be tested. Early detection now provides opportunity for early treatment interven-tion, which includes options in both Western and Eastern/holistic medicine. Further information about the HIV virus and AIDS can be obtained by from a primary physician, a government-sponsored anonymous testing site, a counselor, or by calling the National AIDS Hotline (1-800-342-AIDS).

In many countries, including the United States, having an HIV antibody test or a physician's diagnosis of AIDS may invalidate life or health insurance. Even if a test is negative, an insurance company may cancel a policy on the basis of the belief that having a test may be regarded as a declaration of an unaccept-able or risky lifestyle. This does not mean that individuals who suspect that they have come in contact with the HIV virus should avoid HIV antibody testing. Privacy can be assured by having an anonymous HIV antibody test done, by privately paying for the test through a different physician, or by seeking assis-tance from an HIV support organization.

AIDS and the Transgender Individual

Transgender individuals frequently have questions about whether the HIV virus can be transmitted during electrolysis and surgery, or if HIV-positive individuals are even permitted to have surgery. Where electrolysis is concerned, occasionally minute amounts of blood may emerge during the procedure. However, the amount is so insignificant that no known cases of HIV transmission have oc-curred to either operator or patron when needles are discarded after single use or "individualized." (Individualization of needles requires proper labeling and steril-ization by use of an autoclave. An autoclave is a device that sterilizes with super-heated steam.) Individuals are advised to ask an electrolysis operator about dis-posable, single-use needles and needle individualization.

HIV transmission should be a concern to any individual seeking surgery. The blood supply in the United States is relatively safe; however, many individ-uals still choose to make arrangements to receive their own blood. This may be done by making arrangements through the surgeon or hospital before actually undergoing surgery. Individuals undergoing surgery in underdeveloped countries are strongly urged to do the same, where any uncertainty exists about sanitation or blood screening processes.

HIV viral transmission to surgeons and surgical staff within operating thea-ters is highly unlikely where universal blood and body-fluid precautions are fol-lowed. Some surgeons and surgical staff are hesitant to perform surgery on HIV-positive individuals, unless the procedure is considered life-saving in nature. This is especially so for Genital Reassignment Surgery, where large volumes of blood are involved.

Providing surgical and other support services for an HIV-positive transgender individual introduces numerous questions and uncertainties, particularly since up to this point, there have been no recommendations available to provide informed guidance to all concerned. In this modern era where physicians are viewed as miracle workers who can even transform biological males into females or females into males, their powers seem hopelessly shackled where treatment of HIV disease is concerned. To some extent, these views can be attributed to our unrealistic expectations of Western medicine. The public at large is conditioned to believe that Western physicians can always prescribe magic bullets to treat diseases like polio and herpes. Unfortunately, these successes have diminished the public's understanding of the true nature of disease; few people recognize that diseases are conditions created by more than one causal factor or that many are treated with multilevel approaches.

A transgender individual who has tested positive for HIV or has been diagnosed with AIDS faces what may seem a devastating dynamic tossed into an already difficult situation. We strongly advise that ongoing support be made available for these individuals. Support needs for a transgender HIV-positive individual can vary greatly, depending on the individual's background as well as ability to interact with and place trust in a support team. Not surprisingly, a large proportion of such an individual's support needs resemble those of any individual dealing with a life-threatening illness. They may move through various cycles of denial, despair, anger, and acceptance. Additionally, they may have fears about abandonment, disclosure to others, finding support, burdening others, and becoming ill and dying. It can be hoped that, with the acceptance of disease (including HIV disease) as an inescapable part of human life, the individual will seek out mainstream and alternative supports, and invest in positive, life-affirming lifestyle changes. These factors are the hallmarks that long-term survivors have in common.

At present, no cure for AIDS (or the newer and broader term *HIV disease*) exists. However, an HIV-positive test result, an HIV-related opportunistic infection, or an AIDS diagnosis should not be misperceived as a death sentence. Early detection through HIV testing provides an excellent opportunity for an individual to build a medical and emotional support team. This multilevel support team, as well as any subsequent medical and emotional treatment or support, must reflect the true nature of HIV disease in order to be effective. HIV disease, like other medical conditions, has more than one cause. Testing positive for the HIV virus is only one of several factors individuals who have HIV disease have in common. To reframe AIDS away from its stereotypes, HIV disease denotes a chronic medical condition that is best managed by the use of multilateral medical care. Recently, protease inhibitors have offered short-term benefits in improving health; however, their long-term side-effects are not fully studied.

Numerous medical options are available to help prevent and treat the many opportunistic infections characteristic of AIDS or HIV infection. Western medicine has discovered no magic bullet to cure HIV disease or completely restore an individual's immune system, but it has had moderate success treating many of the opportunistic infections that accompany AIDS. Additionally, alternative or holistic medicine, which includes traditional Chinese medicine, acupuncture, herbs, mega-vitamin therapy, massage, meditation, and so forth, has succeeded in minimizing opportunistic infections as well as maintaining (and in some cases increasing) an individual's immune function. HIV-positive individuals are encouraged to explore healing alternatives in both Western and Eastern medicine without indiscriminately valuing one over the other, particularly when one or several medicinal practices may be combined so as to improve one's quality of life and longevity.

Support concerns regarding hormone administration, aesthetic surgery, and Genital Reassignment Surgery are the common denominators that set HIV-positive transgender individuals apart from the remaining HIV-positive population. No other HIV-positive population is subject to so many surgical procedures. Because many years may pass between an individual's testing positive for HIV and having a fully progressing case of HIV disease, surgeons, Gender Specialists, and the consumer need to understand that although gender transition is possible, caution is encouraged with regard to both hormones and surgery.

Sex hormones alone are not recognized as immunosuppressive in HIV-positive individuals. Hormone administration in these individuals should follow the same prescription regimens as is recommended for individuals unaffected by the HIV virus. Although no formal studies exist at this time, some practitioners believe that hormone administration in HIV-positive transgender individuals may have an immune-enhancing effect. Providing the means for these individuals to bring body in line with psychological and emotional needs is also likely to alleviate their feelings of disparity, depression, and suicidality.

Setting these views aside, it should be clearly recognized that although sex hormones are powerful chemicals that can provide desired physical transformation, they should never be viewed as a panacea. Nor should they be indiscriminately taken or irresponsibly prescribed. Responsible hormone administration reflects up-to-date recommendations, including regular blood-level monitoring and physician follow-up.

The risks associated with hormone administration increase significantly if an individual has a history of any of the following conditions: high blood pressure; heart, kidney, or liver dysfunction; blood cholesterol and clotting disorders; migraine-type headaches or seizures; respiratory difficulties; a family history of breast cancer; obesity; or heavy tobacco use or other chemical consumption.

All hormones may temporarily cause or aggravate depression, moodiness, or even euphoria until the body adapts to chemical changes, which takes anywhere from several weeks to several months. HIV-positive transgender individuals who may already be dealing with significant issues are particularly susceptible to these conditions. Accordingly, physicians are advised to maintain contact with the individual and the referring Gender Specialist so that the individual's emotional state may be closely monitored.

Aesthetic and Genital Reassignment Surgery carry the deepest concern for transgender HIV-positive individuals, particularly when an awareness of gender incongruity drives an individual toward surgery to resolve gender-identity issues. There does not appear to be any evidence that aesthetic or elective cosmetic surgeries present any greater risk than other medical procedures to the HIV-positive individual having fair health. Numerous HIV-positive individuals have had breast implants, mastectomies, as well as facial masculinizing or feminizing procedures. Minimal quantities of blood are involved, and a number of surgeons have safely performed elective procedures on HIV-positive individuals.

Surgeons are not hanging up a shingle that reads "Will Operate On HIV-Positive Individuals." In fact, for the HIV-positive individual, locating a reputable surgeon willing to perform Genital Reassignment Surgery is virtually impossible. During the research for this book we were unable to speak with any surgeons who had operated on HIV-positive individuals, though several sources indicated that there are several respected surgeons who operate strictly on a case-by-case basis.

The decision for an HIV-positive individual to have Genital Reassignment Surgery or for the surgeon to provide the procedure raises several critical questions:

- What is the risk to the surgical candidate?
- How much will surgery improve the quality of life for that individual?
- Will surgery ultimately send the candidate's immune system in a downward spiral?
- Is the operating surgeon liable if the candidate becomes ill as a result of the surgery?
- Will performing this surgical procedure utilizing universal blood and body-fluid precautions place surgical staff at a higher level of risk of contracting the HIV virus than their risk of exposure to any other viruses?

Owing to lack of adequate clinical research on the effects of aesthetic surgical procedures or of Genital Reassignment Surgery on HIV-positive individuals, the Guidelines can neither endorse nor disqualify individuals from seeking (nor encourage or discourage surgeons from performing) these procedures. Universal blood and body-fluid precautions should be standard operating-room procedure and thus far have proven largely effective where other transmittable diseases are concerned, but many surgeons are nevertheless unwilling to put themselves or their staff at risk of contacting the HIV virus. At this point all we are left with are questions, particularly with regard to Genital Reassignment Surgery. Are the surgeons' decisions based on a common belief that this is an elective procedure and that the individual's quality of life should be ignored? Are their decisions influenced by the social stigmatization of HIV and AIDS? Ultimately, are the contractual risks that surgeons and other medical personnel take with the HIV virus any different from those associated with hepatitis B or other hospital-acquired infections?

While surgeons and medical staff remain at minimal risk of contracting the HIV virus and other infectious agents when following proper procedures, individuals undergoing any major surgery (including genital reassignment) place themselves at considerable risk of contracting hospital-acquired infections. For immunocompromised individuals, that risk is amplified, to include the possibility that surgery itself may spark any number of infections laying dormant in the surgical candidate. With this in mind, it is of little wonder that gonad-removal procedures have become the surgical procedure of choice for many HIV-positive individuals and are widely supported both by consumers and surgeons. Primarily performed on MTF and less frequently on FTM transgender individuals, gonad removal may provide a satisfactory sense of completion to the psychological processes of transition.

HIV Interviews

This section contains a selection of brief interviews with several transgender persons living with HIV disease, as well as interviews with their friends and community leaders. Gianna Israel interviewed these individuals during late 1991: follow-up regarding the status of each person as well as commentary is provided at the end of this section. Some names have been changed for the sake of privacy.

Violet—A Survivor

Violet is a thirty-eight-year-old pre- or nonoperative transsexual who simply self-identifies as a transgender woman. She has been living with HIV disease for the past six years and remains asymptomatic of any major opportunistic infections. Violet has been living as a woman for eight years now. She has finished her electrolysis, had breast augmentation, and has both a pleasant personality and appearance. While visiting my office twice, she looked remarkably healthy and attractive. Violet has left the workforce to take care of her health needs; however, she occasionally does paralegal research for law firms and volunteers as a home healthcare aid. Her best friend, Marguerite, has also agreed to be interviewed and comment on how HIV affects their friendship.

Ms. Israel: Thank you for having the courage to interview, Violet. You said earlier that you would interview only under the condition of anonymity.

Violet: Yes, when you first asked me to interview I was hesitant. We are living in changing times, and I don't really care to talk about my health unless it directly affects a person close to me. Right now I see this as a time for taking good care of myself. I don't like the idea of being thought of as a radical AIDS activist or having additional labels attached to me by others. Even though AIDS is a medical problem, too many people become uncomfortable when they find out someone has it. If I tell others about my condition, the way they think about me may change, and they may spend too much time focusing on how I will die. I want people to see me for who I am today. Alive, in good health.

Ms. Israel: When did you first realize you were infected with the HIV virus?

Violet: About ten years ago. I actually wasn't tested for the HIV virus until three years ago when I started having trouble keeping things together, especially with going to work regularly. Even though I was certain something was wrong, I was terribly frightened of getting tested because of the stigma attached to AIDS. Getting tested meant taking on things I wasn't ready to accept.

Ms. Israel: Can you tell me a little more about what getting tested was like?

Violet: When it came right down to it, the act of getting tested was quite easy. Emotionally, I had a real struggle deciding to go in; however, once I saw my health was not improving, I thought I better get tested. So, I called my public health department, who referred me to an anonymous testing site. My first thoughts were that it would be filled with sick, dying people, drug addicts, or people who were screaming and pulling out their hair. I was surprised that the clinic was filled with ordinary-looking people. There were, in fact, several attractive men I wouldn't have minded dating, except a testing site isn't a match-making service. Back to the subject. I was called after a short wait, and went into a small office where I told the counselor I wanted to take the AIDS test. She talked to me about my reasons for wanting to take the test, talked about what I could expect if I turned out to be positive or negative. Then, a nurse came in and took some blood. Afterward, the counselor talked with me about safe[r] sex guidelines. Before leaving I made an appointment to return later in the week. On the day I returned I spoke with the same counselor. She told me I was HIV-positive, and I became so upset I got up and walked out without saying another word. I went home feeling as if I was going to die, and considered ending everything. Later, after I could cry no more, I decided to keep enjoying life since I'm not dead yet.

Ms. Israel: The people who read this interview will benefit from hearing your story. I want to thank you for talking about what obviously was an extremely difficult experience.

Violet: I felt like my mind was going crazy. I hope my telling about it does help someone, even if only to let them know that there is life after taking the test.

Ms. Israel: I noticed you went to an anonymous testing site rather than seeing your family physician.

Violet: Absolutely! I was not sure how my doctor felt about AIDS. Lots of people think it means you are a sick, horrible freak. My doctor also knows many of my coworkers. I felt it was best to be tested anonymously. This was so that I could decide who to tell now. Telling others can wait until I am actually dying.

Ms. Israel: You mentioned safe sex guidelines. There appears to be plenty of information in the media about safe sex. However, what the term means to different people can vary. For the sake of clarity, would you tell me what safe sex means to you?

Violet: Safe sex means always using protection when licking, sucking, or fucking. It's an easy to understand concept. Even hookers make their tricks wear condoms.

Ms. Israel: Your definition for safe sex sounds accurate to me. However, I am wondering, between the time you suspected you were HIV-positive and was actually diagnosed, did you always have safe sex?

Violet: No. I've always told sex partners that I thought I may be HIV-positive, but for most of them it didn't matter. They simply put on the condom I handed them, and we got busy. On several occasions my regular partner and I agreed not to. It was a personal choice. After several times we decided to always use protection because it didn't make sense to put someone I care about at risk. Later, my acupuncturist told me that there are different types of HIV viruses, and that having unsafe sex also put me at risk of catching additional types.

Ms. Israel: Do you feel comfortable sharing where you feel you caught the HIV virus originally?

Violet: No, not really, I hate thinking about the subject. [*long, uncomfortable pause*] Isn't it obvious that it must have gotten passed through sex? Particularly since I do not inject drugs into my body with needles that have been used by others. There, I said it; let's just say as an adult, I love getting mine. I have a lot of trouble talking about sex as the route of transmission because there are a lot of so-called moral people out there spreading herpes, chlamydia, and gonorrhea. There are a lot of people who would judge me as dirty and untouchable because of this disease. For example, my mother told me it was God's will that I die a horrible death from AIDS. According to her, homosexuals and their cohorts deserve punishment for being lower than human. I think all variations of human sexuality and gender are natural, and other people's ignorance and bigotry pisses me off!

Ms. Israel: I sense you have a lot of anger over this subject. Tell me more.

Violet: You're damn right I feel angry. [*more silence*]. I feel hurt and alone. I don't just feel angry; sometimes I feel afraid for my future, very sad at some of the things I have either lost or had to set aside. I was talking with my own therapist just the other day, discussing my fears of becoming involved in another long-term relationship. It seems unfair to ask the man I am currently interested in to get involved with me, knowing that someday I may not be able to take care of his needs. If I get sick, I would also become a burden on him. After a long conversation with my therapist, I came to the understanding that one of the qualities of a person who loves you is that they will have the patience to look beyond the small inconveniences to enjoy the "bigger" you.

Ms. Israel: Violet, I have met you twice in person and your T cells have been under 200 pg/mL since you were tested. It would be difficult to guess that you are HIV-positive just from looking at you. What is your secret for staying so healthy?

Violet: Rest and reduce stress. Now is the time for me to be taking good care of myself. I eat a lot of healthy food and try very hard to cut down on high sugar—no-nutrition junk foods. My eyes tell me that pecan pie and vanilla fudge ice cream look good, but my mind tells me I need to eat vegetables. This is quite a change, since I normally would never consider even looking at something green that grows in dirt. I also try hard to avoid bad relationships that don't help me. Since I last saw you in person, I have also started doing simple, healing meditations and visualizations. I've never really been interested in meditating, but I think visualizing that little Pac-Man-style helpers are running around chomping down HIV viruses helps tell my immune system to do its work. Meditating and visualizing also has helped me feel calmer. My friend Maggie has also been very supportive. She has become part of my "chosen" family, and promised to help me out in time of need no matter what. This gives me some hope that someone will be around to help me if I need it.

Ms. Israel: Are you currently taking AZT, and what other treatments have you sought?

Violet: No, I went on AZT shortly after I was tested and began losing weight. However, four months into trying it, I decided the side effects were killing me. Since going off AZT, I have decided that unless I am actually in the process of falling apart completely, I'm not taking any drug without it having been successful on other people for at least seven years. I have been exploring alternative medical healing. What I found was really helpful is receiving a weekly massage. Marguerite and I get together weekly and give each other massages. If she can't, I find someone who can. Massage is really nice, intimacy without sexual intrusions. I was never touched as a child, so it was difficult at first to allow others to touch me. In trying something new, I found I benefited. Also, I feel very fortunate to have discovered acupuncture. That, combined with good diet, helps me relax and helps keep my body in balance. I am blessed to have good health for so long. Part of that blessing is due to the love I get from my friends I don't think anyone can survive long without attention.

Ms. Israel: As you are aware, your closest friend Marguerite has also agreed to be interviewed. Please tell me how you see HIV as affecting your friendship.

Violet: I think my telling Maggie about my condition has brought about a stronger friendship. Shortly after I was diagnosed, I had to choose which friends I felt I could really trust. A lot of them just don't need to know my business. However, Maggie is such a caring individual. I wanted her to be part of my life on a long-term basis, and I felt she had the right to know. Most of the time our friendship feels good, but other times it feels a little sad because there are dreams we may not be able to pursue together. I know Maggie will always be there as a friend, even should we grow apart. Sometimes it is not easy telling her I am having trouble keeping up with her. But through it all, sometimes I feel our friendship is close enough that we can sense each other's needs without having to speak about them all the time.

Ms. Israel: If your limitations should increase, what do you feel your best friend's needs will be?

Violet: That is something I think you should ask her. We haven't talked a lot on that subject, so I can imagine even reading her interview will bring up some new conversation between us. [*silence*] I would hope that she realizes I care very deeply about her as a friend and that she can feel comfortable talking with me about her needs.

Ms. Israel: What changes in yourself do you see since coming to terms with your HIV diagnosis?

Violet: I see myself as having becoming a lot more focused in what I want to get out of this lifetime. I almost sense that my purpose is basically just in being here . . . and I often find that I am giving myself permission to live and do things I don't think I normally would have done if my life didn't appear limited.

Ms. Israel: Violet, Genital Reassignment Surgery is difficult to obtain for persons infected with the HIV virus. Can you describe for me how you have established a quality life as a woman?

Violet: Initially, I was devastated when I realized I may never have a surgery. It sure as hell set aside any fantasies becoming reality when it comes to being complete physically. But I still have my fantasy life. Perhaps it is possible, if this homophobic society could move away from sexually politicizing this disease, that with medicine it may be reduced to a treatable life disorder. A year ago I went to Belgium with Marguerite to be her cheerleader and helper after surgery. At first I anticipated that witnessing the surgery would be very depressing, but it wasn't, and I met some very nice people. The whole experience left me feeling good about myself, and I realized I am not any less desirable or likable because I am unable to have surgery. Several years ago I had castration [*orchidectomy*] done so that the feminizing benefits of hormones will not be reversed in the event I become ill and unable to take hormones. I also had breast implants. I'm just about finished with my electrolysis, which I have really taken my time doing because I don't tolerate the pain well and am allergic to most painkillers. Except for [*genital-reassignment*] surgery, no one would ever guess that I am not complete. I can still live a womanly lifestyle beyond that old, tired subject of genitals.

Ms. Israel: Tell me about your future.

Violet: Well, I'm dating a real special guy right now. Telling him about my HIV status was the hardest thing I have ever done in my life. We had known each other for about three months, and one evening I decided I better tell him before we became to intimately involved. All along I've been telling him that I had hesitations in forming a long-term relationship . . . and after telling him, he understood why. I ended up taking a taxi home to be alone and sort through my thoughts. He called me to make sure I got home all right and told me he'd be there for me as a friend and that my being HIV-positive didn't matter to him. He told me he always thought that I had a lot of spark and didn't see me as someone giving up and just dying. So, anyway, we are still friends, I think in part he may be my future. Oh, and he and I have committed ourselves to practicing safe sex.

Ms. Israel: I want to thank you for sharing your experiences with me in this interview. Do you have any closing thoughts?

Violet: Not really, except perhaps to say I hope people will practice safe sex, enjoy life, and don't allow themselves to believe that AIDS means an immediate death sentence.

Marguerite—A Friend of a Person with HIV

Ms. Israel: I can imagine that having a friend who is HIV-positive must at times be difficult for you. If this is your experience, what things have been difficult and how do you cope?

Marguerite: The first thing that comes to mind with this question is that Violet doesn't appear to be sick most of the time; and, being in good health myself, I don't always remember that she doesn't have the stamina that I do. She tires easily, and when she gets tired, she does have a tendency to get a bit cranky. Unless I keep her health issues in mind, it can lead to misunderstandings between us. But then, even when that does happen, we are such close friends that those misunderstandings get resolved.

Ms. Israel: Currently, Violet appears healthy, although in her interview she stated she sometimes has limitations in her stamina. There may come a time and place where she is going to need more assistance and may be less able to fulfill your needs as a friend. Would you care to talk about that?

Marguerite: Yes, as I said, her appearance of health now belies her actual condition. As to the future and future needs, one cannot make predictions with any real certainty, but I consider Violet to be more than just my friend; she and I are in a true sense family to each other. In that family sense, she will not want for care from me. To take care of her is the same as taking care of myself.

Ms. Israel: What changes have you seen take place in Violet since she was diagnosed?

Marguerite: I have watched her grow as a person. Not that she wouldn't have if she didn't have HIV disease, but with the thought of one's own certain mortality, the focus is on those things that are really important. For Violet, this means having her own life in order and having true and honest relationships with the people she loves. It has not only been gratifying to watch these changes in her, but they have also been a good part of my own growth process.

Ms. Israel: There would appear to be a greater likelihood of her predeceasing you. What are your thoughts and feelings around this? Has her illness brought on a greater awareness of your own mortality?

Marguerite: Of course. It has reinforced in my own mind the thoughts of mortality that have come with middle age. Violet's health issues have made me aware how special my own life is and what a gift good health is to me.

Ms. Israel: What other issues and feelings have been brought up as a result of witnessing your friend's experiences?

Marguerite: There are many things that her health has brought up for me. First, there are the political issues that revolve around AIDS and what is and is not being done about it. There is also the issue of the cultural homophobia and the lack of understanding about all the issues of gender, and . . . well, just the general patriarchal repression of the culture. On a personal level, I feel that the time that I spend with Violet is all that more special, just because of the finite feeling that our time together has.

Ms. Israel: Certainly you are not alone in having a friend with an HIV infection. What supportive advice can you offer to others who may have a friend with an HIV infection?

Marguerite: Enjoy your time together, be those times good or bad. You have an opportunity for one of the most profound relationships that you can ever have because the imminence of mortality demands of each a complete honesty both to one's self and to the other. That kind of exercise in honesty can only extend itself into all other parts of your life, and an honest life is what it's all about, isn't it?

Jasmine—A Success Story in Recovery and HIV Survival

Gianna Israel met Jasmine at a meditation workshop she facilitated during the summer of 1991. She is an extremely attractive preoperative transsexual woman living with an HIV infection for the past five years. She has been asymptomatic so far. A former prostitute, she has been working forty hours a week at a "yuppie" technical job for the last two and a half years. She lives in a downtown area of Los Angeles and commutes to work. Her T-cell count is under 200, and she has been taking AZT for the past two years. One would never know she is living with an HIV infection by looking at her.

Ms. Israel: It is community knowledge that you are a recovering substance abuser. In what ways do you view your recovery from chemicals as part of your healing journey?

Jasmine: First of all, I have good reason to believe that my infection came as a direct result of my addiction. By abstaining from drug use, including alcohol, I am lessening the likelihood of putting myself in a situation where I could become reinfected with the virus. Furthermore, by staying clean and sober, I am giving my immune system the best possible chance of fighting this disease. Many drugs, especially alcohol and amphetamines, are major immunodepressors and could lead to a bout with ARC [*AIDS-related condition*] or AIDS. Finally, I think being in recovery has given me a healthy emotional and spiritual outlook that gives me the will to live and stay healthy. It is my belief that my love for myself and the will to manifest that love is just as important as maintaining my physical well-being.

Ms. Israel: It must be extremely difficult being triply labeled, as transsexual, lesbian, and HIV-positive. What can you tell me about your experience?

Jasmine: While labels may describe aspects of who I am, I needn't become a label or a stereotype. I can retain my humanity in my own eyes despite labels. One of the things I learned in recovery is that my self-esteem comes from within and that only I have the power to diminish my self-esteem. Ego, on the other hand, is a weak, externally defined view of myself that is extremely fragile and susceptible to undermining by others. By loving myself unconditionally, I build my self-esteem and minimize the importance of my ego.

It is sometimes difficult being a lesbian when many other lesbians have trouble accepting transsexuals as "real" women, and being HIV-positive increases this difficulty. Unfortunately, many lesbians don't see HIV as an issue that directly concerns them, so my being infected sometimes serves as another barrier to assimilation into the lesbian community. Fortunately, awareness of these issues is increasing among lesbians, and the barriers are slowly coming down.

Ms. Israel: It is obvious you expect to continue living with HIV. What wisdom would you wish to pass on to other transsexuals dealing with this disease?

Jasmine: As a former sex worker with ties to people still in that industry, I would suggest that TS [*transsexual*] prostitutes find another line of work, or at least one that doesn't involve sexual contact that would serve as grounds for arrest for PC 647b [*prostitution*] and place one at risk for reinfection. First of all, California has an oppressive law that permits nonconsentual HIV antibody testing of those convicted of prostitution, and provides for felony prosecution of those who test positive and are arrested for 647b again. Secondly, even condoms can't guarantee 100 percent safety, and they won't protect you from the mandatory testing law either. Finally, prostitutes often lead an unhealthy lifestyle that excludes exercise, sufficient sleep, good dietary habits, and it often involves drugs. By switching to exotic dancing, domination, phone sex, or other jobs, it is possible to stay in the sex industry and be more safe.

No matter how you support yourself, I would suggest living as healthy a lifestyle as possible. That includes abstaining from all drugs, including alcohol, caffeine, and nicotine, or at least cutting down to a minimal level. I would also recommend cutting hormone dosage to as low a level as is still effective. Hormones put a strain on the liver, as do many of the AIDS drugs such as AZT. By cutting your hormones to a minimum, you improve your overall health. Since I am a year away from being financially ready for my surgery, I had an orchidectomy [*castration*] so that I could reduce my estrogen dosage to a bare minimum without becoming masculinized.

I can't stress how important my recovery from addiction has been to me. It has contributed to my spiritual and emotional health as well as having had physical benefits. Aside from acquiring a spiritual belief system that is the source of untold strength, I have the support of fellow recovering addicts and alcoholics who provide me with yet another reason to be alive. In general, my recovery has given me so much of a desire for life that I believe it is the principle reason I continue to stay healthy.

Robin—A Letter of Compassion

After hearing that she was interviewing transgender individuals dealing with the HIV virus, Robin—one of Ms. Israel's ongoing clients—expressed interest in participating by writing a letter. Robin is an inspiring preoperative transsexual living with an HIV disorder. Her life-long struggle has been in dealing with an overwhelming sense of depression.

Dear Reader:

The first time I elected to approach the issue of being transgender I was only fifteen. Needless to say, although the doctors admitted that I was more woman than man, they decided that I was to learn to consider myself homosexual. For many years I hid my gender problem not only from others but from myself as well.

Today I am in my thirties and because I am HIV+, I have decided that it is now or never in dealing my gender issues, so in November of 1990 I began.

The first thing I needed was to seek the guidance of a good counselor. Lucky for me I was able to find an excellent one. The second thing I needed to do was get in touch with the real me, the girl who got lost in a shuffle of misguidance by a group of doctors who began to lead my life into a mass of drugs and confusion. This where I am at now.

In a sad way, Being HIV+ and on AZT has helped me to realize how important it is to live my life to its fullest. I now take one day at a time and if I may add, it is often very hard to do even that. I have to constantly remind myself that who I am today is just that, and, if I am here tomorrow then tomorrow is who I am. Hopefully each day will bring me closer to getting reacquainted with and learning to love the woman I know I was meant to become.

Sometimes I find the only ways I can deal with these struggles in my life are in self-destructive ways. Often-times I will take just enough barbiturates to knock myself out. Then there are other times I will drink alcohol. Sometimes I have even combined the two. Thankfully I am learning more healthy ways to deal with my life.

I am blessed with the understanding of certain family members and a handful of loyal friends, so I now have the opportunity to talk to one of them if needed. I have also joined groups with others who have similar issues.

One very important thing for me is having an honest and caring psychiatrist on hand to help me with my depressions. I'm not saying that everyone need seek professional help or medications because everyone's situation is different. However, if it were not for the healthier ways of living I have learned, and also perhaps the various medications I am now on, I doubt if I would be writing this letter.

Another form of help and guidance is through meditation, self-hypnosis, and visualization. In these ways I can actually enter into my own body and attempt to pull out some of the sickness, tossing it into a pit of imaginary crimson fire where it is destroyed forever. I also have a spirit guide or if you prefer a Higher Power. He is there when ever I call and has helped me through a lot of troubles in my life.

I realize that there is only so far I can go with my gender issues because of my HIV status, but with a lot of help and a little more hope, each day may bring more answers to those of us who are ready to ask.

Sincerely,
Robin L.

Dallas Denny—A Public Person Speaks Out

Ms. Dallas Denny is the director of AEGIS, the American Educational Gender Information Service, and publisher of *Chrysalis,* a nationally respected magazine serving the transgender community. Ms. Denny is licensed in Tennessee as a psychological examiner. She has twenty years' experience in the mental health field and has worked with transgender persons since 1989. She is a prolific author and is currently completing the Ed.D. degree at George Peabody College of Vanderbilt University.

Ms. Israel: Any preliminary thoughts?

Ms. Denny: Perhaps the term "conspiracy of silence" is too strong a term to describe what has happened with AIDS in this country—and perhaps it isn't. When I think of how things have been and continue to be—the past and present foot-dragging in Washington; the eagerness of the general public to treat a disease which affects us all as "gay-only" and to blame gay men for its spread; the resistance of the populace to the distribution of condoms and to sex education; the fear of and hostility toward persons who are infected; the current hysteria about mandatory testing of health care workers—I am diminished.

Ms. Israel: Presently the majority of the transgender community and its publications appear to be silent on the issue of AIDS. Silence appears to be broadcasting the message that this is a "gay-only" disease, yet in my counseling practice I have encountered growing numbers of HIV-positive individuals who are transgender. Do you see AIDS as the catalyst that will uncover internalized homophobia within our community? Do you have any thoughts you wish to share with your fellow community leaders and educators?

Ms. Denny: I do see AIDS as a divisive force within the transgender community. I also see it as a force that helps maintain the separation between transgender and nontransgender persons.

The majority of gender-conflicted persons would seem to be less sexually active than average. There is data which indicates that crossdressers are less sexually experienced than other men, and many transsexual people are so conflicted that they avoid sexual activity entirely. Yet there is a small but highly visible segment of the transgender community which is highly sexually active.

Transsexual prostitutes are not uncommon. The high costs of physical maintenance associated with transition coupled with the inability to find work in the gender of choice leads some transsexual people to rely upon their bodies for their livelihood. One doubts that safe sex is a high priority for someone who, in desperation, turns to prostitution.

The majority of transgender persons lead quiet lives. They are, for all practical purposes, invisible to the general public. However, the transgender people on the streets are very visible and very vocal. And many of these people are notoriously promiscuous, and so at high risk for AIDS. They serve as negative press agents. They are what many people think of when they hear the word *transsexual*. Their behavior reinforces negative stereotypes and helps to maintain the "freak" status of transsexual people. Other transsexual people know this, and dislike them for it. This will no doubt become more of a problem as the AIDS epidemic escalates.

You are right in your observation that transgender publications rarely mention AIDS. Certainly they should. I think editors often deal with the issue by not dealing with it. The readers certainly need information, especially as it relates to gender issues. They need to realize, for instance, that thinking of oneself as a female in a sexual relationship does not reduce the risk of transmission of the virus during anal intercourse. They need to learn safe sex techniques and to know that sharing of needles is extremely risky. And they need to learn tolerance and love for persons who are HIV-positive.

I suspect that the segment of the transgender community most in need of information is the sexually active group I mentioned earlier. These people typically do not read transgender publications. They are usually heavily involved in the gay community, and I suspect they might best be reached in the same ways that gay men and women are reached.

Ms. Israel: What thoughts do you have on proposing a "Publisher's Standard," which would mean including AIDS-prevention guidelines in all books, magazines, and other materials with the purpose of providing education surrounding the issues of gender or sexual identity?

Ms. Denny: I think your suggestion for a "Publisher's Standard" is an excellent one, and AEGIS will support any such standard. In fact, we'd be happy to be the first to print it and will help you to develop the standard, if you're interested.

I'm not sure that all educational materials need to address the issue of AIDS, but certainly many, and perhaps most, do. It might not be appropriate, for instance, to have a long digression on AIDS in a booklet that purports to help the individual to speak in a feminine or masculine voice. But it would certainly be inappropriate to leave AIDS information out of a booklet which was a general discussion of transsexualism. I think that every publisher should address the issue in the most appropriate place or places—placing public-service advertisements in magazines, for instance, and publishing articles about AIDS. We've spoken about AIDS in *Chrysalis,* but the thought of running an AIDS ad hadn't occurred to me until I just said what I did.

Ms. Israel: As a mental health professional who is involved with the transgender community, I can imagine that you also have received calls from transgender individuals living in isolated parts of the country, many of which have few resources. This state of aloneness can be compounded for the individual dealing with an HIV infection. What words of support and encouragement can you give to our brothers and sisters living in isolation?

Ms. Denny: I recently received a letter from a young lady you are acquainted with. She desperately wants Genital Reassignment Surgery, but her HIV-positive status makes it highly unlikely that she will get it. My heart went out to her.

Those with AIDS may have to look a little harder, or may even have to take the initiative and start something themselves. They are, after all, a minority within a minority. HIV-positive status is an additional burden.

It can be tough if you live in an isolated area. The cities have always been a gathering place for minorities, and the transgender are no exception. If there is a major city nearby, there may be resources. But for those who aren't able to travel, there are alternatives. Publications like *Transgender Tapestry* feature nonsexual personal ads. It's possible to strike up friendships through the mail. Pen pals can become real pals, especially if you're lucky enough to find someone who lives in the same general area. Once you have become friends, an occasional telephone call can be of benefit.

Those with computers and modems will find that there are a number of computer bulletin boards available to them. Logging on to these systems is like joining a social club. There are messages, announcements, fantasies, short stories, and ongoing discussions of all types. It would be very easy to start a discussion of AIDS on a computer bulletin board.

It has been my experience that a good deal of the isolation of transgender persons is self-imposed. Fear and guilt and denial are very effective barriers. And they can be torn down only from the inside of the wall. Learning to be comfortable with yourself will help others to become comfortable with you.

Kim Elizabeth Stuart—On HIV Education and Employment

Ms. Kim Stuart has established a distinguished career as an employment counselor, noted political commentator, and widely respected author of *The Uninvited Dilemma,* a guidebook for anyone dealing with transgender issues.

Ms. Israel: How do you see AIDS affecting the transgender community in the future, and what resources does that community need to create for itself in order to support transgender individuals living with AIDS?

Ms. Stuart: I think AIDS will have a devastating effect on any community whose members place themselves in a high-risk category. The gay community is an example of how members of a group can change the course of events through the education of their own members. When the gay community started practicing safe sex, the infection rate dropped dramatically.

Any person—gay, heterosexual, or transgender—puts himself or herself at risk if he or she practices unsafe sex or takes drugs intravenously and uses paraphernalia that has not been properly sterilized.

My answer to the second part of your question is that I see no need to duplicate effort and support for those who are HIV-positive. This disease is not confined to the gay population. Transgender people and others need to provide ongoing support within network that already exists and work for more funding to increase and expand that network. Education should be an ongoing priority to prevent the spread of AIDS.

Ms. Israel: Ms. Stuart, you have long been an employment specialist within the transgender community I wonder what wisdom you wish to pass along to the transgender HIV-positive individual who is able and looking for work?

Ms. Stuart: AIDS is a public-health issue which has become politicized. When this happens, not only do those who are HIV-positive suffer, but the entire nation pays a price. Homophobics like Senator Jesse Helms of North Carolina are only dividing the country instead of uniting it against a disease that can affect any citizen. Senator Helms and his ilk are simply out to get gays, not to solve the problems. Their priorities are punishment, not health care or prevention. I would advise any person, transgender or not, to resist any and all efforts for mandatory testing.

Having a negative HIV test only provides people with a false sense of security. Subsequently, I would strongly urge all people who are HIV-positive not to reveal that knowledge to employers. Health providers who take appropriate safeguards pose a minimal risk to patients, despite recent publicity. I know of only one case where a health provider has been implicated in infecting patients, and after careful scrutiny, investigators now believe he passed on the infection by means of a dental instrument that was not properly sterilized—not by means of blood-to-blood contact.

Until AIDS is recognized as a public-health problem and removed from the political arena, I would advise all HIV-positive persons to make sure they protect themselves as well as others, and resist all efforts to make testing mandatory.

Commentary

Despite San Francisco's central role as the area hardest hit by the AIDS epidemic within the United States, as recently as the early 1990s it was extremely difficult locating HIV care services in that city that were sensitive to the needs of transgender women and men. During the summer and fall of 1991, as she began laying the foundation for this resource section, Gianna Israel attempted to interview a variety of large local AIDS organizations and several therapists regarding transgender issues and HIV disease. While doing so, she was repeatedly told that the organizations were not aware of transgender persons or that she would be better off abandoning the interviews as "too controversial."

Fortunately, as transgender persons have become a more visible population, San Francisco's HIV care services have responded accordingly. There are now a variety of clinics, support groups, and programs that specialize in or are at least aware of the unique needs of transgender persons. We, the authors, however, are concerned that in other locations where transgender persons are less visible, specialized HIV care may be difficult if not impossible to locate.

"Violet" is doing well. Five years after being interviewed, her T cells remain low; and she has not developed any opportunistic infections. With advances in science, she now also has the option of having HIV-cell "viral load" checked to see how active the virus is, but she prefers to depend primarily on Eastern medicine for her medical care. During our contact with her, she felt optimistic about the new protease inhibitors that are being developed to combat HIV replication. Currently, Violet is no longer in a close relationship with Marguerite; however, she has developed other family-oriented relationships.

"Jasmine" did not respond to our request for an update. However, as recently as six months ago she spoke with Ms. Israel. During that time she appeared in good health and said she was doing well. Over the past five years she has been a source of inspiration to those who know her. This is particularly so, as she remains clean and sober.

"Robin" passed away nine months after submitting her letter. Her last month in life was difficult. She found it challenging to begin living in role full time as a woman, particularly as she battled several major infections. On a positive note, she stated several times that her last months were her best. After spending a lifetime struggling in San Francisco's harsh Tenderloin neighborhood, she met a boyfriend who invited her to live in his penthouse overlooking the city. She stayed there as he took care of her to the end.

Robin's experiences serve as a reminder that our noblest efforts at being human are when we help others. Transgender men and women can help those dealing with the HIV virus by donating money to local HIV care organizations that are inclusive of transgender persons or by volunteering their time as a home care assistant. The latter service provides the means for individuals living with AIDS to remain secure in the comfort of their own homes.

Recommended Guidelines for Hormone Administration, Aesthetic Surgery, and Genital Reassignment in HIV-Positive and Immunocompromised Individuals

Caution: A full understanding of these guidelines is not possible without reading the material in the preceding sections of this chapter. Readers are reminded that hormone administration, aesthetic surgery, and Genital Reassignment Surgery can each effectively produce intended psychological and physical outcomes with a balanced consideration of the patient's surgical preparedness, variable risks associated with all medical procedures, and recognized medical and consumer recommendations. Additionally, all care providers are reminded when working with HIV-positive individuals that confidentiality is essential, and in some locations confidentiality is protected by law or required by liability insurance policies. Care providers are advised that overlooking patient confidentiality is likely to endanger the individual's psychological, medical, social, family, and employment circumstances.

1. Hormone administration for HIV-positive individuals should follow the guidelines at the end of Chapter 3.

2. Individuals utilizing physician-prescribed self-injected hormones should follow the physician's advice in the handling, cleaning, and disposal of syringes. Needle sharing is strongly discouraged.

3. HIV-positive and immunocompromised individuals are commonly prescribed prophylactic treatments or medicinal, antidepressive, dietary, and other regimens that may impair liver functioning. Physicians should be especially mindful of the monitoring of liver function.

4. Physicians (as well as both MTF and FTM consumers) are advised to review gonad-removal options because such procedures require individuals to utilize lower postsurgical dosages of hormones, thus placing less stress on long-term liver functioning. Intravaginal removal of organs in FTM surgical patients is advised over other procedures that might involve increased surgical invasiveness.

5. Evaluations regarding surgical appropriateness for aesthetic and Genital Reassignment Surgeries should follow the guidelines found at the ends of Chapter 4 and 5.

5a. To date, numerous HIV-positive individuals having a stable "fair" or better health condition have undergone aesthetic surgical procedures with no known untoward effects. Such procedures include mastectomy, breast augmentation mammoplasty, facial cosmetic surgery, and other minor elective procedures.

5b. A handful of HIV-positive individuals have undergone Genital Reassignment Surgery performed by reputable surgeons. The surgical recommendations herein are the first ever proposed for these individuals because, at present, no case studies document how Genital Reassignment Surgery affects the immune system postsurgically. However, extensive studies have been done on general, cardiac, orthopedic, and other medically necessary surgical procedures. These operations have not adversely effected immune systems of stable HIV-positive patients. Furthermore, the ethical guidelines of the American Medical Association state that physicians may not withhold medically necessary therapy because of the physicians' fear of contracting the patient's diseases.

6. Surgeons are advised to consult with a surgical candidate's primary physician to verify the individual's current health status and the medical appropriateness for *any* surgical procedure. Candidates having "fair" or better health conditions may be considered medically appropriate, particularly when an aesthetic surgery or genital-reassignment procedure is deemed psychologically beneficial to the individual's quality of life.

7. "Fair" health or better shall be inclusive of the individual's being free of associated diseases and major opportunistic infections for three months with regard to aesthetic surgeries and for six months with regard to Genital Reassignment Surgery. Such diseases would include Kaposi's sarcoma and *Pneumocystis carinii* pneumonia. Examples of major opportunistic infections would include systemic candidiasis, systemic or chronic mucocutaneous herpes simplex, aspergillosis, cryptococcal diseases, cytomegalovirus infection, nocardiosis, strongyloidiasis, toxoplasmosis, zygomycosis, and tuberculosis.

8. Surgeons are advised to evaluate the appropriateness and role of individualized pre- and postsurgical prophylaxis. This may help prevent the development of hospital-acquired illness or the reactivation of a latent disease.

9. Surgeons unwilling to perform surgical procedures on individuals designated as medically appropriate by the candidate's primary physician are advised to refer such individuals to reputable surgeons familiar with operating on HIV-positive individuals.

10. Surgeons and primary physicians who view an individual as medically inappropriate for the extensive invasiveness of Genital Reassignment Surgery yet recognize the individual as appropriate for the lesser invasiveness of gonad-removal surgery are advised to inform the individual that such procedures are available. MTF gonad removal (orchidectomy) and FTM gonad removal (oophorectomy, via intravaginal methods) do not have the extreme invasiveness or graft complications associated with more complex genital-reassignment procedures.

Numerous orchidectomies have been performed on MTF transgender individuals who are HIV-positive, with no known contraindications for those established as being in a stable "fair" or better health condition. Little information is available regarding HIV-positive FTM response to gonad removal. Gonad removal is reported to provide individuals with some psychological sense of completion, whereas not having any procedure leaves the individual in the limbo of transition and may contribute to gender dysphoria. Pharmacologically, gonad removal enables the administration of lower dosages of hormones, thus lowering long-term risks of liver damage and other side effects.

11. Being deemed medically inappropriate for any one or all surgical procedures carries a heavy psychological burden for transgender individuals. Surgeons declining to perform surgical procedures as well as primary physicians discouraging individuals from seeking these surgeries are advised to refer or provide psychological support when turning an individual away.

12. Being crossdressed or living in role provides no one protection from the HIV virus. Individuals who anticipate having sex or having a fantasy fulfilled are strongly advised to carry prophylactic protection.

Cultural Diversity

Chapter 7

_____

*1784—Deborah Gannet, a black female, serves as a man
in the 4th Massachusetts Regiment and later is cited for bravery
in action*

Being transgender and experiencing crossgender needs is a human condition that is present in all cultures and societies. One would hope that this would be cause for a proud celebration of individual and community diversity, and in some societies it is. However, even though it would be erroneous to say that all transgender people of color are struggling and downtrodden, the odds are badly stacked against those who are easily identifiable as members of "dual minorities." Such persons are subject to the compound stress of transphobia and racism.

Providing background information about and promoting understanding in support of transgender people of color are difficult propositions, as each ethnic group presents its own set of cultural values, relationships, social dynamics, communication styles, and even language. Moreover, no individual transgender consumer can ever represent all of the variables characteristic of her or his ethnic minority group. Thus, the Guidelines present broad themes regarding cultural diversity, to provide a frame of reference for supporting transgender individuals in any ethnic minority.

Providing support to ethnic minority individuals can give both care providers and consumers an opportunity to examine and celebrate crosscultural or intracultural dynamics. Taking the time to reflect upon crosscultural differences provides one the opportunity to expand one's empathic skills and to fine-tune one's cultural competency in meeting the needs of all people.

Crosscultural Differences and the Provision of Transgender Care

The informed care provider will develop approaches and attitudes relevant to most environments. First, *assume nothing*. Even if a care provider feels that he or she knows a great deal about a particular ethnic group or culture, it is best to remain open to learning something new. Second, approach questions from an acknowledged position of inexperience and as someone interested in hearing about the individual's distinct cultural experiences. This approach can be a helpful ice-breaking tool and signal that the care provider does not fear disclosure of racial or cultural concerns. A specific request should be made for dialogue about the individual's cultural experiences, perceptions, and emotional responses.

Drawing out relevant information in support of the individual's gender issues can be especially difficult for individuals of certain cultural backgrounds. For them, the difficulty of crosscultural communication in a formal or professional support setting can be acute. Transgender people of color may feel uninhibited and open to the discussion of sensitive, personal issues in a casual or familial relationship whereas their white American counterparts may be more culturally familiar with psychotherapeutic environments and talking to strangers about the most intimate details of their lives. The reluctance to open up across racial and cultural barriers is common in ethnic minority cultures because of a mistrust of persons identified with the dominant culture. Moreover, even when the care giver and consumer share the same racial or ethnic background, the consumer's comfort with personal disclosure may be limited by his or her perception of (or actual) differences in their acculturation to the dominant racial culture. Acculturation factors might be considered for the care giver and the consumer according to the following: the greater the difference between their degrees of acculturation, the care giver and the consumer, the greater the need to inquire about and negotiate cultural differences.

> The greater the difference between the degrees of acculturation of the care giver and the consumer, the greater the need to inquire about and negotiate cultural differences.

The degree of acculturation can be described as follows: The *assimilated* person has largely adopted the values and characteristics of the dominant racial or ethnic culture. For example, in the United States, most white people would be considered highly assimilated to the pervasive, institutionalized European cultural norms.

The *integrated (bicultural)* person has socially or professionally adapted to the dominant racial culture; however, the person also identifies selectively but strongly with a racial or cultural minority culture. For example, such a person typically moves comfortably between the dominant white American culture in their workplace or in the health care setting, while adopting the more familiar language and behavior styles of an ethnic minority group when among family and peers.

The *separate (culturally immersed)* person has limited contact with the dominant culture and is exclusively identified with a racial minority culture. This distance from the dominant culture may be by choice or may be the result of exclusion via racism. The person typically feels validated only by close association with other persons who share the same racial or ethnic culture.

The *marginalized* person is distant both from the dominant, majority culture and the culture of origin. These persons are at a particularly high risk of despair and are particularly vulnerable to multiple oppressions because they lack support from any social group. Tragically, too many transgender people of color end up in this state of alienation from both society and their culture of origin, lacking both vital cultural group identification and social support.

One of the care provider's first tasks is to pursue a cultural assessment by discussing cultural values, beliefs, and loyalties with the consumer. It may well be determined that, whether in crosscultural or intracultural dialogue, there are major differences between the two with regard to cultures of origin and degrees of acculturation to the majority culture. Such differences are common and must be respected. Time must be allowed for building trust, exchanging cultural information, and anticipating more gradual disclosure. Initially, this means that some individuals may feel extremely uncomfortable when questioned about sex, sexual practices, and intimate feelings. Others may have great difficulty discussing negative family dynamics. Finally, some individuals may reject or feel uncomfortable with physical contact, such as touching or hugging. These cultural differences *must* be respected by all care providers, whether support counselors or medical professionals.

When providing support, it is often best to first ask individuals how they feel about discussing sex, talking about family members, and whether they would like nonsexual physical contact if appropriate. These dynamics should also be kept in mind when asking individuals with cultural differences to fill out intake forms and questionnaires, as some individuals may reject the idea of writing down their most intimate experiences and thoughts. Because of the additional time that may be required to build the trust necessary to transcend cultural differences, the care provider should invite the consumer to raise issues of cultural significance at any time.

Cultural competency (that is, highly skilled cultural knowledge, sensitivity, and experience) should also be extended to immigrants and foreign visitors who come to the United States or western Europe to seek out expertise and services for their transgender needs. As international travel expands, it has become all the more commonplace for the specialized care provider to encounter transgender persons from as far away as Cairo, Moscow, or Tokyo. In these situations the care provider would be well advised to research the cultural and religious values of the individual, particularly in light of the fact that some foreign-born individuals may have survived under the threat of societal ostracism, unlawful imprisonment, sexual abuse, and physical torture, abuses "justified" solely on the basis of transgender identification.

Working with an interpreter can also prove challenging as the care provider strives to meet the needs of immigrants, or those who may be visiting for a short time. It is highly recommended that the provider strongly encourage non-English-speaking individuals to come prepared with a list of focus items or inquiries, since working through an interpreter can be a time-consuming process. Another option, if appropriate, is to refer these transgender individuals to multilingual, culture-specific agencies that serve transgender individuals.

Ethnicity, Race, and the Transgender Experience

The experience of a person of color as an African American (or being of African descent), Asian or Pacific Islander, Latina or Latino, or Native American can vary widely, depending on age, family generation, and economic background. As an example, the experiences and needs of a first- or even second-generation Japanese American may differ sharply from those of a fourth- or fifth-generation Japanese American. The latter may have a greater proportion of Westernized ideals, yet still retain concerns about racial discrimination or varying family structures and values. Similarly, differences due to generational factors or socioeconomic class may also intrude on the provider-consumer relationship.

An example of one common support theme that differs among ethnic groups is the reaction of peers within an ethnic community to an individual's transgender identification. In an African American, Asian or Pacific Islander, or Latin American context, for example, heterosexual males and females commonly will stereotype gay males and lesbians as not being a part of their ethnic community because they assume that all people of color are or should be heterosexual. This ostracism carries over to transgender individuals, who are then stereotyped as gay or lesbian because many communities fail to distinguish between gender identity and sexual orientation.

Transgender people of color are unwilling, in fact unable, to divide their identities along race and gender lines, though the racial or ethnic community or the transgender community may demand, "Which are you first, transgender or black?" (or Latino, Native American, Asian-Pacific Islander, as may be the case). The answer can never be to choose between one inseparable aspect of self and another. That would be as if to say that the oppression of one targeted aspect of oneself, such as gender identity, is more or less important than discrimination against another aspect, such as race. One must strive to build a positive self-image that embraces the concept of a whole being, self-satisfied with one's personal attributes, including race and gender.

The transgender community must also come to understand that transgender people of color do not "check their culture at the door." Culture and race must be viewed as having equal importance to an individual's identity and presentation. Community services and events should recognize cultural diversity in their planning, administration, and implementation. In particular, every possible effort should be made to involve people of color in planning and providing services so as to reliably ensure cultural competency—a step beyond cultural sensitivity that includes the added elements of knowledge, skill, and implementation.

Just as there is certain to be transphobia among individuals of any race, it is essential to recognize that racism exists within the transgender community. For example, an African American drag queen who was attacked along with his friends by police during the 1969 Stonewall Rebellion in New York City was later referred to in the community as a "nigger" and subsequently denied entrance to gay community meetings. It is no wonder that many transgender people of color either remain isolated within their ethnic minority communities or exiled from the white dominant culture of the transgender community and community services.

When visiting professional or transgender community support groups, one is often left wondering why few persons of color are in attendance. Is it that they feel unwelcome? Are they aware of support and social groups? Do they not see such groups as realistically supporting their needs? To gain some perspective on individuals of color within the transgender community, we can consider San Francisco's model of community and support services.

San Francisco is by far one of the most ethnically diverse cities in the United States and in many respects compares favorably with other large international gateway cities, such as New York and Los Angeles. Aside from the fact that ethnic diversity has been evident in the general population for many years, it was only recently that African Americans and Asians or Pacific Islanders became visible in the Bay Area's largest transgender social organization, Educational Transvestite Chapter (ETVC). In the past, ETVC events so rarely included people of color that one African American guest at an ETVC social function remarked in a television interview that he felt he must have been the only African American crossdresser around.

The 1995 ETVC Cotillion made advances in welcoming and recognizing transgender people of color. Two African American transgender women, Sheri Webb of the Tenderloin AIDS Resource Center and Doris Robinson of the Brothers Network agencies, served as talent contest judges. Kiki Whitlock, an Asian-Pacific Islander transgender woman, received commendations and an award for her legislative endeavors.

People of color constitute the majority of the population in San Francisco, which leads to several crucial observations. After comparing a primarily white-attended and middle-income-funded social organizations such as ETVC with the city's mental-health and social services, one quickly comes to recognize that the further down one looks on the socioeconomic ladder, the more evident African American and other ethnic minorities become. Tragically, once people of color realize this, they recognize that obtaining professional and social support suddenly has become "their" problem. Mainstream transgender organizations can do much more than they are doing now to reach out to transgender communities of color. "Going through the motions" cannot mask the facade of racism, elitism, and sexism that many transgender people of color regularly face.

Nationally, the mental health and social services support for transgender individuals of color is minimal, at best. Under constant threat of budget cuts and overburdened by a diversity of needs, these agencies face an ongoing struggle to survive, much less provide specialized services to transgender individuals. Like culturally sensitive and gay or lesbian bisexual populations, transgender persons face intense competition when they pitted against other populations.

Although not all transgender persons of color are trapped on the lower rungs of the socioeconomic ladder, it is imperative that professionals and transgender community alike recognize that people of color sometimes face disproportionately higher rates of victimization, unemployment, substance abuse, HIV infection, prostitution, and other difficulties. In addition, many go for years without mental health support for their transgender needs and have little money available for electrolysis, hormones, or reconstructive surgeries. As a result, some people of color from lower socioeconomic levels are more likely to seek out illicit medical services, such as silicone injections, "back room" breast implants, or hormones from black-market supplies. In addition to health risks they pose, many of these illicit services cost more than the same services from established resources.

Recommended Guidelines for Transgender People of Color

1. Hormone administration, aesthetic surgery and Genital Reassignment Surgery advice for transgender people of color should observe the Guidelines found at the ends of Chapters 3, 4, and 5.

2. Given the fact that HIV disease and AIDS are disproportionately found among people of color worldwide, it is important to observe the Guidelines at the end of Chapter 6.

3. The decision-making process of any gender-confirmation procedure needs to allow for the following critical factors:

- Informed consent obtained in the language of greatest fluency of the transgender consumer.
- The degree of cultural difference between the care provider and the transgender consumer.
- Family and traditional ethnic community perspectives.
- Frank discussion between care provider and consumer regarding the effects of racism and cultural difference upon their work together.
- The care provider's level of knowledge regarding the consumer's cultural background.

4. Care providers should endeavor to ensure that professional services are equally accessible to people of color, and that selection criteria do not contain racial bias.

5. The Guidelines advise that both transgender status and racial or ethnic minority identification be viewed as complementary and integral aspects of an individual's identity.

6. Care providers should seek to identify and make referral to support services that focus upon issues concerning transgender people of color. Two such national resources are the Black Gay and Lesbian Leadership Forum and National Task Force on AIDS Prevention.

7. Transgender people of color face compound stressors resulting from transphobia and racism, which may result in a need for additional emotional and social support services, as well as possible legal redress of discrimination. The San Francisco Human Rights Commission has resource listings of a variety of international resources that may prove of use. (See the listing of resources in the Appendix.)

Transgender Youth

Chapter 8

_____

No single group has gone more unnoticed by society, or abused and maltreated by institutional powers, than youth with transgender needs and feelings. With the exception of its attention to child labor and child abuse or neglect law, our society has relegated children to a class virtually without voice or rights in society. Even the most disenfranchised group of adults can usually seek out information and mobilize to effect positive change. Complicating these concerns are the fact that most transgender youth remain invisible; most of those experiencing crossgender feelings are indistinguishable from other youth. With few exceptions, they do not publicly crossdress or appear feminized or masculinized; as adolescents, they have a significant investment in appearing indistinguishable from their nontransgender peers. The overwhelming message from family, adult society, and youth peers says that gender nonconformity is a sick, mentally unstable condition to be feared, hated, and ridiculed. Transgender youth quickly give in, suppressing their transgender identity rather than face ostracism. Care providers and parents interested in supporting transgender youth will duly note that it is _imperative_ that the adult establish that discussion regarding gender identity concerns is appropriate, and that the adult is an empathic and nonjudgmental individual in whom the young person can confide.

The Transgender Experience in Adolescence

Experiences of transgender feelings or of a desire to crossdress often reach a peak during puberty, when these young adults are in their junior-high and high-school years. According to Luanna Rodgers, MFCC (Marriage, Family and Child Counselor), a Gender Specialist familiar with youth issues, approximately

3 percent of the general population experience concerns about gender identity. This means that three of every one hundred young adults may have transgender feelings. Also, it is of equal interest that Kim Elizabeth Stuart, author of *The Uninvited Dilemma,* found that approximately 75 percent of surveyed adults felt that "gender discomfort" had caused social problems during their youth.

Because isolation and ostracism are key components of transgender youth experience, it would be irresponsible to overlook the associated mental health concerns of substance abuse, self-abuse, depression, and suicide or suicidal ideation. Although statistics may vary, the difficulty these individuals face is evident when we consider that approximately 50 percent to 88 percent have seriously considered or attempted suicide. When a young adult commits suicide, the loss is final; no opportunity remains for others to step in and help. Fortunately, young adults experiencing depression and suicidal ideation, as well as those who have become involved in substance abuse, more often than not display warning signs that an attentive adult will hopefully notice.

The Warning Signs of Troubled Youth

- A significant change in sleeping or eating patterns.
- A dramatic loss of interest in presentation and personal hygiene.
- Drastic changes in mood, attitude, and reactions.
- A sudden loss of interest in all previous social activities and hobbies.
- Skipping classes.
- A rapid decline in grade point average.
- Quick changes in friends, especially to those who seem dishonest, or poor influences.

Family Responses

Dealing with a young individual who has questions about gender or who has expressed interest in crossdressing can be very difficult situation for most parents. Panic is frequently one of the first responses caring parents experience when they perceive something is amiss with their child. They ask: "What did we do wrong? Is my child mentally ill? What will others think if they find out? How do I deal with this shocking news?" Regardless of the child's age, most parents feel confused, angry, self-doubting, and deeply worried when they learn of their child's crossdressing or gender identity issues. These feelings are frequently exacerbated by the parents' belief that there is no place to turn for help.

During this time of crisis, parents typically make incorrect assumptions, such as "Oh, no, my son or daughter must be gay or lesbian!" Others may believe they did something wrong, or that the child must be mentally unbalanced. In their search for answers, many parents turn to a school counselor, local therapist, or their minister, priest, or rabbi. Unfortunately, in most circumstances these persons are not familiar with gender-identity or sexual-orientation issues. The fact is, even most mental health professionals are not familiar with gender issues. This is because, with the exception of actively practicing Gender Specialists or clinical sexologists, the vast majority of mental health professionals receive no formal training in this specialty, and what little information they have is erroneous. As a result, parents may assume or be misled into believing that their child's behavior is deviant and unhealthy, or that the child is being "difficult." Frequently, they are told they must work to suppress the child's behavior.

While it is true, particularly during puberty, that a young person is likely to ask questions about gender and sexuality, it should be noted that these are separate components of self-identity. Some parents who lack the insight and awareness needed to accept human nature may attempt to control the behavior. Others seek to have the crossgendered feelings and behaviors "cured" through punishment or by endlessly seeking mental health treatments. In extreme situations, if a young individual is not physically abused, he or she is locked into closets and bedrooms or denied opportunities to socialize and lead an ordinary childhood. Some are shipped away to boarding schools, behavioral camps, or institutions where rigidly enforced social conformity further represses their needs. In any event, minimizing, controlling, punishing, or attempting to "cure" a transgender identity tragically does more harm than good, no matter how well intentioned the regimen.

As there are no treatment models for curing transgender feelings, needs, or behaviors, one is left to wonder what types of treatment transgender youth have endured at the hands of parents and professionals. The latter, despite being licensed, have no actual background or training in supporting transgender individuals, much less any recognized affiliation with professional gender education and support organizations.

Furthermore, youth are the most disadvantaged of all transgender persons, lacking funds and autonomy. As a result, they have little say about the types of treatment they receive. Parents with resources large or small will spend their last penny trying to help their young son or daughter conform to their concept of what is "normal." As with sexual orientation, most parents are inherently biased by their own self-identity, religious beliefs, and ideas about social norms.

Society's Responses

Before homosexuality was reclassified by the American Psychiatric Association and the American Psychological Association, lesbian and gay youth were professionally victimized and faced many long hours of psychoanalysis and behavioral modification, personal intimidation, hostile questioning, and other ill-founded treatment approaches Because gender-identity conflicts are still perceived as a mental health disorder by uninformed care providers, today's transgender youth still are at risk of being treated in the same manner gays and lesbians encountered years ago. Sadly, these treatment approaches are little more than abuse, professional victimization, and profiteering under the guise of support for parents' goals.

The Guidelines condemn such practices, particularly since Gender Specialists now recognize that a transgender identity is a primary element within an individual's self-identity and psychological make-up. Additionally, healthy psychological options do exist where a child's gender identity can be safely explored or current status prolonged until a decision-making age has been reached.

In addition to making individual counseling and support available to youth, group modalities provide socialization opportunities that can substantially help reduce their feelings of isolation, ostracism, and victimization. It should be noted, however, that youth typically have difficulty with notions of "confidentiality" within their peer group; thus, group modalities that include visits by positive transgender role models who as individuals can provide a reality check of what the transgender experience is like are particularly beneficial. Groups also frequently benefit from one-time visits by a gender-specializing professionals, such as a psychologist, cosmetologist, or a voice coach.

> In additon to making individual counseling and support available to youth, group modalities provide socialization opportunities that can substantially help reduce their feelings of isolation, ostracism, and victimization.

What happens with transgender youth who are perceived as overtly feminine boys or masculinized girls? Infrequently, some transgender youth successfully live in role or present an androgynous persona during their school experience. However, even they encounter the same verbal and physical abuse from peers encountered by others with gender issues. Criticism and ridicule often increase as the individual approaches puberty and then adulthood. Masculine females are often tolerated more than feminine males are, however, as most of Western society's power structure is sexist and endorses maleness over femaleness, the "tolerance" is not an expression of fairness or understanding.

In the school setting where "closeted" transgender individuals receive no attention at all, those who are "out" frequently receive far too much attention. Children with gender issues frequently are regarded as unruly or disruptive in the classroom and more often than not are punished, expelled, or otherwise made an example of by school administrators. This is tragic, particularly when we consider the plight of young individuals who receive substantial parental and peer support, yet receive none at all from the very place they spend most of their daytime hours. When encountering transgender youth, school administrators are advised to seek gender-specialized consultation and learn about the needs of these persons, just as they would for other minority groups.

Interestingly, those youth who are most integrated within an established transgender identity are also those who function best within their general peer groups. As an example, in institutional settings "punk" or "sissy" boys may stick together in groups, transform their shirts into feminized styles, and sashay about, to the consternation of insensitive administrators and care providers uninformed about gender and sexuality issues. Although they are disliked by administrators, typically these individuals receive far less harassment from their peers than those who remain closeted and isolated, according to mental health specialist Ruth Hughes, who has spent the past fifteen years providing professional support for gender and sexual minority youth at San Francisco's Center for Special Problems. Ms. Hughes often sees transgender individuals who have been in trouble most often because they have been abandoned by parents, society, or even the mental health system. At present, very few gender-specialized youth resources exist in mental health systems across the country, although several do exist under the auspices of gay and lesbian youth services.

Helping Young People with Gender Issues

Care providers and parents are frequently at loss for direction when it comes to providing assistance to transgender or gender-questioning youth. First, it is important to be supportive of those who are asking questions about gender, sexuality, and defining one's sense of self. Asking these types of questions is a healthy part of self-development and may be engaged in by males and females of any age. Because gender issues are frequently confused with sexual orientation, it is important that youth have access to easy-to-understand information about these subjects. In the simplest of terms, sexual orientation refers to those people a person finds attractive for *sexual interaction*—persons of the same gender, the opposite gender, or both. *Gender identity* refers to how a person identifies his or her role (male or female), and how he or she presents it to the world. Most adults are comfortable with their "birth" gender and sexual orientation, but there are individuals who find themselves dealing with personal questions concerning these matters during different stages of life. Such questioning, often rooted in the feeling that their own outward physical appearance does not match their gender identification, for individuals going through puberty.

Some young adults will adopt androgyny for a while, although as most progress toward adulthood, they will adopt a firmer gender orientation, leaving only a small proportion who permanently self-identify as *androgyne* individuals or as members of the transgender community. There are also persons who feel perfectly comfortable with their gender yet need to crossdress in order to relieve anxiety, reduce stress, or to get in touch with their opposite-gendered feelings. Within transgender youth populations, crossdressers are the least visible individuals. Most are unlikely to express their needs openly to family or friends, and few are likely to go out in public crossdressed. Youth who are caught crossdressing are frequently humiliated. As a result, they are likely to keep their needs deeply hidden so as not to be found out again. Because the issue is not dealt with during childhood, these crossdressing needs are more likely to reappear in adulthood, when the individual can no longer hold back and often when he or she faces times of crisis or major change.

Generally, young adults find themselves examining many questions as they develop a separate identity rooted in their own needs and experiences. This dynamic also holds true for children who have questions about gender identity. Most gender-questioning youth do not make firm transition-oriented decisions until close to adulthood or later. This group of young persons will be tomorrow's transsexuals, transgenderists, crossdressers, persons attracted to transgender individuals, those who repress gender issues, as well as persons who develop non-transgender identities. (See Chapter 1 for detailed definitions of these terms.)

This dynamic raises the frequently-asked question, "Is this a phase?" When parents ask this question, it is usually based in denial, a cry, "No, not my child!" Most parents really do want the best for their child and do not want to see their children suffer unnecessarily; moreover, they do not care to have friends and family question their efficacy as parents. Parents of adult children are also likely to ask whether the emergence of gender issues is a phase. When parents cling to the belief that this is only a phase and that their child couldn't possibly have gender issues, it is most likely that the parents are having serious difficulties with allowing their child to build a self-identity and experiences that are different from family or social stereotypes. Nearly all parents fear the awful stereotypes that the media uses when characterizing transgender persons. Most are not aware that transgender persons are, with the exception of being differently gendered, much like other persons they may know.

Several criteria help determine if the child really has crossgender issues or is going through a phase.

- Do the child's questions about gender arise regularly?
- Does the individual consistently express his or her gender issues or adopt an opposite-gender identity?
- Are attempts to crossdress made regularly?

An affirmative answer to any of these questions suggests a strong possibility that this is not a phase and that the individual likely has special gender issues and needs. These criteria apply generally to both youth and adults, except for closeted crossdressers, who are the least likely to bring gender questions to the forefront unless actually in crisis or caught in the act.

If there is any "cure" for children or youth with gender-identity issues, it can be found in the key words *acceptance, androgyny, compromise,* and *communication.* It is important for parents to recognize that all children need to be accepted for who they are, not for what others believe they should be. This also holds true for children with gender-identity issues. Having a transgender identity or crossdressing needs is not mentally disordered, mentally diseased, or pathologic. Once that fact is recognized, it becomes clear that the majority of difficulties transgender persons face do not originate internally or from their own question-asking process; rather, the origin of their difficulties is external, resulting from the abuse, harassment, and violence transgender persons face from people who cannot accept differences in others. Parents can play a major role in teaching children how to communicate effectively and counteract abuse from others who cannot accept differences.

To look at gender issues from a larger perspective: all cultures have varying degrees of acceptance and permissiveness toward individuals who embrace androgyny. Adopting a unisex or bigendered presentation is a safe option for children and adults who need to explore gender-identity issues, who are in the beginning stages of transition, or who are unable to crossdress publicly because they have not built sufficient opposite-gendered presentation skills. Many adults are locked into gender-specific social stereotypes, but youth often embrace androgyny as a form of self-expression, whether or not they have questions about gender identity. Remarkably, those youth who do adopt an androgynous presentation, as well as those who openly explore issues of gender and sexuality, frequently have an advantage over their peers who simply conform to stereotypes. In establishing independence in dress and presentation, they also build communication skills and coping strategies that will be advantageous later in life.

Many parents are surprised initially when they hear a gender-specializing care provider state that compromise is the best approach to supporting children or youth who have strong transgender needs and feelings. After all, don't parents know what is best for their child? Not always. Parents are not provided a training manual when they have children, whether their children have gender issues or not. Building mutually acceptable compromises can include asking the child to dress in original gender clothing for formal events such as weddings but allowing the child to dress androgynously for school and peer activities. Children who insist on using opposite-gender names can be encouraged to adopt an androgynous name until they are old enough to be certain they want to change their name permanently. Examples include Mickie, Bobbie, or Chris. More fully developed gender-transition plans or crossdressed presentations should be adopted only after both parent and child have consulted with a gender-specialized therapist or sexologist.

Communication is the final key for a healthy relationship between parents and children and is a crucial component to dealing with gender-identity issues. Even if parents cannot fully understand what their child is experiencing, children of all ages need their parents' love, acceptance, and compassion. Children also need to be reminded that their parents' love is unconditional, even when they find the child's experiences or identity difficult to understand or initially accept. Relationships are most fragile when talking stops, becomes unproductive, or one-sided. Although parents may be charged with the responsibility of caring for their children, they also need to recognize that letting go is part of parenting. As children move through youth and into adulthood, they need the opportunity to build social skills and a separate identity in order to survive independently.

The price of not talking about these processes or encouraging children to become independent is very costly. Youth who are continually forced to comply with social stereotypes may develop behavioral problems or depression. Like adult transgender persons, they may also become estranged from family relationships. Youth who become disillusioned with their families may end up homeless and at risk of victimization and disease. Some may commit suicide, leaving others with no explanation or insight into the pain they were suffering. As adults, those youth who were not permitted to give voice to gender-identity issues may find themselves in tremendous anguish later in life. These children frequently become examples of the very stereotype the parent had hoped to prevent, a gender-conflicted adult. Tragically, in an effort to find herself or himself later as an adult, such an individual may end up destroying his or her own family, career and friendships.

Regrettably, far too often transgender youth face horrific abuse during childhood. If not actually thrown out of their home, they are likely to run away, typically to larger cities. Most feel that there is no place or person to turn to where their needs and feelings would be understood. Many end up homeless and unable to finish school. With few financial resources or employment skills and little maturity, these individuals face an increased likelihood of becoming victims, manipulated by sexually predatory adults and exposed to sexually transmitted and other diseases. In San Francisco more than 17 percent of homeless youth test HIV-positive, according to the Larkin Street Youth Center, which serves homeless youth. A high proportion of these individuals are gender and sexual minorities.

Occasionally, parents respond with sincere dismay or shock upon finding out that a son or daughter has gender-identity issues or crossdresses. Though some parents may have suspected and denied it, most never imagined such a possibility. This is particularly true in situations where the now-grown children have adopted stereotyped roles and socially acceptable gender behaviors in order to mask their gender-identity issues or crossdressing needs. Though it may be difficult for a parent to accept that a child has these issues, and it may not be possible to offer validation or acceptance, children need a parent's love and compassion. Parents should make every effort not to reject a child, as this may result in unresolvable differences.

Some parents believe that their child is not well and needs help; others think they themselves need help. In addition to looking for a cure, these parents frequently ask, "What did we do wrong?" Chances are, nothing. After all, if a child is asking self-examination questions, a parent is likely to have done more right than wrong. Though continuous parental self-doubt is not useful to anyone, asking questions of oneself is healthy. The following are some useful questions to start with:

- How can I keep communication lines open even though I am not familiar with gender issues or crossdressing?

- Where can I send my son or daughter for support and validation, particularly when I don't know how to offer it right now?
- Which is more important, fulfilling social stereotypes and other's expectations or giving my child an opportunity to develop a healthy, gender identity?

Recommended Guidelines for Transgender Youth

Caution: A full understanding of these guidelines is not possible without reading the material contained in the preceding sections of this chapter. Additional information and guidelines on hormone administration, aesthetic surgery, and Genital Reassignment Surgery may be found in the recommendations at the end of Chapters 3, 4, and 5.

1. Hormone administration and aesthetic or genital reassignment procedures should not be broadly limited by age but evaluated on a case-by-case basis with the individual, the physician, and a Senior Gender Specialist. For all minors, with the exception of those who are legally emancipated, the written consent of one parent or legal guardian is required for hormone administration and all surgical procedures.

2. The decision-making processes for any gender-confirmation procedure needs to include consideration of the critical factors of age, maturity, and physical development. All Guidelines regarding decision-making processes for transgender individuals apply equally to youth and adults, except as amended below.

3. A two-year wait is recommended for transgender youth between the initiation of hormone administration and either Genital Reassignment Surgery or gonad removal (castration).

4. Schools, social-service, mental health systems, and churches are all likely to encounter gender-questioning as well as self-identified transgender and androgynous-identified individuals. These providers and organizations are advised to make individual counseling and support groups available to these persons. When gender-specialized questions arise regarding these individuals, a gender-specialized care provider should be sought for consultation or inservice training.

5. Support services designed for transgender, androgynous, and gender-questioning youth are advised to operate within a sensitive-services structure or model, emphasizing a confidential atmosphere that does not require parental consent. Other sensitive-service models can be found in youth-counseling centers and family-planning clinics.

6. Community-based counseling and support services are advised that youth in general do not have the financial resources to pay for support. Accordingly, these services should be made accessible either by being free or based upon donations or sliding-scale fees.

7. Youth support services and care providers are advised to make youth-oriented literature containing information about HIV and AIDS, safe sex and abstinence, alcohol- and drug-abuse prevention, and access to mental health and social support. Information about telephone numbers and the services of youth-support hotlines should also be readily available.

8. Youth support services and care providers are advised to remind young individuals that their search for self-identity and other processes of inquiry about identification as a transgender or androgynous person are natural and healthy.

9. Gender Specialists are advised to offer transgender youth a "courtesy disclosure letter," primarily because these individuals are at high risk for victimization and frequently interact with persons in authority. (A sample of the courtesy disclosure letter may be found in Chapter 9.)

Transgender Youth Encountering Difficulties May Contact:

For child abuse concerns

    National Child Abuse Hotline   1-800-540-4000

For runaway concerns and shelter referrals

    National Runaway Hotline   1-800-621-4000

                                  1-800-843-5678 (alternate number)

    Children of the Night   1-800-551-1300

For concerns around gender and sexual identity*

    Lyric Youth Talkline 1-800-246-PRIDE (nine-county Northern California Bay Area)

    Hetrik-Martin Institute 1-212-647-2400 (Greater Metropolitan New York City)

    Out Youth Often 1-800-96-YOUTH

    Indianapolis Youth Group 1-800-347-TEEN

* These excellent resources come under the auspices of gay and lesbian youth organizations, although each appeared sensitive to transgender issues. Individuals seeking more localized transgender organized resources may contact AEGIS, IFGE, or another adult service organization listed in the Appendix.

Support Tools

Chapter 9

—————

This chapter provides the means for professional and consumers to fully explore and analyze issues and needs associated with having a transgender identity. In the past, researchers and clinicians relied heavily on traditional diagnostic tests designed to detect mental disorders. We discourage the practice of arbitrarily requiring such testing of transgender men and women except in circumstances where a true mental disorder appears evident and diagnostic assessment is necessary. The tools provided here are designed for clinical and personal use, and they can be individually tailored to suit a wide variety of transgender support applications, including assessment, issue analysis, and subpopulation comparisons. The sample letters in this chapter provide reference for educational purposes only.

Advantage-Disadvantage Analysis

Being transgender frequently creates situations and personal decisions that can be confusing to the individual. Advantage-disadvantage analysis is a classic tool borrowed from cognitive therapy to help individuals more fully understand and refine their decision-making processes when they are faced with choices between alternative courses of action.

When the issues are laid out in a visible format, an individual can more fully address hard questions. Should I start hormones now? Should I disclose my transgender status to my spouse? Should I have genital-reassignment surgery? What will my employer's response be if I make an on-the-job transition? In Figure 9.1, the basic form one can use to do an advantage-disadvantage analysis

	Option 1	Option 2
Advantages		
Disadvantages		

Figure **9.1** *The Advantage-Disadvantage Analysis Form*

is shown. (Fill in each box with at least three well-thought-through responses.) In Figure 9.2, an example of the use of the form is shown.

In our example, Ryan, an FTM individual, is looking at the advantages and disadvantages of asking his physician now for a testosterone prescription. Ryan's example reveals some unfinished business: For example, he needs to talk about his intention to take hormones with his spouse. Telling his employer about starting hormones isn't really necessary; however, if he does make an on-the-job transition, he certainly will want to think that through and plan accordingly.

First Contact Information

Care providers, group facilitators, and interns are frequently interested in knowing what type of information is most useful to provide at first contact with a person who is questioning his or her gender identity. This is a particularly important concern, since gender-questioning persons may not show for follow-up sessions or group sessions. Coming out is a very difficult process for some and is often accompanied by fear and denial. The following information will help the individual confront stereotypes and correct any misinformation that hinders the

	Start Hormones Now	**Wait 3 Additional Months**
Advantages	• Will reduce feelings of gender incongruity	• Would give me time to tell my significant other and boss.
	• Will be able to speed up transition time.	• Would be able to talk to more tg'd. men about their experiences.
	• Voice will deepen, and I will get facial hair. All right!	• Can find out more information about the effects of hormones on my liver.
Disadvantages	• I fear my significant other may reject me if I start hormones.	• Would feel like a setback.
	• May discover I am wrong about this whole transgender thing.	• Reintroduces questions of doubt, "Am I intentionally sabotaging my own plans?
	• Would need to disclose to my employer before things became obvious.	• Would feel like I am doing this to please my significant other.

Figure **9.2** *Ryan's Question: What If I Ask for Hormones Now? What If I Wait?*

coming-out process. This information is based on the principles established in the Recommended Guidelines for Transgender Care.

There Is No Cure

Before coming to terms with who they are, many people invest a great deal of time and resources in the search for a cure for their crossdressing desires or transgender identity. These individuals may also attempt to escape their needs through denial, addictions, overwork, moving, changing relationships, purging or throwing away a transgender wardrobe, or by seeking a more "masculine" or "feminine" job. They need to know that all these strategies have been tried before, and they do not work. Unresolved gender issues will return time and time again, until the person takes responsibility for his or her life and transgender needs.

There Are Others with Similar Needs

Transgender men and women, as well as persons who crossdress, come from all walks of life. There are transgender physicians, lawyers, engineers, homemakers, construction workers, and politicians. In most respects, they are like anyone else, with their families, children, and friends. By planning carefully, maintaining a support system, and building up transition resources if needed, transgender persons can safely incorporate the means to meet their transgender needs into their lives. In many circumstances it is also possible to minimize impact upon family and other important relationships.

Get Support and Stay in Touch

Coming to terms with crossdressing or gender-identity issues takes time. Although there are established paths for making the transition, finding individual resolution takes more time for some people. This is particularly so for men and women who are involved in complex relationships and employment situations.

Consider Maintaining an Androgynous Presentation

Because educational information about transgender persons is becoming more available to the general public, fewer transgender persons are losing employment while making on-the-job transitions. However, many still do. Prior to transition, maintaining an androgynous presentation in the workplace can buy the time required to finish electrolysis, allow hormones to begin their work, and learn crucial disclosure skills. If a person finds himself or herself unemployed before he or she is ready to live in role full-time, a compromise of seeking employment in the original gender may be advisable in order to build up transition resources. However, even new employment situations from the first interview onward can be good environments in which to maintain an androgynous presentation. If a person is perceived as different from the beginning, people are going to be less surprised to learn that she or he has a transgender identity.

Not Everyone Can Provide Validation

During first-time gender-issue disclosures, some people will respond with support and acceptance, but others will not. Some will be indifferent. For example, a crossdresser's wife may tell her husband to go ahead and crossdress on his own, but not to expect her to participate or to attend social functions with him when he is crossdressed. A few individuals will simply not be able to understand the turmoil and pain transgender persons experience. Transgender individuals can gain acceptance and validation through support groups, discussing their needs with a gender-specialized care provider, or through knowledgeable and compassionate friends. Receiving validation and acceptance through these persons, as well as resolving crisis situations before disclosing within important relationships, will enable a person to appear more stable and less needy.

Transgender Men and Women Need to Be Cautious Consumers

Regrettably, there are merchants and care providers who prey on transgender individuals who are closeted or unaware that other resources exist. The unscrupulous take advantage of a transgender person's sense of desperation. Examples include retailers who under the mask of privacy sell ordinary or even cheap clothing and shoes at dishonest prices to people who have not yet learned how to shop discreetly, vendors who sell herbal hormones and estrogenic creams that offer "immediate" breast growth to persons who are not ready for or do not know how to obtain a physician's prescription, and care providers or gender clinics who portray their services as a client's only route to treatment. Frequently, providers in this latter group characterize the clients as "disordered" in order to make them believe they need treatment.

Having a Transgender Identity Is Not a Mentally Disordered or Medically Diseased Condition

With the exception of hormone administration and surgeries, which are medical interventions to help transgender persons bring body in line with gender identity, transgender men and women do not need "treatment." They are not more medically diseased or mentally disordered than the general population. After coming to terms with who they are, most transgender persons find that the difficulties they confront come from unsophisticated people who cannot tolerate differences in others. Knowledge of these facts is helpful in combatting self-doubt, shame, discrimination, and social stereotypes on personal and public levels.

Basic Support Group Pointers

Start-Up

If for reasons of location, timing, or specialized interests, an individual is unable to find a support group, there always remains the option of starting one. Locating members for a group may be done by running a classified ad, posting notices in places frequented by transgender individuals, or even on a computer bulletin board. Before venturing out on their own, new group facilitators are encouraged to have had experience co-facilitating a group with an experienced facilitator, or at the very least to maintain consultation with an experienced Gender Specialist.

Confidentiality

The feelings, thoughts, and experiences that individuals talk about should stay within the group. This makes it a safe place, without the fear of being found out or embarrassed at a later date. Sensitive information presented by group members should not be discussed in their absence without their permission.

Speak from Ones' Own Experiences

Being criticized, ridiculed, humiliated, or bullied is inappropriate, harmful to participants, and threatens the life of the group. Disagreement is acceptable, but the best way to advise others of alternatives is to share one's own experience. Speaking from one's own perspective diminishes the tendency of individuals to take on the role of instant expert.

Facilitation

Establishing a format helps groups run smoothly. Start out with group member introductions, allowing time for each individual to mention his or her name, as well as any pertinent questions or concerns for the group to explore. Advise new group members of the group's focus. Provide each member with time to talk. Encourage questions and discussion on topics of mutual interest. Move toward closing time by asking if anyone has any questions or concerns that have not been raised. Close with affirmations of time well spent, as well discussions of any disappointments. Announce the next group meeting date and time, and any other relevant community announcements. Following meetings should begin with the introduction of new members and inquiry into whether there is any unfinished business from the last meeting.

General Courtesy

After group, members and facilitators should clean up. This includes straightening chairs and removing refuse. Many groups are located in environments which will later be used by others. If donations are requested from group members, facilitators should allow time for collection of funds at each group meeting as well as remind group members that their donations help offset expenses.

Information-Age Resources

Today's world offers more group environments for transgender men and women on the Internet, both with mainstream servers such as America Online (AOL) and Compuserve, as well as on local bulletin board services. Many of these service providers not only provide forums for groups of individuals to chat in "real-time" mode, but also maintain databases of transgender-oriented materials. These typically are located in the sexual minority or human sexuality sections.

Current transgender Internet resources include a variety of World Wide Web (WWW) pages, newsgroup forums, and regular digest format mailing lists. When accessing these resources as a newcomer, make certain to inquire how you may obtain each site's Frequently Asked Questions (FAQ) file. This way, you can quickly learn all you need to know about a resource without unnecessarily interrupting group process.

Group Focus Survey

Group facilitators can use this survey to help a transgender support or therapy group find a focus. The survey presents a listing of common themes. The facilitator asks participants to circle the top three issues they would like to see discussed within group. Space is also provided for group members to write in additional concerns.

Transphobia	An irrational fear or hatred of transgender individuals by others; *internalized transphobia* is the same fear or hatred from oneself.
Isolation	Being alone; limitations upon socialization
Job discrimination	Being harassed, fired, or not hired
Family	Loss and reconnecting
Relationships	Conflicts, communication difficulties
Sexual orientation	MTF issues include a relationship to women's communities; sexism; lesbian issues; bisexual and heterosexual issues FTM issues include a relationship to men's communities; gay issues; bisexual, heterosexual, and reverse discrimination issues
Anger	Self-destructive behavior; constructive ways of releasing anger; alternatives to suicidal ideas
Substance abuse	Coping mechanisms and support
Politics	Self-empowerment in a society geared toward suppression; maintaining self-identity within political models
Surgery	Preoperative issues, including economics, information, and referrals

Codependency	Relationship models based upon family and past relationships; the impact of the past upon current and future relationships
Health issues	Medical concerns; mental health; HIV; health of others
Child abuse	Physical, sexual, and emotional; discrimination during childhood, such as rejection by family and other children
Discrimination	Against those who are HIV-positive, women; racism; classism; other "isms"
Violence	Verbal and physical assault
Denial	Unhealthy behaviors; unprotected sex
Write in _____	

Postsurgical Follow-up Letters

Occasionally overlooked by surgeons, postsurgical courtesy letters are an important means of communicating a patient's surgical outcome and postoperative needs to the primary Gender Specialist. Frequently, the postsurgical follow-up letter contains medical information about the individual (or about the actual procedure) which the care provider was previously unaware of. The Guidelines for genital-reassignment surgery advise surgeons to provide these letters (see Chapter 5). Gender Specialists who do not receive follow-up information after recommending a client for surgery are encouraged to request such letters from surgeons.

Follow-up Letter: Sample 1

April 21, 1995

To: Donald E. Tarver, II, M.D.
295 Fell Street, Suite A
San Francisco, CA 94102

RE: YVONNE CHAPMAN

Dear Dr. Tarver:

Yvonne as you recall is a 38-year-old white male-to-female transsexual who underwent male-to-female Genital Reassignment Surgery with a skin graft on April

8, 1995. She tolerated the procedure well, and her postoperative course was uneventful.

On April 16, 1995, the vaginal pack was removed, and the patient was instructed to dilate frequently to keep the neo-vagina patent. She was discharged on that date with instructions to take ferrous sulfate 300 mg t.i.d. and Ceftin 250 mg b.i.d. and to return to her regular physician for regulation of her hormones.

Thank you for the excellent evaluation and recommendation work-up that you provided. Thank you also for the referral. If you have any questions regarding Yvonne, please feel free to contact me.

Sincerely,
A. Surgeon

Follow-up Letter: Sample 2

Surgeons occasionally forward a copy of the operative report in lieu of an actual letter. Care providers requiring additional postoperative care information should request such information directly from the surgeon.

OPERATIVE REPORT

PATIENT:	Daugherty, Stephen
SURGEON:	A. Surgeon, M.D.
DATE OF ADMISSION:	5/08/95
PREOPERATIVE DIAGNOSIS:	Female to male transsexual
POSTOPERATIVE DIAGNOSIS:	Same
PROCEDURE PERFORMED:	Bilateral mastectomy and nipple areolar reconstruction
ANESTHESIA:	General

FINDINGS: This patient is an established female-to-male transsexual undergoing gender-specialized therapy and hormonal therapy. He was referred for a mastectomy by Gianna E. Israel, a practicing Senior Gender Specialist. The breasts are female in appearance; there is no evidence of intrinsic breast disease.

PROCEDURE: The patient was preoperatively marked in the sitting position with preliminary markings to identify the amount of skin for removal. Patient was administered general endotracheal anesthesia in the supine position and prepped and draped. Both breasts were treated similarly.

Appropriate-sized areolar grafts were delineated over the right areola. Hemostasis was facilitated with local injection of 0.5% Xylocaine added adrenaline 1:200,000. The areolar grafts were taken as well as the right nipple and preserved in saline for later use. Both inferior incisions were made and dissection carried to the pectoralis major fascia. A suprapectoral pocket was developed under the entire extent of the breast. This was carried laterally as well to obtain additional fat lateral to the breast tissue. The superior incision was made and at a plane that would correspond with the inferior incisions' degree of adiposity of the breast dissected free to its superior, medial, and lateral extents. Entire breast tissue and overlying skin was excised. Hemostasis was obtained by electro-coagulation and ligature, where indicated. The skin flaps were retracted inferiorly and additional excess skin was excised. Hemostasis was assured. Bilateral Jackson-Pratt drains were placed and sutured into position through separate stab incisions.

The incisions were then approximated in multiple deep layers using interrupted and inverted 3-0 Vicryl and 4-0 Vicryl. The skin incisions were approximated with interrupted and continuous 5-0 nylon sutures.

Measurements were taken and appropriate new nipple areolar positions identified bilaterally. Circular portions of these of appropriate size were de-epithelialized. The preserved areolar grafts were defatted and sutured into position on the new beds with interrupted 5-0 silk sutures left long and 6-0 nylon suture for approximation of the skin edges. Areas of appropriate nipple size at the centers of the areolar grafts were removed. Segments of the preserved right nipple of appropriate size were taken and sutured into the center of the areolar graft with fine nylon sutures. The grafts were dressed with Xeroform gauze, mineral oil saturated cotton in the form of a stent, and tied into position with long silk sutures. The wounds were cleansed, dressed with Xeroform gauze, bulky cotton, and a thoracic binder.

Estimated blood loss was 250 cc. The patient tolerated the procedure well and left the operating room in a stable and satisfactory condition.

A. Surgeon

Gender Identity Profile

The Gender Identity Profile was developed during the mid 1980s by Gianna E. Israel. Over the years it has undergone significant refinement through consumer use and mental health peer review. It has been used as a model by several Gender Specialists and mental health clinics as a means to better understand gender-identity issues. It provides an excellent resource for Gender Specialists seeking guidance in developing a repertoire of gender-oriented questions that enhance history taking and provide a structure to help transgender individuals further understand their gender-identity development and experiences.

This tool was not designed for clinical research purposes. It is best utilized for documentation, dialogue building, and a means for transgender individuals to assess their own knowledge of transgender experiences. Some questions are intentionally presumptive, to help the Gender Specialist identify when the individual is aware only of stereotyped transgender-oriented information that she or he misapplies to his or her situation instead of developing independent self-identification and presentation dynamics. Several questions are repeated, since it has been found that repeating a question later within the process commonly draws different responses.

Individuals personally familiar with gender-identity issues may ask why question 17 ("What do you feel causes your transgender identity?") and 36 ("What is the difference between gender identity and sexual orientation?") are included, when they are seemingly unnecessary? With regard especially to question 17, it could be pointed out that non-transgender individuals are rarely asked questions about the causation of their gender identification. Asking transgender individuals what they feel causes a transgender identity provides the Gender Specialist with an opportunity to assess an individual's deductive, self-identifying abilities and communication skills, as it is a question unlikely to elicit "textbook" responses from whichever theory is currently in fashion. Many individuals encountering gender-identity issues for the first time may think they know what the difference is between gender identity and sexual orientation, when in fact they, too, may be misinformed by socially stereotyped information.

> The key factors that distinguish the individual who has successfully moved beyond gender dysphoria into self-identifying as a transgender individual are these:
>
> * An accurate description in one's own wording of the difference between gender identity and sexual orientation, and how those constructs apply to the individual's experience;
> * The ability to provide an easy-to-understand explanation of why he or she has self-identified as transgender;
> * The ability to describe how one's presentation fits in with a perceived sense of gender identity and self-defined goals.
> * Consistently staying within one's chosen presentation.

Experienced mental health workers should be able to locate questions that screen for depression as well as those that help gauge an individual's depth of knowledge about gender-identity issues. Additionally, questions that reveal potential malingering or medical concerns are included.

Many of the questions are very personal and may not be suitable for intake screening at a first appointment, when individuals may feel nervous about attending a counseling or therapy session to discuss gender-identity issues for the first time. In most cases, introduction of the Gender Identity Profile is best delayed until confidentiality and trust have been fairly well established, typically by the time of an individual's third or fourth office visit. In cases where the individual has been suicidal or in crisis, it is best to introduce the Gender Identity Profile after those crucial issues have been appropriately addressed. Some individuals may have great difficulty disclosing information of an extremely personal, sexual, or intimate nature, even after several office visits. In situations such as these, it is often best to first address how the individual feels about discussing and disclosing such information before proceeding with the Gender Identity Profile.

GENDER IDENTITY PROFILE

INSTRUCTIONS: The purpose of this profile is so that your experiences and support needs may be more fully understood. There are no "right" or "wrong" answers. Complete it as neatly and accurately as possible. Please ask for help if you have any questions.

Legal Name (first) _____ (middle) _____ (last) _____

Preferred Name (first) _____ (middle) _____ (last) _____

Date of Birth ____/____/____   Today's Date ____/____/____

1. Are you interested in: _____individual counseling _____group support

   other? _____

2. What is your transgender identification: (check one)

   _____ TRANSSEXUAL—a person interested in *permanently* changing gender through cross-gender hormones and various surgeries. This often includes crossliving part time, with the end result being living full time in a newly established gender identity prior to Genital Reassignment Surgery.

   _____ TRANSVESTITE / CROSSDRESSER—a person interested in wearing clothing of the opposite gender privately and/or socially as an opportunity to explore masculinity or femininity. Typically not interested in hormones, aesthetic surgeries, castration, or genital reassignment.

   _____ TRANSGENDERIST—a person interested in crossdressing and crossliving part or full time. Typically not interested in Genital Reassignment Surgery. Possibly interested in hormones, aesthetic surgeries, or castration.

   _____ ANDROGYNE—a person interested in taking on the characteristics of both or neither gender role(s), i.e., male/female or occupying a middle ground. Not interested in genital-reassignment surgery. Possibly interested in hormones, aesthetic surgeries or castration.

   _____ UNSURE   OTHER (*please describe*) _____

3. What is your gender identification, as determined by your biological status? (*circle one*)
    Male to Female   Female to Male
    Male*   Intersex or hermaphrodite
    Unsure   Female*
    (* wish to remain the same as biological sex or not currently in transition)

4. Do you crossdress for sexual excitement and fulfillment? (*circle one*)   Yes   No

Explain _____

_____

_____

5. How long have you been experiencing transgender feelings? _____

6. Have you lived part or full time as a man or woman before, starting and then stopping?

    (*circle one*)   Yes   No

If yes, please indicate dates and lengths of these experiences.

_____

_____

7. I am sexually attracted to: (*circle appropriate response*)

        Men   Women   Both   None   Uncertain   Transgender Individuals

8. While crossdressed or living in role, my sexual orientation and fantasies change. (*circle one*)

        Yes   No   Sometimes

Please explain _____

_____

_____

_____

9. My sexual fantasies differ from my actual sexual experiences. (*circle one*)

        Yes   No   Sometimes

Explain _____

_____

_____

_____

10. How frequently are you sexually active with self or partner? _____

Do you always practice safe sex (using condoms or other latex barriers) (*circle one*)

Yes   No

11. What are your present *gender-oriented* counseling, transition, or support needs?

_____

_____

_____

12. What past counseling or group support have you received regarding *gender issues?* (*List clinic, therapist or counselor, or group by name, location, dates.*)

_____

_____

13. If in the past you have received counseling or group support regarding gender issues, what caused you to stop?

_____

_____

14. Hormones (*please read **all** selections and check responses*)

_____ I am not interested in hormones
(*In space provided below, please explain.*)

_____ I am interested in obtaining hormones
(*In space provided below, list what changes you expect as a result of taking hormones and when you anticipate starting.*)

_____ I have used hormones in past or am currently using them.
(*In space provided below, list prescribing doctor, start and stop dates, and your reason for stopping, if applicable.*)

_____ I have a hormone imbalance where my body acts irregularly.
(*In space provided below, describe your condition.*)

_____ I am on hormones now.
(*In space provided below, give the name and dosage.*)

_____ I have a medical condition restricting my use of hormones

(*space for answers to question 14*)

_____

_____

_____

_____

15. Electrolysis (*check one*)

_____ I have already begun electrolysis.

_____   _____

Date started   Completed

_____ I am not interested in electrolysis.

_____ I am interested in electrolysis information.

16. Surgeries

_____ I am interested in Genital Reassignment Surgery (vaginoplasty, phalloplasty). If so, specify approximate amount of time you anticipate waiting between beginning crossliving full time and actually having surgery: _____

_____ I am not interested in Genital Reassignment Surgery.

_____ I am unsure if I am interested in Genital Reassignment Surgery.

_____ I have a medical condition which may restrict my eligibility for surgery.

State your reason(s) why, for the surgery item checked: _____

_____

_____

_____

_____ I have already had Genital Reassignment Surgery.

_____

(date completed, hospital and doctor's name)

_____ I have had or I am interested in aesthetic surgeries *(specify types and when)*.

_____

_____

17. What do you feel causes your transgender identity? _____

_____

_____

_____

18. When did you begin experiencing transgender feelings? _____

Describe those feelings in detail: _____

_____

_____

_____

_____

19. When did you most recently begin crossdressing or living in role? _____

What activities do you take part in while crossdressed or crossliving? _____

_____

20. Which bathroom(s) do you use while crossdressed? _____
Do you fear being "discovered"? (*circle one*)

    Yes   Sometimes   Occasionally   Never

21. What is your occupation? _____

22. What is your intended occupation after gender transition (*answer if appropriate*)

    _____

    Do you currently appear crossdressed or in role at work? (*circle one*)

    Yes   Sometimes   No

    If no, would you like to do so? (*circle one*)   Yes   No

23. Are you single, married, or divorced, and for how long? _____

24. Do you have children and what are their ages? _____

25. Have you disclosed your transgender status to parents, siblings, spouse, children, friends, employer or co-workers? If yes, who?

_____

_____

26. Have you had or are you currently receiving counseling, therapy, or treatment for any mental illness or other personal issue? If yes, please list therapist, location, dates, and reason for counseling.

_____

_____

_____

_____

27. With the exception of transgender issues, have you experienced any major life transitions, crises, decisions, or changes in mood within past two years? If yes, please describe.

_____

_____

_____

_____

28. Are you currently having any difficulties eating, sleeping or concentrating? (*circle one*)

    Yes   No   Sometimes

29. Do you have any major underlying medical conditions? If yes, please describe:

_____

30. Are you currently taking any medications prescribed by physicians? (*circle one*)

    No   Yes

    If yes, please list: _____

_____

31. Have you been depressed within the past three months? (*circle one*)   No   Yes

    If yes, please describe your depression and for how long you were/have been depressed:

_____

_____

_____

32. Have you ever considered committing suicide in the past, or are you presently feeling suicidal?

        (*circle one*)   Yes   No

33. When standing in front of a mirror nude, how do you feel about your body?

Be specific: _____

_____

_____

34. In addition to dealing with your transgender issues, what interests, goals, or hobbies do you have?

_____

_____

35. Have you ever attempted self-inflicted bodily or genital mutilation?

    Yes   No   Unsure

    (If yes or unsure, please describe incident on line below.)

_____

36. What is the difference between gender identity and sexual orientation?

_____

_____

37. How do you imagine your life will be seven years from now? Visualize and write a creative description.

_____

_____

_____

_____

38. Whether acknowledged or unacknowledged, how have your parents, family, and spouse reacted to your being transgender? Please describe in detail.

_____

_____

_____

_____

39. Listed below are statements made by transgender individuals in support counseling. Please read each statement carefully and check statements you find similar to your own experience.

_____ While playing alone during my childhood, I would play with opposite gender-oriented toys such as dolls (for girls) or trucks (for boys).

_____ I have secretly crossdressed with a family member's or spouse's clothing.

_____ During my childhood, siblings or friends would assign or address me in a crossgendered role while playing.

_____ My parents allowed me to crossdress until I reached puberty.

_____ I suspect that during her pregnancy with me my mother really wanted a child of a different gender from what I was born. (Example: If you were born a boy, your mother wanted a girl.)

_____ I was abused as a child.

_____ My parents forced me to crossdress as a punishment.

_____ My brother or sister received more attention than I, so during my childhood I really wanted to be a person of the opposite gender so that I also could receive more attention.

_____ As a child I crossdressed at school.

_____ Being crossgendered is part of my spiritual life-journey.

_____ The reason I am crossgendered is that during a past life I was a different gender.

_____ The real reason I want to crosslive is to gain social status.

_____ As an adult, crossdressing is a safe way to explore my attraction to the same sex.

_____ My crossgendered behavior feels compulsive, I think about it obsessively and feel frustrated.

_____ I was labeled a disturbed child.

_____ I understand that exploring and developing my transgender identity will take some time.

39. Give a brief history highlighting your experiences to date with crossdressing, crossliving, and being a transgender individual. Use the remainder of this page; continue writing on back of previous page.

_____

_____

_____

_____

_____

_____

_____

_____

_____

_____

_____

40. Listed below are issues common to transgender individuals.

   INSTRUCTIONS
   1. Circle the one (1) item that is presently most concerning you. (*circle only one*)
   2. Check other items you would like to examine in the future. (*check any number*)

   _____ Find out about surgery

   _____ Find out about hormones

   _____ Find out why I'm transgender

   _____ Found out about support, social, talk groups

   _____ Talk about presentation skills

   _____ Explore my feelings about being transgender

   _____ Find a cure for my being transgender

   _____ Talk about spiritual issues

   _____ Cope with my depression

   _____ Explore options for disclosing to others

   _____ Build skills for making an on-the-job transition

   _____ Find supportive resources for my partner, spouse

_____ Talk about difficulties with a personal relationship

_____ Talk about fear of being discovered

_____ Talk about fears surrounding coming-out

_____ Talk about being single

_____ Find out about safe-sex or HIV/AIDS information

_____ Find out cosmetic and clothing resources

CONGRATULATIONS! YOU HAVE SUCCESSFULLY
COMPLETED YOUR GENDER PROFILE.

Courtesy Disclosure Letter

Individuals who crossdress or who are at the beginning stages of living in role may have concerns about appearing in public, being stopped by law-enforcement officers, or interacting with social service agencies. A courtesy disclosure letter provided by a Gender Specialist may in some cases smooth over communication difficulties that may arise over the individual's transgender status. Gender Specialists are advised to tailor courtesy disclosure letters to suit an individual's circumstances and special needs.

Counseling Practice of Gianna Eveling Israel
P.O. Box 424447, San Francisco, CA 94142
Telephone (415) 558-8058
June 10, 1996
Dear Sir or Madam:

Ms. Denise Noble (also known as, or, formerly, David Noble) has been an individual counseling client of mine since November 10, 1994. During our work together we have focused on helping Denise build support for her gender-identity issues and establish permanent transition goals.

Her crossdressing and/or living in role is necessary to this individual's self-integration process. Therefore, it should not be misconstrued as an attempt to impersonate the opposite gender or perpetrate wrongdoing. In growing numbers of locations, transgender individuals are protected from employment, housing, and services discrimination.

Please feel free to contact me if there is any way I can be of assistance regarding Denise.

Regards,
Gianna E. Israel
GEI/bms

Support Scenarios

Chapter 10

Recognizing and fathoming their own gender-identity issues are particularly perplexing tasks for transgender individuals who are in the coming-out and initial self-integration processes. Psychiatry and psychology professionals, family and youth counselors, crisis workers and social service providers, though proficient within their respective fields, commonly find themselves at a loss for knowledge when encountering a transgender individual's basic support needs. At times, both transgender individuals and support organizations find themselves desperately searching for answers in this relatively new field. This chapter attempts to answer basic support questions. Specialized or individual questions that are not covered here should be directed to an experienced Gender Specialist.

Care providers encountering transgender issues for the first time are advised to remember that it is the provider's responsibility to follow the ethical and professional guidelines established for his or her specialty, and to ensure that the transgender individual is treated with the same dignity, respect, and quality of care extended to others, regardless of how unusual an individual's needs and feelings may seem. In the past, immeasurable damage to transgender people has been inflicted by insensitive care providers who, in so doing, compromised their professionalism.

Examples of actions not helpful to the transgender individual would include minimizing or avoiding the individual's concerns or ridiculing the individual's behavior and feelings as disgraceful or bizarre. Situations such as these sometimes happen because the care provider has distorted or incorrect information; others act shamefully out of ignorance. Much harm can be prevented by making available staff sensitivity training regarding transgender issues.

In Chapter 1, the reader has been provided with detailed descriptions of correct usage of appropriate terms. This chapter provides examples of most of those terms in use. Be advised that the options suggested by these scenarios are provided only as a frame of reference; they should not be misconstrued as the only "right" alternative for similar circumstances. Readers are encouraged to draw their own conclusions, be creative, and choose options that are most applicable to the real-life situations they encounter.

Gender Differentiation and Placement in Residential Treatment Settings

The Situation

Tracy is a twenty-two-year-old, self-identified MTF transsexual woman applying for temporary residence at a city halfway house prior to being released from a two-week stay at a psychiatric hospital following a suicide attempt by drug overdose. Tracy meets eligibility criteria for the halfway house, yet the program's staff is unsure whether to place her in men's or women's housing. Tracy's actual presentation ranges from mostly androgynous to occasionally feminine; she self-identifies as female and becomes hostile or despondent when referred to as male or with male pronouns. She has recently reported taking female hormones she obtained through a friend. Tracy has asked for placement in the women's section, as she feels vulnerable around males. Concerns arose during the intake interview that many of the women would have difficulty identifying Tracy as female and therefore would find her presence unsettling, particularly since many of the residents had been victims of sexual violence.

Discussion

Whether it be to a homeless shelter, a rape treatment or domestic-violence program, a mental health ward, or a halfway house, the issue of placement of transgender individuals poses a real dilemma for care providers. Placement in an institution raises concerns regarding both the individual's and other clients' well-being, as well as a number of ethical questions. Tragically, many transgender individuals who would otherwise meet a program's eligibility criteria are either flatly turned away or are, at best, forced into situations that do not provide them with transgender-specific support and follow-up. Placement of any transgender individual should be based on an evaluation and recommendation provided by a Gender Specialist or other counselor with gender-identity qualifications. If this is not possible, than the burden of making the placement decision falls on the program. The following are pointers that can assist in that process:

Motivation behind an individual's actions should always be carefully considered. In this scenario, Tracy consistently referred to and presented herself as female, so it should be no surprise that any reference to her by her male name or a male pronoun is perceived by her as provocative and offensive. Highly functioning individuals are the least likely to use social and mental health support services, but those with reduced coping and communication skills are frequently dependent on them. Regardless of actual placement, an individual's name and pronoun preference should be respected. At the same time, transgender individuals should be advised to discuss their needs in a straightforward, constructive manner so as not to inflame hostilities. There will always be individuals whose limited levels of understanding and opinions will be the reason they neither appreciate nor respect the transgender situation. Those individuals should be ignored unless their behavior becomes intolerant and requires staff intervention.

Client safety is another factor of concern in placement decisions. In this scenario, Tracy has expressed fears over being placed with males. Does placing Tracy in a male housing unit place her in a high-risk situation? Does she have previous victimization issues involving men? Will placing her in the female facility truly aggravate other's victimization issues, or simply make some women and staff uncomfortable with a new situation that requires education and tolerance? The latter question introduces a particularly significant issue if an agency employs both male and female support staff for female clients yet suddenly finds itself unable to provide support to an MTF transsexual or androgynous individual solely because of biological male status. All of these are important questions that should be considered in the light of the individual's background, consistency of presentation, and personal needs.

In the San Francisco model of support services, it is likely that Tracy would be placed in women's facilities because the city's providers have become accustomed to responding more frequently to issues of diversity. Decisions are typically made on a case-by-case basis and commonly involve creativity on the part of care providers. As an example, in addition to staff and peer sensitivity training, the individual may be paired up with a companion in a "buddy system." That is, whether Tracy is placed in a male or female facility, she would be paired up with a peer-client who is interested in and would benefit by helping Tracy become more adjusted and accepted within the facility. In some cases placement is made on a temporary or probationary basis, and weekly, biweekly, or monthly review is provided, where program staff and the transgender individual can gauge the success of the placement decision and make changes as needed.

As a final note with regard to the Tracy scenario; she reported having recently taken female hormones. This claim should be further investigated, and if she intends to continue taking hormones, she should be referred to a physician familiar with hormone administration so that her blood levels may be monitored and an appropriate prescription given. See also the Guidelines at the end of Chapter 2.

Gender-Identity Issues and Alcohol Dependency

The Situation

Lin is a forty-seven-year-old biological female who is entering a short-term sub-stance-abuse treatment center in a small town. During her intake, she tells a troubling tale of nearly destroying her whole life as she knows it. She fears losing her professional career of eighteen years because she finds herself unable to resist drinking alcohol between appointments, and she worries that others secretly laugh at her. She says her husband has grown to hate her because she has manip-ulated him financially and she verbally abuses him constantly. Nearly three years ago she introduced sexual role-play into their sex life. During sexual activity she acts out her fantasy of "being a man making love to another man"; now, only this role satisfies her. She worries that her husband would rather maintain tradi-tional sex roles, although he has never voiced opposition to what she describes as her "unnatural desires."

Lin states that for as long as she can remember she has felt that she ought have been born a man. She despises her female body and says that daily use of alcohol seems to be the only thing that can numb her anger and confusion. During intake, as well as in individual and group sessions, she repeatedly reflects that although she is aware that transsexualism exists, she could not possibly live "like those people do" because she would lose everything, including the husband whom she loves, despite her history of exploiting him. Staff at the substance-abuse treatment center are completely uncertain as to how to support Lin. Should her alcoholism or gender-identity concerns be dealt with first? Finally, center staff are uncertain whether to diagnose her for alcoholism or transsexual-ism for insurance billing purposes.

Discussion

At a glance, Lin's situation appears to be a simple case of alcoholism masking an FTM transsexual identity. After all, her ongoing attachment to identifying with gay male role play and the hatred she expresses toward her female body image must certainly prove that she is transsexual. Right? Not necessarily. Although alcoholism certainly seems to be masking potential gender-identity and sexual-orientation issues, no thoughtful Gender Specialist would be so careless or pre-sumptive as to label an individual transsexual without a great deal more informa-tion. There appears to exist, however, relatively clear evidence pointing to a current state of gender dysphoria. We will thus informally identify Lin as gender dysphoric in the absence of further information. After having done so, we will further look at whether alcohol treatment or exploration and support of gender-identity issues should take place first.

Lin's case provides a brief illustration of how gender-identity concerns can be masked by alcoholism or other addictions. Addictions to substances, sex, work, or relationships form a common theme running through various transgender populations. In some circumstances, addressing the addiction reveals hidden gender-identity issues. Addictions are most frequently used as an anesthetic to cover the pain, isolation, and loss that can accompany an individual's actual development of a transgender identity or, their fear of doing so.

Although the causality of addiction in transgender individuals may hold some common themes, other contributing factors can differ sharply, depending on an individual's experiences, socioeconomic status, relationships, and other dynamics. These individual differences are a primary reason why concurrent conditions and methods of support need to be assessed on a case-by-case basis. Lin's scenario highlights the complex dynamics that can be experienced by transgender individuals, and it introduces the primary assessment question; determining where support is needed most. That is to say, where is the individual's support system most in jeopardy?

Is Lin's support system most in danger due to her gender-identity issues or her alcoholism? It is hoped that care providers would recognize that although her gender-identity issues can and should be addressed, focusing on her alcoholism may be the one thing that will ultimately help keep her support system intact. Without a support system in place, it would be difficult for anyone to address both long-term alcohol and gender-identity issues without becoming so overwhelmed that the individual sees little choice but regression into further denial.

Since Lin sought help primarily for her alcoholism, either alcohol dependence (*DSM*-IV 303.90) or alcohol abuse could be used for diagnosis and insurance billing purposes. A concurrent or provisional diagnosis of gender-identity disorder in adolescents or adults (302.85) would not be applicable in this scenario, because its presence would have little bearing on insurance authorization in a clear case of alcohol dependency. Furthermore, the possibility exits that the claim may be rejected; some insurance companies contain exclusionary clauses that routinely reject claims bearing gender-identity disorder as a diagnosis. Situations such as these raise the question as to why gender-identity disorders are included in the *DSM*-IV at all.

■ _____

> Care providers are advised that careless application of the gender-identity disorder label perpetuates the excessive pathologizing of transgender populations and is likely to bar individuals from receiving treatment for a recognized mental health disorder. Further material regarding this issue and insurance billing information can be found in Chapter 2.

In summary, Lin's scenario is particularly challenging, since without further consultation and exploration of gender issues, one could not simply identify her as transsexual. Thus far she has experienced many transgender feelings, which present a wide variety of possible explanations and outcomes. For example, some of the same dynamics that an inexperienced care rovider might mistake for a case of transsexualism may, in fact, support a "transgenderist" identity, or they may indeed prove to represent transsexualism after Lin has had the opportunity to actually explore crossliving alternatives. On the other hand, despite the current fantasy of male-to-male sex play, a dominant lesbian identification may be an underlying issue.

In contrast to Lin's fears of losing her relationship as a result of her being a transgender individual, the experienced Gender Specialist would see the probability of her continuing in that relationship. Clearly, her manipulative and verbally abusive behavior needs to be addressed; however, it is also clear that if the relationship is to survive, her husband's acceptance of her needs must be addressed as well. Couples therapy would provide an excellent setting in which to address these and other relationship issues.

Sexually, Lin's worries may not be as catastrophic as she believes them to be, particularly since her husband has been a willing participant in their sex role play. Classically, a woman who finds herself attracted to males, then comes to later self-identify as an FTM transsexual, may later identify as a gay male. On the other hand, a woman who self-identifies as a transgenderist or crossdresser may maintain her sexual orientation by strictly viewing her activities as "fantasy" or "role play." Lin characterized her role play activity as an "unnatural desire." Obviously, she would benefit from basic sex education focused on the importance of role play in intimate relationships, as part of her support process.

Gender Specialists are advised that not all FTM transsexual, transgenderist, and crossdressing individuals identify as or become gay males. Most FTM individuals are attracted to and become involved with women, identifying as heterosexual males. Prior to recognizing their transgender identity and transitioning to male gender identification, some FTM individuals identify as lesbian, while others find themselves attracted to women yet are unsure how to approach relationships until after they have resolved their gender-identity issues. Long-term support for FTM individuals can introduce a variety of dynamics, some of which may concurrently exist in their nontransgender counterparts. For example, heterosexually identified males may spend a great deal of time struggling with social gender constructs in a world where males have a great deal of social responsibility placed upon them. Individuals who were previously lesbian identified may find that many of the woman-oriented politics they once identified with no longer apply now that they are male. Finally, a gay transsexual male may find the additional process of coming out as a gay male yet another challenge, one that is particularly challenging in a heterosexually oriented world.

When Resources Are Difficult to Locate

The Situation

Frank is a twenty-eight-year-old biological male living in a very small and isolated town. He is employed as an assistant manager at a small logging company, where he enjoys his work and is well liked. The town's population is well under 600 and is located at least three hours from the nearest small city. He says he is single by choice because of "a problem that just won't go away." Since early childhood, he has been interested in wearing clothing of the opposite gender and has wished he had breasts.

Frank stated that until recently, "the problem" left him feeling very isolated. He knew of no one else who felt the way he did, and in fact, he didn't even understand why he was having these feelings. This all changed one afternoon while he was watching a television talk show featuring men who dressed as women and women who dressed as men. Tearfully, Frank says that for the first time in his life, he is beginning to understand that there are others like him. There are even some who live completely as women and have had genital-reassignment. Before seeing this television show, the only reference he had seen about sex changes was in a grocery store tabloid. Now that he knows such a thing exists, Frank would like to know where he can turn for help. There are no therapists, other transgender people, or support groups in his area. Finally, his finances limit his choices; he cannot afford to travel frequently or move to another area.

Discussion

Isolation, as is clearly portrayed Frank's case, can work on many levels. Although we lack enough information to be certain what type of transgender individual he is, we can be certain that his feelings of isolation are acute. Like many others, Frank has spent a great deal of time unaware even that support exists for his "problem." Now, that he has been able to self-identify as transgender, he recognizes that no support resources are likely to exist in his location.

Situations like Frank's are typical of individuals living in rural areas, although most transgender individuals face some degree of isolation, even when they reside in metropolitan areas. The misinformation and stereotypes that surround transgender individuals only intensify their isolation. In some circumstances, having a transgender identity is considered "worse than being gay or lesbian." We should not be surprised that some nonintegrated transgender individuals burst into tears upon receiving validation for their transgender needs.

Tragically, the same negative stereotypes that prevent transgender individuals from coming out are also carried into the mental health profession. It is not uncommon to hear of licensed professionals' advising clients against crossdressing or exploring transition options. Media portrayals of transgender individuals play a large role in society's view of them as being unusual, sensational, or freakish, when in fact most are creditable, healthy individuals. In fact, transgender individuals can be found in and may prosper in all levels of society.

Although face-to-face support does not appear to be available for Frank, there are means available to put him in contact with specializing professionals and other transgender individuals. Through them, he can obtain more detailed information regarding transgender individuals, needs, and concerns. With access, it is possible for him to arrange telephone consultation with a Gender Specialist in a metropolitan area. That form of consultation could be supplemented by monthly, quarterly, or biannual office visits, depending his ability to travel.

Support for the individual in a rural location need not be limited to specialized professional contact. Therapy cannot provide the social interaction and peer feedback provided by association with transgender social organizations, educational organizations, and friends. Individuals like Frank should be encouraged to contact a nationally recognized education organization such as the American Educational Gender Information Service (AEGIS) or the International Foundation for Gender Education (IFGE). Both organizations provide at reasonable cost pamphlets, magazines, and books covering a wide variety of transgender subjects. AEGIS is particularly noteworthy for its journal *Chrysalis,* which features comprehensive educational articles written by transgender consumers and professionals. In addition to written materials, national organizations also serve as clearinghouses for referral sources. IFGE's *Transgender Tapestry* magazine features in each issue an up-to-date resource directory containing well over 300 national contact points. In Frank's case, there are four contact points for locating social organizations or specialized care providers in his state. Frank was encouraged to make contact, not only to determine what support they might afford him but also to see if those individuals were aware of any care providers, support groups, or other transgender individuals near his location.

Support groups are one of the most important resources for transgender individuals. Numbering well over one thousand nationally, most are facilitated by social organizations located in metropolitan areas, although some do exist in suburban or rural areas and may be organized by individual care providers or transgender individuals. Support groups can vary widely in structure and targeted participation. If by chance one support group is not appropriate for an individual's needs, a suitable alternative group may exist nearby. Support groups are not only a place where one can meet others with similar needs and feelings; they are also an excellent means for the dissemination of information about available hormone and surgical treatments and for sharing experiences with coming out, communication, social stereotypes, relationships, and victimization.

For example, one crossdresser's support group in Northern California invites participants to socialize together over midweek lunches. What looks like an ordinary business lunch is actually a support group of crossdressers meeting "in drab" (not crossdressed). The only thing that may seem out of the ordinary would be the placement of a sugar container atop a napkin holder as a signal to others. Any group of individuals with common interests can strive together to create a sense of community. (See sections on support groups in Chapter 9.)

Employment Concerns for the Transgender Individual

The Situation

Elizabeth, formerly Marcus, is a thirty-six-year-old self-defined transsexual woman who has been crossliving for almost nine months. During this time she has been receiving counseling support for her transgender issues, established hormone treatment, and made a good start on electrolysis to the point that facial hair has become sparse. Elizabeth recently announced in counseling that she felt it was time to make an on-the-job transition so that she could meet the requirement that she must be employed while living in role in order to have Genital Reassignment Surgery.

Elizabeth works as a training specialist at a large savings bank, where she is responsible for training new bank tellers. She feels quite certain that her employer will ask her to resign, since maintaining a "professional image" is a requirement of her position. Additionally, she feels there is bound to be tension over bathroom use and hostility from coworkers, since, to her knowledge, no other transgender individuals have ever worked in her district. Elizabeth's Gender Specialist, being new to this type of situation, has sought consultation.

Discussion

Whether an individual crossdresses solely within the confines of her or his personal life (as many crossdressers do), or desires to live in role full time, employment issues frequently remain a source of concern because so much may be at stake. For most people, employment provides both a source of income as well as a place where much of one's social life takes place on a regular basis. Depending on the position and individual, one's place of employment may also provide a sense of belonging and achievement. All these are the benefits employees receive in compensation for their time, skills, and dedication, yet in most circumstances, employers hold the trump card, with license to hire, promote, demote, lay off, or fire.

Crossdressers, pretransitional transsexuals, and others who have kept their transgender status private frequently fear having their transgender status found out. Sometimes these fears revolve around having one's transgender status discovered during an inconvenient time or under inappropriate circumstances. In other situations, those actually wanting to make an on-the-job transition may have fears about the actual disclosure process or negative responses from management and coworkers. Yet with all this, some transgender individuals do choose to come out in the workplace in various stages. Employment issues are not exclusive to any one transgender group, but shared by all.

It should be noted that those with no intention of crossdressing at work disclose to others primarily in order to reduce feelings of isolation or fears of being found out. In addition, they may have a genuine interest in sharing a private part of themselves with others in an effort to gain understanding, respect, and support. It is evident, however, that such choices beget consequences, and any transgender individual considering disclosure in the workplace would be well advised to invest substantial forethought into disclosure, as well as to refine and practice his or her disclosure skills. Finally, the individual should consult with several people experienced in workplace disclosure before proceeding.

> Bringing transgender issues into the workplace should be considered only by those willing and prepared to face potential risks and make necessary changes.

Reflecting back to Elizabeth's scenario, we have what appears to be a preoperative transsexual individual's desire to make an on-the-job transition. The fears she raises about such a transition are familiar enough, although the reasons behind her motivation are open to question. Is Elizabeth interested in making an on-the-job transition on the basis of a desire to experience living in role and thus further develop her identification as a transgender individual? Or is she motivated only because she sees it as a requirement for surgery? If the latter, Elizabeth, with the help of her counselor, would be well advised to examine further her reasons for seeking Genital Reassignment Surgery and for making an on-the-job transition.

Genital Reassignment Surgery is a confirmation of a permanently established gender identity, which should include substantial experience living in role. It is not a reward for jumping through hoops. Frequently, individuals assume that fulfilling a real-life test requires making an on-the-job transition. This is based in part on a misinterpretation of the HBIGDA Standards of Care, principle 5.2.4. ("The patient must have been living in the genetically-other sex role for at least one year"). Though many individuals do make on-the-job transitions, success at living in role is not limited to this one option. Some individuals might be better suited finding new jobs, transitioning in those positions, or living in role full-time. Others, lacking adequate socialization and employment skills, may find volunteer work best fits their needs.

Assuming that Elizabeth's motivations are for the best, her fears about remaining at the same place of employment are justifiable, even if her presentation is well planned. As an example, her concern regarding bathroom issues is quite common. Does Elizabeth use the women's bathroom? Should she be allowed to use the women's bathroom only postsurgically? What effect will her using the women's bathroom have on others? How do other companies provide for their transgender employees?

This is a type of decision which for the most part is beyond Elizabeth's power, although she can play a key role in the decision-making process by developing a dialogue about the issue as well as encouraging her supervisor (or personnel department) to seek the advice of a Gender Specialist familiar with this issue. When appropriate dialogue between the individual, management, and other coworkers takes place, transgender individuals typically then use a restroom that is consistent with their actual presentation without incident. Staff meetings on this issue can go far in helping set aside concerns others may have. Some companies ask the transgender individual to post a note on the restroom door stating they are using the restroom facility, thereby accommodating those who do not want to use the restroom at the same time. Finally, some companies have gone so far as to create one or two unisex restrooms with lockable doors, thereby eliminating any need for concern.

This is just the beginning of the issues Elizabeth may encounter. Any individual considering going to work in role should not overlook the following before that first day:

Does the Individual Have Adequate Disclosure Skills? Crossdressers and transgenderists who choose disclosure typically share their transgender status and experiences with one or more trusted friends in the workplace. Individuals told are also usually asked to maintain privacy and not tell others. Those interested in making on-the-job transitions may find that predisclosing to one or more trusted coworkers may help build confidence and supportive alliances prior to informing management. Others find themselves going to management first, if difficulty or harassment from coworkers is anticipated. In either circumstance, disclosure is a judgment call, and the individual is advised to do so in a manner that she or he finds least threatening. Taking transgender issues into the workplace requires disclosure skills, so much so, in fact, that individuals should not disclose in the workplace until they have had sufficient experience doing so in personal relationships.

Responses to an individual's disclosure of transgender identity can vary. Some may find it interesting and be supportive; others have no opinion or interest and could not care less. Some find the topic alienating or sensational. The transgender individual should be familiar with all these response types prior to attempting a workplace disclosure.

What Is the Individual's Physical Presentation Like? There are a variety of options where presentation is concerned. The androgynous look is commonplace and effective for transsexuals who are in an in-between state or who desire to gradually pace their transition, thus creating a space for building social, communication, and presentation skills. Others, including transgenderists and even some crossdressers, opt for an androgynous presentation because it does not require disclosure yet helps afford a feeling of integration. One common draw-back individuals presenting androgynously should be aware of is the potential confusion and questions such a presentation may create when others are unsure how the individual wishes to be addressed in title or pronoun. Additionally, there exists the potential that some individuals may find an androgynous presentation so disconcerting that they become hostile.

Transsexuals (and even some transgenderists) such as Elizabeth who wish to initiate crossliving full time by carrying their transgender identity into the workplace should, in all circumstances, have refined their presentation so that their appearance lends few clues to their actual inexperience presenting in the workplace. Style of dress and mannerisms should be appropriate to the individual's position. Unless one is working at a nightclub or within the sex industry, individuals typically are not well served by adopting a flamboyant or overtly sexual manner of dress. Attire designed to make an activist or political statement should also be reserved for social or political activities until one's identity is relatively well established.

What Backup and Security Plans Does the Individual Have? Some employment positions may not be suitable for an on-the-job transition, not because of a lack on the transgender individual's part, but rather from an employer's unwillingness to support his or her employees' individual needs and concerns. If this is the case, finding an equal or better position utilizing one's skills may be appropriate. Although transgender individuals are encouraged to pursue discrimination complaints against unethical employers, they also are reminded not to pursue retribution so far that it prevents them from moving on toward a better employment position where their skills will be appreciated.

Those actively pursuing an on-the-job transition would be well-served by having three to six months' cost-of-living savings securely set aside in the event of a surprise firing. Though transgender individuals are advised to avoid self-sabotaging thoughts and actions, they should be aware that an employer may occasionally wait as long as several years to fire an employee for being transgender, so as to build a case for firing the individual as well as to avoid discrimination suits.

There are some positions where making a transition may be intolerable, not as a result of a change in the individual's skills, but because some coworkers may attempt to make life unbearable for the individual or simply have great difficulty understanding the individual's needs. Many of these issues can be addressed through coworker sensitivity training. However, the individual may wish to look at employment alternatives. For example, Elizabeth might consider an interdepartmental transfer within her own company. Larger corporations can make departmental transfers, and this alternative works best when the individual, management, and personnel are in agreement. In many situations this provides an opportunity for a fresh start in a new department where establishing a new identity may be less difficult.

An individual's decision to change employment often means a change in career fields, which could mean that an individual will need retraining. Those who cannot afford retraining may find that Social Security disability benefits will cover some, if not all, costs. For example, in California transgender individuals may apply to the Department of Vocational Rehabilitation for retraining assistance. Individuals located in other areas are encouraged to see if their federal, state, or local government assistance programs offer similar assistance.

Has the Stage Been Set for an On-the-Job Transition? Making preparations for an on-the-job transition or preparing for the eventuality of finding a new position does not end with the initial disclosure, particularly when this is one of the most important social steps a transgender individual can face. Individuals themselves, employers, personnel departments, and even novice Gender Specialists sometimes feel at a loss for the words (or skills) to address such a change.

Tools to Ease the Workplace Transition

The following is a brief overview of tools that can ease the transition in the workplace.

Pictures. Pictures really are worth a thousand words. These can be used in situations where a crossdresser or transgenderist wishes to share his or her special secret with others. Those making an on-the-job transition may use pictures to give management an idea of what the employee's new presentation will be like.

Disclosure Letters. Writing a disclosure letter can help an individual pull her or his thoughts together. A good disclosure letter validates the relationship, states facts and needs, reassures continued reliability, welcomes inquiry, and finally, closes with a revalidation of the relationship in addition to an expression of gratitude. Brevity generally is best when dealing with business; sharing more personal details is more appropriate to personal relationships. Review and rewrite disclosure letters over a period of several weeks to allow for revision. Share these drafts with a knowledgeable friend or care provider for additional input.

Introduction or Business Cards. Cards presenting the new names and title help in setting first and follow-up impressions. They are particularly useful when coworkers and associates accidentally forget a new name or pronoun. Including a title ("Ms." or "Mr.") will help identify gender role, particularly where the individual may be presentable but not pass perfectly.

Letters of Introduction. Written by the employer, a letter of introduction can be distributed in a timely manner several weeks before the actual transition date. A well-written letter provides introduction and support of the individual and his or her transition, as well as support for coworkers' needs and questions. The letter should contain a company statement of sexual harassment policy and may announce upcoming sensitivity training dates for staff. The letter should also reflect the individual's and supervisor's willingness to address inquiry within the boundaries common courtesy.

Sensitivity Training. Sensitivity training provides opportunities for the transgender individual, coworkers, and management to meet in a safe, structured environment. These meetings can provide forums for presenting the individual's transition and needs as well as coworkers' needs. A company may have two meetings, the first providing space for the individual to speak and answer questions, the second, held in the individual's absence, providing coworkers with an opportunity to direct questions toward management that they may have felt uncomfortable asking in the presence of the transgender individual.

> Most individuals who make a concerted effort in making an on-the-job transition should have little if any reduction in work performance.

Fears about Victimization and Coming Out

The Situation

Marti is a self-identified crossdresser who called to request a counseling appointment to sort out fears about attending one of the Bay Area's social organizations. He said this was his first time going out crossdressed, and he was particularly afraid of being physically attacked or harassed by the police. Toward the end of the telephone conversation, Marti came across as uncertain whether he would be able to make his appointment. A week later, he failed to keep the appointment or follow through with a twenty-four-hour preappointment confirmation message.

Discussion

Although Marti's scenario is brief, it can help us better understand the many support concerns that affect transgender individuals. Care providers and transgender social organizations should bear in mind that first-time coming-out experiences, including going out dressed in role, are frequently the most frightening rites of passage that a transgender individual faces.

Will I be victimized by hostile strangers? Will I be arrested? Will my family and coworkers discover? Will I be suspected of homosexuality? Which bathroom should I use? Do I have to go to a support group crossdressed? If I go crossdressed, will I be rejected by other transgender individuals because of my appearance? These are typical of the questions that run through the transgender individual's mind. It was not surprising that Marti canceled his counseling appointment. Sometimes fears over coming out or even seeking help may cause individuals to remain closeted for many years.

Self-identified transsexuals and some transgenderists feel strongly motivated about defining a major element of their identity and eventually find their way out of the closet, but this is not always the case with crossdressers. Many crossdressers are more likely to take a few initial steps toward satisfying their momentary crossdressing needs; then, having done so, they slam the closet door shut until these feelings arise again.

The effects associated with these cycles are easily recognized by seasoned Gender Specialists. They include:

- MTF purging, that is, cyclically purchasing, using, and then throwing away opposite-gender clothing. This pattern is rarely associated with FTM individuals, who may typically maintain male clothing without drawing attention.
- Periodically calling for information or appointments and then not following through with commitments.
- Seeking exaggerated gender-stereotyped activities or roles in an effort to reaffirm masculinity (or femininity, in the case of FTM crossdressers), or simply denying crossdressing needs.
- Use of addictive substances, or involvement in dependent relationships or work addictions, in an effort to compensate for unresolved gender identity issues.

These unhealthy cycles are not only frustrating but demoralizing, and they need to be brought to the attention of the individual caught in them, if at all possible. In Marti's case, when he began coming across with uncertainty over keeping his appointment, he was gently informed that his uncertainty might suggest that such a cycle existed. He was then told that if, for some reason he was not ready or chose not to deal with his crossdressing needs, an appointment could be made for him at a future time. Sometimes an individual must truly want help to seek it. It should come as no surprise that no transgender persons, whether transsexuals, transvestites, transgenderists, or others, begin taking steps forward until they are sufficiently motivated.

Fears regarding victimization remain at the heart of the coming-out process and may continue throughout a transgender individual's lifetime. The best defense against victimization is to be prepared by putting sufficient forethought into crossgender activities. Beginners are encouraged to attend social functions with a companion or in groups until confident doing so alone. Carrying a letter from a Gender Specialist or disclosure card from a transgender social organization can help relieve some of the anxiety over being stopped by law enforcement officers. (See the Courtesy Disclosure Letter in Chapter 9.)

In our scenario, Marti identified his primary fear as one of being attacked while crossdressed in public. Although he did not say whether he had actually attended any previous transgender social activities "en drab" or wearing male attire, this remains a viable option for individuals who wish to test the receptiveness of a social organization, build self-confidence, and receive social support until they are ready to take their crossdressing outdoors. Within counseling and social support environments, individuals are encouraged to talk about their fears, as doing so will help minimize risks of developing long-term situational anxieties. Support groups provide an excellent opportunity to hear how others have avoided and confronted their victimization.

Postsurgical Concerns

The Situation

Val is an individual who had Genital Reassignment Surgery and breast augmentation two and a half months ago. She had surgery out of state, and upon her return she has been recuperating at home with the help of her boyfriend, Matt. Upon her return home, her therapist called to check in and see how Val was doing. During the conversation the therapist discovered that Val had failed to schedule a postsurgical medical follow-up appointment with her primary physician.

For the most part, all seemed well to the client; however, she was concerned with redness and chafing around the area of the postsurgical site. The client called to schedule a medical follow-up appointment but was unable to get one until two months later. Subsequently, her therapist called the physician, stressed the importance of postsurgical medical follow-up, and was able to obtain an appointment for the client three days later. At her medical appointment Val was found to have no serious medical complications, although an antifungal cream was prescribed to help counter the redness and chafing that had developed as a result of the surgery.

At her postsurgical mental health check-in appointment, Val reported feeling fine. To the therapist, Val looked tired and weak, and her skin color was somewhat gray when compared with her presurgical appearance. Overall, though, Val appeared fine and reported no complications or pain. Not surprisingly, she reported experiencing some discomfort (or healing pains), none of which could be described as acute discomfort. Val reported that she was following the physician's instructions to dilate her vagina four to six times daily for a half hour. He had provided her with three dilation stints (small, medium, and large sizes). She had no difficulty dilating with the small, had some discomfort with the medium, but found herself unable to use the large stint.

When she returned to regular couples therapy one month later, Val's condition had much improved. Her skin color had returned to normal. Her vaginal sensitivity had begun returning quickly, almost pleasurably. She reported having returned part time to work and was picking up her usual social activities. She also reported that the redness and chafing had virtually disappeared with use of the antifungal medication. Her breast augmentation surgery was healing successfully, although she had been somewhat unprepared for the cost of purchasing new soft-support undergarments needed during the healing process.

Her boyfriend Matt, appeared to still be tired after having spent a great deal of energy over the preceding several months supporting Val. Part of the couples session was devoted to acknowledging Matt's commitment to Val and exploring options to help him get his life back to normal, since he was having difficulty sleeping. During the remainder of the couples session, Val and Matt invested their time exploring Val's concern about having vaginal intercourse for the first time. She primarily had concerns that having intercourse might be painful, given the fact that she was still unable to use the large dilation stint during dilation exercises.

Discussion

The circumstances presented in this case scenario will not match every individual's experience. If postoperatively an individual feels any acute discomfort or pain or senses that something is not right, he or she should contact the surgeon or physician immediately. Val's scenario is representative of an individual who has successfully undergone Genital Reassignment Surgery without any major medical complications. It came as no surprise to the therapist that Val had failed to schedule a medical follow-up appointment. Many individuals set that task aside, thinking they will do so once they return home, or they may simply remain unaware of its importance. Subsequently, these individuals may find the physician's schedule completely booked, and unless the importance of the situation is stressed, the individual may not obtain a follow-up appointment for several months.

Delaying the follow-up medical appointment for several months risks complications' remaining undetected, if they do exist. It is for this reason that the Guidelines for Genital Reassignment Surgery (see Chapter 5) urge that individuals have postoperative medical follow-up appointments within two weeks of hospital discharge. At the time of the appointment, the individual's physician will examine the surgical sites and provide preventive treatment for any minor symptoms that indicate the possibility of a future complication. For Genital Reassignment Surgery patients, the physician also provides a new hormone regimen.

Val's difficulty using the large dilation stint raises questions that cannot be answered without her physician's assessing the vagina's breadth and depth. After an examination, Val was told that the breadth and depth of her vagina were simply insufficient to permit entry of the large stint, but that over time and with upkeep of her dilation exercises, this may improve. It was particularly promising that by the second month of recovery Val's vaginal sensitivity had returned almost completely and that at times it felt pleasurable. Many times individuals have concerns about whether orgasm is possible postsurgically. Return of the majority of an individual's genital sensitivity is a good indicator that at some point orgasm will be possible, although this is not always the case.

Val was instructed by the surgeon not to have intercourse until sixty days after surgery. After a physical examination, and with the knowledge that Matt's penis was approximately the same size as the medium dilation stint, she was told by her physician that intercourse did appear possible after sixty days. Her fear about having intercourse for the first time, although primarily based on her concerns about not being able to accommodate the large dilation stint, may have been augmented by other concerns. Will she find intercourse pleasurable? Will she find Matt pleasing? Will Matt find her pleasing?

Concerns like these are best addressed in couples counseling with a therapist familiar with clinical sexology. In regard to practical matters, Val and Matt were encouraged not to rush into intercourse or set heavy expectations upon their first attempts. Their therapist encouraged them to gradually reinitiate sexual intimacy by starting with massaging, holding, and mutual masturbation. Additionally, usage of the small dilation stint or a dildo might help Val to relax and explore penetration in an intimate setting with maximum self-control. Usage of extra lubrication would also be helpful. Anal intercourse, which may have been part of the couple's routine sexual activity prior to genital reassignment, may continue to yield pleasure once enough time has passed to allow for healing of the vaginal wall.

Part II

Essays

Ethical Implications for Psychotherapy with Individuals Seeking Gender Reassignment

Barbara F. Anderson, Ph.D., L.C.S.W.

Chapter 11

Some individuals are so dissatisfied with their genetic sex and with the societal imposed gender roles associated with it that they seek the dramatic resolution of gender reassignment. In the course of this process of transformation from their genetic sex to their perceived true gender, they may choose to utilize many resources—endocrinologists, surgeons, electrologists, image consultants, lawyers. However, if they wish treatment by physicians who adhere to the only currently accepted standards for the care of such individuals, they will be required to consult with at least two mental health professionals. One will provide psychological treatment, and, if merited, a recommendation for the desired procedure. The second serves to confirm the first opinion prior to surgical reassignment.

The "Standards of Care: The Hormonal and Surgical Sex Reassignment of Gender Dysphoric Persons" (Walker et al., rev. 1990) was the first, and until now, the only document of its kind. It was designed to lay the best possible foundation for a successful transformation as well as to weed out the poorest risks for reassignment (Bolin, 1988, p. 49). Requirements that candidates live "full-time in the social role of the genetically-other sex" for a minimum of one-year (Walker, Standard 9) and that they obtain an evaluation of their mental state as well as the attitudes and beliefs upon which their requests are based (Standard 1), are obviously supportable toward that end. In addition, the Harry Benjamin Standards of Care require that applicants have had a "psychotherapeutic relationship" of at least three months' duration prior to hormonal sex reassignment (Standard 6) and one of six months' duration prior to surgical reassignment (Section 5.2.2), with each being "preceded by recommendation . . . by a clinical behavioral scientist." (Standard 4, hormonal sex reassignment; Standard 11, surgical sex reassignment). Finally, prior to surgical reassignment, an applicant must obtain a recommendation from a second mental-health professional (Standard 7).

It is the requirement that clients obtain permission from their therapists that raises an ethical dilemma for the clinician whose philosophy is to treat clients in an open-minded, nonjudgmental manner. Such therapists see their role as one of accompanying the individual on a journey toward increased awareness and self-actualization motivated by the client's desire to transcend her or his present level of functioning to one that promises greater contentment. Such therapists bring their expertise on the human condition to the therapeutic relationship without influencing the direction of choices made by the client.

However, in the case of the therapist who serves the multiple functions of healer, evaluator, and gatekeeper to genital reassignment, an adversarial attitude between client and therapist is created within their relationship which makes a travesty of the process of therapy. Rather than a joint venture between the two in which both seek the best solution, that relationship becomes one in which the client, eager for permission to proceed with the desired medical procedures, may fear rather than trust the therapist. The client may be reduced to reciting the "party line"—that which the client believes will maximize the probability of gaining access to the desired treatment. Reflexively, the therapist, aware of the client's effort to manipulate the outcome, may interpret this behavior as evidence of underlying psychopathology that might impede the client's satisfactory adjustment after reassignment. The more skeptical the professional becomes, the more desperate the applicant feels, as she or he accelerates efforts to convince the therapist that emotional survival is dependent upon being granted a recommendation for the desired procedures.

A hypothetical situation as follows might arise: Joseph makes an appointment to meet with mental health clinician Dr. X for the purpose of beginning a therapeutic relationship as recommended by the Harry Benjamin Standards of Care, to which his future endocrinologist and surgeon adhere. He understands that he must get approval for each procedure from his therapist, who will want to know all about his past and present as well as his expectations and plans for the future. The materials that Joseph has read have forewarned him that therapists are most inclined to endorse those applicants who demonstrate mental and emotional stability, unwavering purposefulness in pursuing reassignment procedures, a family and/or social support network, and physical attributes that facilitate "passing." Joseph becomes quite anxious as the date of his first meeting with Dr. X approaches. He is worried about whether he will meet the criteria he imagines that Dr. X holds up for clients pursuing gender-reassignment procedures. His life flashes before him, punctuated by images of himself as a boy rejected by his family and peers, as an adolescent school drop-out and loner, and most recently, as an adult holding and losing a series of jobs with no future, several suicide attempts, and an ongoing battle to conquer one or another addiction. Joseph cannot align his image of a successful candidate for reassignment procedures with his life experiences. He begins to consider his options—find physicians who do not adhere to the Harry Benjamin Standards of Care; modify the facts of his life to conform more closely to what he believes is required; tell all and then throw himself on the mercy of the therapist, stressing his desperation and willingness to do anything, including suicide, if not granted an endorsement; or give up his pursuit of the only life-affirming solution to his problem of gender discordance. Under such circumstances Dr. X doesn't have a chance to get to know Joseph, to work with him in a therapeutic milieu, or to make useful interventions that might prepare her client to accept and adjust to the benefits as well as the limitations of hormonal and genital reassignment.

A second hypothetical situation might be one in which another client, Melissa, being less sophisticated than Joseph, but having the same historical life experiences, goes to Dr. Y. Although for the last five years she has lived a stable life, built a small community of friends in the transgender world, and worked regularly in a position requiring little contact with others, she recounts the same early difficulties that Joseph experienced and also admits continuing bouts of depression, occasional lapses of sobriety, and an inability to engage in intimate relationships. Dr. Y expresses concern that Melissa is suffering from several mental disorders, including chronic depression, alcohol abuse, and schizoid personality. He suggests that treatment will most likely be lengthy and does not know if or when he will ever be able to endorse Melissa's request for hormonal or genital reassignment. Melissa, who initially saw herself as having come so far in her growth into adulthood, suddenly feels as if the road yet to be traveled is far longer than the distance she has traversed. She feels defeated, depressed, and without motivation to continue striving for her goal of reassignment, and she slips back to her earlier level of marginal functioning, without benefit of psychotherapy. Again, Dr. Y finds himself unable to help an individual who has sought him out and was amenable to therapy, but was discouraged by the process imposed upon each of them.

The Harry Benjamin Standards of Care allude only briefly to the possibility of difficulties arising in the role of the therapist as judge in stating that "clinical behavioral scientists must often rely on possibly unreliable or invalid sources of information (patients' families and friends) in making clinical decisions and in judging whether or not a patient has fulfilled the requirements." The document then changes tack and goes on to express concern that such professionals "given the burden of deciding who to recommend for hormonal and surgical sex reassignment . . . are subject to extreme social pressure and possible manipulation as to create an atmosphere in which charges of laxity, favoritism, sexism, financial gain, etc. may be made" (Principle 19).

The authors of the Harry Benjamin Standards of Care seem more concerned about professionals' ability to resist "social pressure" and avoid charges of malfeasance than of the more immediate pressure exerted by clients desperate for a procedure that promises relief from their gender dysphoria. Though there is some awareness that information elicited from clients who desire reassignment might be tainted, there is no suggestion of how to resolve this matter. And there is no recognition of the potential harm therapists could do in their murky roles of healer, judge, and jury.

Little has been written on either the recognition or resolution of this dilemma. Wardell Pomeroy's article "The Diagnosis and Treatment of Transvestites and Transsexuals," which predates the Harry Benjamin Standards of Care by four years, discusses the mental health professional's role.

[T]he first task for the therapist in dealing with a transvestite or transsexual is the establishment of rapport. . . . transsexuals insist that their gender role confusion is biologic, and that because . . . their psyche cannot be modified to conform to their body[,] the only alternative is to have their body changed to conform to their psyche. In the light of present knowledge they are correct. A therapist can be of help to them, however, by giving them support, helping them with social problems, counseling their relatives about their condition, and by referring them to knowledgeable . . . [professionals] who can help them to accomplish a conversion operation, if this is indicated. (p. 222)

Pomeroy is quite clear in his position that the therapist must not let transsexuals make their own diagnosis [*sic*] . . . . Also, even if they are bona fide transsexuals but are obviously recognizable as a member of their anatomic gender, one might rightfully reject the idea of a conversion operation. A tall, heavy, deep-voiced, heavily bearded, tattooed man who is, indeed, a transsexual can become a ludicrous woman, and I, for one, would not recommend an operation in such a situation." (p. 221)

Pomeroy, without either recognizing or acknowledging the dilemma, simply ignores the paradoxical situation of attributing to the therapist the tasks of establishing rapport, extending emotional support and information about resources, and deciding if genital reassignment "is indicated" (p. 222).

Bolin identifies the problematic aspect of the Harry Benjamin Standards of Care's recommendation as creating "an inequity of power relations such that the recommendation for surgery is completely dependent on the caretaker's evaluation. This results in a situation in which the psychological evaluation may be, and often is, wielded like a club over the head of the transsexual who so desperately wants the surgery" (p. 51). She goes on to suggest that living for a year in the desired gender role may be far more useful than a similar period of psychotherapy as a gauge in diagnosing the true transsexual (p. 53). She posits that mental health professionals' importance may reside instead, in their roles as care providers and gatekeepers throughout and following a successful period of cross-living (p. 54). Bolin, an anthropologist studying transsexualism, recognizes the dilemma, but from a sociocultural perspective (p. 5), and as such, suggests a resolution that negates the greatest skill that the therapist has to offer—an understanding of the human condition and a mastery of the tools to facilitate individuals' growth, development, and self-awareness.

Drawing from both Pomeroy and Bolin, one could synthesize their recommendations to arrive at another solution. The resolution of the dilemma of the conflicting demands of the roles of healer, evaluator, and gatekeeper to genital reassignment may lie in the diversifying of functions between the two required clinical behavioral scientists. Neither the role of healer nor those of evaluator and gatekeeper need be compromised if they are divided between the two professionals. The applicant for reassignment could still be required to engage in a psychotherapeutic relationship for a minimum of three or six months, depending on the procedure sought. The therapist's singular role would be to counsel, support, interpret unconscious material, and educate and encourage the client in the interest of exploring all possibilities that promise growth and change in a desired direction. At the end of the period of therapy and at a point prior to requesting the procedure, the client could meet with a second clinical behavioral scientist who, furnished with records of the process and outcome of therapy, would evaluate the applicant and ultimately recommend or withhold endorsement. This process does require an additional meeting with a mental health professional, for the current guidelines do not require a confirmatory opinion prior to hormonal reassignment. It may however, minimize the total number of psychotherapy contacts as a result of avoiding the earlier described complications engendered by the therapist's murky role.

References

Bolin, Anne. 1988. *In Search of Eve: Transsexual Rites of Passages*. South Halley, Mass.: Bergin & Garvey.

Pomeroy, Wardell B. 1975. The Diagnosis and Treatment of Transvestites and Transsexuals. *Journal of Sex and Marital Therapy* 1(3): 215–24.

Walker, Paul A., et al. 1990 (rev.). *Standards of Care: The Hormonal and Surgical Sex Reassignment of Gender Dysphoric Persons*. Palo Alto, Calif.: The Harry Benjamin International Gender Dysphoria Association, Inc.

Understanding Your Rights under the San Francisco Ordinance

Larry Brinkin, Acting Coordinator
San Francisco Human Rights Commission

Chapter 12

In January 1995 San Francisco's laws prohibiting discrimination were amended to add protection for discrimination on the basis of "gender identity." This landmark legislation was designed primarily to protect the transgender community in San Francisco from discrimination in employment, housing, and public accommodations. After the San Francisco Human Rights Commission held a public hearing to document discrimination against the transgender community, the legislation was passed unanimously by the Board of Supervisors and signed by the Mayor.

Questions Commonly Asked about the Ordinances

So that readers may understand how the law works, and what it does and does not do, we present here some commonly asked questions and the answers of the Human Rights Commission. These answers are not intended to be used as legal advice; anyone believing that his or her rights have been violated should consult an attorney to determine all possible options.

General Issues

How is gender identity defined by the law? The ordinances define gender identity as "a person's various individual attributes as they are understood to be masculine and/or feminine."

Who is covered under the ordinances? Everyone has a gender identify; therefore, everyone is covered. However, the laws primarily are for the protection of transgender individuals, who we define to include transsexuals (preoperative, post-operative, and nonoperative), crossdressers, intersexed people, drag queens, drag kings, female and male impersonators, masculine women, and feminine men.

Employment Issues

Can I be fired for being transgender? No. Your employer cannot fire you simply because of your status as a transgender person.

Can an employer refuse to hire or promote me because I am transgender? No.

Can anyone harass me or threaten me because of I am transgender? No. You have the right to work in a discrimination-free atmosphere. Harassment, including verbal harassment, whether by a coworker, manager, client, or customer, is a form of discrimination and is illegal. Your employer has the responsibility to provide a workplace that is safe and free of illegal discrimination of any kind.

Sometimes verbal harassment can take the form of deliberate use of wrong pronouns (e.g., referring to an MTF person as "he"). If someone does it inadvertently once or twice, he or she can be gently reminded. If he or she intentionally persists, it is illegal harassment.

Can I present myself at work in my true gender identity? Yes. If you are a transsexual, or living "24-7" (24 hours a day, 7 days a week), you have the right to express your gender identity at work; that is, a male-to-female can present as female, and a female-to-male can present as male.

Do I have the right to crossdress at work? Not necessarily. If you crossdress at home and your employer finds out about it, you cannot be discriminated against. However, employer dress codes typically are upheld by the courts, and your employer probably would have the right to require that you conform to gender codes (unless you are "24-7").

If I am FTM, do I have the right to use the men's restroom? If I am MTF, do I have the right to use the women's restroom? Generally speaking, a transsexual would have the right to use the restroom corresponding to his or her gender identity. For a postoperative transsexual, there is no exception to this rule. For a preoperative or nonoperative transsexual, or a crossdresser living "24–7," the rule is usually true unless there is unavoidable nudity. If there is nudity—for instance, if there are toilets without stalls—the employer can require that you use the restroom corresponding to your genital sex.

The restroom issue can be the most difficult. State health and safety codes require separate facilities for men and women. Though the rules as described above generally hold true, we have to look at each case and determine the best resolution. Sometimes it works before for a preoperative transsexual to use a private restroom, if one is available, until surgery. We require that the employer accommodate the transgender employee as reasonably as possible, meaning that all options should be explored to make sure that the employee is not required to use the restroom of his or her former gender. The Commission would place the burden on the employer to show why such accommodation was not possible.

If I make my transition while employed, can my employer be required to honor my request to use a name matching my gender identity? Yes. This is especially true if you have changed your gender on documents such as a driver's license.

If I have decided to make a transition, can my employer require me to wait to change my presentation until after surgery? No.

What if the discrimination I am suffering is based on my employer's belief that I am gay, lesbian, or bisexual? Many uninformed people believe that being transgender is simply a manifestation of being gay, lesbian, or bisexual. If someone perceives that you are gay, lesbian, or bisexual, whether you are or not, and they discriminate against you, you would be protected by the sexual-orientation discrimination provisions of local and state laws.

Housing Issues

Can I be denied rental of a room, flat, apartment, house, or place of business because of my gender identity? No, that would be illegal. The only exception is that a person can discriminate if he or she is looking for a roommate or housemate in a private home.

Can I be legally discriminated against in real-estate transactions because of my gender identity? No.

In a homeless shelter or a residential treatment facility, can I demand assignment to the section matching my gender identity? For the most part, yes. Generally speaking, a transgender person should be housed according to her or his gender identity. However, if the facility's staff has reasonable doubt as to your gender identity, they can ask for identification showing your gender. This cannot be a blanket policy for all transgender people, and it cannot be done in order to harass anyone. If there is unavoidable nudity in the gender-specific unit of the facility, the staff can legally limit accommodations to only postoperative transsexuals. But the staff would have to provide accommodation to a preoperative or a nonoperative transsexual if there is a reasonable way to do so—for instance, requiring clients to undress in private areas such as bathroom stalls.

Public Accommodations Issues

Can I be denied services as a client of an agency or a customer of a business because of my gender identity? Generally, no. The exception might be a residential treatment facility in which the rules stated above would apply.

Is it legal for the staff of a government agency, nonprofit organization, or business to verbally harass me or make fun of me or fail to treat me with equality or respect because of my gender identity? No. Such treatment is illegal. The Commission could be of help in such cases, except that San Francisco ordinances do not apply to state or federal organizations.

Can a medical provider refuse to provide care, or treat me differently, because of my gender identity? No! There have been many reports of negative behavior by medical providers treating people who are changing their bodies. This not only reprehensible; it is illegal.

Does the San Francisco ordinance require that insurance companies provide coverage for transgender therapies and surgeries? No. Insurance coverage is governed by federal and state law.

If I want to try on clothes in a department store, can I use the facility matching my gender identity? Generally speaking, yes, especially if there are private cubicles for changing. If changing clothes is done in a common, open space, the store might have the right to require that only postoperative persons be accommodated. However, the store would have the obligation to accommodate other transgender customers, such as offering them a private space, if it wouldn't be to expensive or disruptive to do so. They might also be asked to reconfigure the common space to cubicles.

Do I have the right to use the restroom that matches my gender identity in a public agency or business? Generally speaking, yes. The rules above governing employee restrooms generally apply.

Remedies

If you experience discrimination on the basis of your gender identity, you can file a complaint with the Human Rights Commission. The Commission staff would not represent you, but instead would try to resolve the matter as a neutral mediator. If you call the Commission with a complaint, we will first determine whether we have jurisdiction; that is, the discrimination has to have occurred in San Francisco (or it could have happened anywhere if perpetrated by a city contractor). Then we will conduct an intake meeting to get all the facts of the case and decide whether to accept it for handling.

If we take your case, we will send the complaint to the accused employer, landlord, or business owner, and ask him or her to respond. In our complaint letter, we also strongly suggest that the respondent participate in a mediation session on an attempt to resolve the complaint. Mediation is the primary work of the Commission; most of our complaints are resolved this way and are not investigated.

If the respondent company refuses to mediate, or if mediation is attempted and fails, the Commission will then conduct an investigation to see whether there is evidence to support your allegations. An investigation typically consists of interviews of coworkers, supervisors, clients, customers, or anyone who might have information relevant to the allegations. We would also examine any relevant documents such as performance evaluations, personnel files, and the like. The Commission can use a subpoena to get this information, if necessary.

Following the investigation, we would again attempt to resolve the situation through mediation. If that fails, we would then issue a director's finding indicating whether there was sufficient evidence to sustain the allegations. The Commission's powers end with the finding; we do not have the power to order a remedy. However, it is rare that we get to the stage of issuing a finding; the cases are usually resolved before that point.

Examples of remedies the Commission has negotiated include monetary settlements (usually based on back pay or some other formula), continuing health benefits for terminated employees, reinstatement, promotion, gift certificates (when a business has discriminated against a customer), changes in company policies (such as adding "gender identity" to the company's antidiscrimination policy), and training of the company's staff on transgender issues.

The San Francisco ordinance also provides a civil remedy; that is, a lawsuit could be filed in Superior Court. This could be a stronger action in that the court has the authority to order a remedy, including awarding damages. However, it is unclear at this point whether court cases can be heard; the State Fair Employment and Housing Act has a preemption clause providing that only the state can occupy the area of discrimination and that cities cannot. It will take a state Supreme Court ruling to determine whether San Francisco's ordinance can be enforced in court.

Findings and Recommendations

These findings and recommendations of the San Francisco Human Rights Commission are derived from public testimony. Principally authored by Jamison Green, this section of the chapter comes from the San Francisco Human Rights Commission's booklet *Investigation into Discrimination against Transgendered People* (September 1994). These findings and recommendations document the types of discrimination that affect transgender persons, and they illustrate how local government can address the issues. Researchers interested in reviewing actual

changes to city law can do so under City and County of San Francisco Administrative Code Chapter 12a, 12b, and 12c, as well as under San Francisco Police
Code Article 33.

Findings

The Human Rights Commission, having conducted a public hearing on May
12, 1994, to investigate discrimination against the Transgender Community, and
having considered verbal and written testimony, hereby finds:

1. That the City and County of San Francisco, by legislation, policy and practice, has consistently valued diversity and tolerance and has worked to eradicate
discrimination based on prejudice in employment, housing, and public accommodations.

2. That the term transgender is used as an umbrella term that includes male and
female cross dressers, transvestites, female and male impersonators, pre-operative
and post-operative transsexuals, and transsexuals who choose not to have genital
reconstruction, and all persons whose perceived gender or anatomic sex may
conflict with their gender expression, such as masculine-appearing women and
feminine-appearing men.

3. That gender identity is different from sexual orientation, and sexual orientation discrimination ordinances do not protect transgendered persons. Gender
identity is the deeply felt knowledge of an individual that he or she is male or
female; in transgendered persons, the gender identity and the anatomic sex may
not be in alignment. Sexual orientation is not an indicator of gender identity: for
example, a male-bodied person who is attracted to men and has a male gender
identity is not considered transgendered; a male-bodied man who is attracted to
women and who has a female gender identity which is expressed through crossdressing and/or the desire to live full-time as a woman, is considered transgendered. It is the expression of gender identity that results in discrimination because that expression is perceived as conflicting with the expectations placed
upon the individual solely because of the form of his or her body, particularly
the genitals.

4. That actual and legal discrimination do currently exist in the City and
County of San Francisco with regard to gender presentation and transgender or
transsexual status or identity.

5. That existing laws and policies often undermine the dignity and privacy of,
and do not include protections for, transgendered persons. The sovereign dignity
of the individual and his or her right to privacy are cornerstones of American
values.

6. That there are no accurate statistics reflecting the demographics of the transgendered population, but informal surveys of the membership of local transgender organizations and of local community service agencies indicate that there
are approximately 6000 transgendered individuals in San Francisco. This num-

ber is increased substantially by including persons who may be perceived as transgendered and may therefore experience adverse discrimination.

7. That transgendered persons are present in every demographic group: every race, every class, every culture, every sexual orientation, and every epoch of recorded history includes evidence of the existence of transgendered persons.

8. That in the current social climate, persons who are perceived to be transgendered are considered by some as less than human and therefore assumed to be fair game for objectification, violence, and discrimination. Hate violence is perpetrated against transgendered persons as much as, if not more than, any other group.

9. That the efforts of the Human Rights Commission to address complaints involving transgendered persons are seriously hampered by lack of legislation to support and protect the basic human rights of transgendered persons. In some cases, the Commission has been successful in mediating resolution, but without the force of law the power of the Commission to compel humane treatment is severely limited.

10. That some transgendered persons may be driven to suicide in response to the severe discrimination they may face on a daily basis.

11. That many members of the transgender community are afraid to testify at public hearings for fear of retribution against themselves or their families, especially for fear of loss of employment and loss of child custody.

12. That transgendered persons are subject to severe discrimination in employment, housing and public accommodations.

13. That transgendered persons have experienced harassment by members of the San Francisco Police Department and the Sheriff's Department, and that it is possible that crimes against transgendered persons have not always been taken seriously by these agencies.

14. That transgendered persons have experienced great difficulty in obtaining medical and social services from hospitals, public health agencies, rape crisis centers, battered women's shelters, homeless shelters, and other organizations in San Francisco. Many of these providers treat transgendered patients and clients with great reluctance, sometimes pointedly harassing them and embarrassing them in waiting rooms, or condoning harassing behavior on the part of other patients or clients.

15. That representatives of some City and County agencies admit their employees are not uniformly educated about or sensitive to the needs of transgendered persons.

16. That the transgender community is often aligned with the Lesbian/Gay/Bisexual community, but still experiences discrimination within the Lesbian/Gay/Bisexual community and its institutions.

17. That both the news media and entertainment media tend to perpetuate stereotypes in their coverage or treatment of transgendered persons and issues.

The ill-informed biases expressed in the media then become a sanction perpetuating discrimination.

18. That some transgendered women who are raped, battered, homeless, or otherwise in need of services, as well as transgendered men who require medical attention for female anatomy, are frequently denied services from women's support group agencies based on their transgender status or identity. While some agencies providing services for women are working to educate themselves with respect to the transgender community and to combat the internal prejudices that lead to denial of services to the transgendered community, the Commission finds that greater effort must be made to eliminate discrimination based on transgender status or identity.

19. That transgendered youth frequently are unable to find sources of support for their difference. Feminine boys are often harassed and tortured by their peers and by their parents. Masculine girls are usually teased and/or ignored. Both boys and girls are called queer and left alone to traverse the difficult terrain between gender identity and sexual orientation. With no language to talk about their feelings, no social support, and little (if any) education about sex and gender, transgendered youth are at high risk for attempting suicide, being rejected by family or peers, becoming runaways, becoming subject to medical incarceration, getting stuck on the bottom rungs of the economic and social ladder in this society. One agency in San Francisco reported receiving nearly 2000 calls in the past year from transgendered or gender questioning youth. These youth express deep isolation, the desire to connect with other youth who share their feelings, and a desperate need to escape harassment, abuse and rejection because of who they are. The demand for transgender services is roughly 20% of the total demand for youth services at this agency which serves lesbian, gay, bisexual, and transgendered youth. This indicates that comprehensive gender-issues-related social services are necessary for the community-at-large.

20. That once an individual is labeled with the medical diagnosis transsexualism, insurance companies discriminate against them by excluding them from coverage for the necessary treatments and procedures and for any complications or conditions that may arise from these treatments and procedures.

21. That the economic hardship imposed on some transgendered (particularly male-to-female transsexual) persons due to discrimination in employment and in medical and insurance services frequently forces them to live in poverty or to turn to sex work to survive.

22. That the wives, partners, husbands, children, and other loved ones of transgendered people feel the intolerance and harassment shown by people out of ignorance just as deeply as does the transgendered person. They fear for their own safety and security as well as for that of the transgendered person they love and on whom they may depend economically.

23. That transgendered parents live with an often debilitating fear of the loss of custody or contact with their children, and may in fact lose that custody or contact solely because of prejudice. There is no evidence to show that transgendered persons as a class are not fit parents. This discrimination is arbitrary and may unnecessarily damage the relationship between parent and child.

24. That legislation to protect the transgendered community has been enacted in other locations: Minneapolis in 1974, Seattle in 1986, Santa Cruz in 1992, and Minnesota in 1993.

25. That Proposition L did give protection to the employees of the San Francisco City and County government against discrimination based on gender identity. Since proposition L was passed in 1993 by a vote of the People of San Francisco, it is their will to protect transgendered persons.

26. That professionals who may serve the transgender may also become stigmatized by their peers for their association with the transgendered community, and this stigmatization, or fear of it, often prevents attorneys, physicians, nurses, psychotherapists, etc., from treating or serving transgendered patients or clients. Attorneys, in particular, are reluctant to advocate on behalf of transsexuals whose surgical treatment has gone awry.

27. That the Human Rights Commission needs to work actively with employers, businesses, non-profit organizations, and public agencies to educate them as to the validity of the transgender experience and the value of cultural diversity in the area of gender, and to lead the way in demonstrating how the myths and prejudices surrounding the transgender community can be broken down to reveal the human beings who are struggling for their civil rights.

Recommendations

1. That the City and County of San Francisco develop and enact legislation amending the City's Human Rights Ordinances to add "gender identity" as a protected class with the intention of granting specific human rights protection to persons who are transgendered, and empower the Human Rights Commission to serve as the administrative agency to investigate and mediate discrimination claims that arise.

2. That the City and County of San Francisco budget for a position with the Human Rights Commission for the purpose of coordinating education and investigating and mediating claims, and that outreach be done to the transgender community in the hiring process for this position to ensure that transgendered applicants are considered.

3. That the Human Rights Commission ensure that its staff is adequately trained in transgender issues to enable them to perform transgender sensitivity training in San Francisco and to investigate and mediate discrimination claims.

4. That the Human Rights Commission produce and distribute information and resource materials for transgendered persons, their families, and their associates concerning their legal and civil rights.

5. That the Human Rights Commission serve as a clearing house for the general public and the media to contact for information regarding transgender education and human rights.

6. That the City and County of San Francisco conduct sensitivity training for its employees to demystify the subject of transgender experience and prepare both management and front-line employees to appropriately handle situations that may arise involving transgendered persons or the reactions of others to them.

7. That employees of the City and County of San Francisco are made to understand that discrimination against transgendered people is grounds for disciplinary action.

8. That the San Francisco Police and Sheriff's Departments conduct transgender sensitivity training for all personnel to ensure that transgendered persons are treated with respect, that their complaints are taken seriously and acted upon with reasonable dispatch, that if a transgendered person is detained or incarcerated he or she is housed in a manner which is consistent with the individual's gender identity, that his or her prescribed medication is provided, and that if the transgendered person's safety is compromised or at risk, he or she will be immediately protected and not subject to any physical or psychological harm perpetrated by other inmates or officers. Transgender persons should have the right to be placed in protective custody upon request.

9. That the San Francisco Police and Sheriff's Departments use terminology that is appropriate to an individual's gender identity on departmental forms and police reports, and refrain from insulting or compromising the privacy and dignity of persons who may have physical anomalies. It is respectful to ask a person whose gender identity is in question which gender they prefer; it is not respectful to ask "What are you?" or to make assumptions and enter descriptions of physical anomalies as part of a report, except when such anomalies are material to an investigation.

10. That the Office of Citizen Complaints conduct transgender sensitivity training for its personnel for the purpose of improving relations with the transgender community and improving the Office's ability to comprehend and process complaints filed by transgendered persons.

11. That the Department of Social Services conduct transgender sensitivity for its personnel to ensure that transgendered persons are treated with respect, that their complaints are taken seriously and acted upon with reasonable dispatch, that their fitness as parents is not judged solely on the basis of prejudice against transgender persons, and that transgendered clients do not endure physical or psychological abuse in the process of obtaining services.

12. That arbitrary gender-specific dress codes should not be imposed where they are not necessary: employers approached by employees who are undergoing a gender transition should assist the employee by accepting their gender identity as expressed by their clothing and helping other employees to understand the transition process. In such instances in which there is a reasonable requirement for a dress code or for specific gender separation in facilities (such as locker-room dressing areas, etc.) then reasonable accommodations should be made so that the transgendered person's dignity and privacy are preserved, and the concerns of others are also considered. All of the parties should work cooperatively to address the issue.

13. That employers, businesses, and public agencies not restrict the access of transgendered persons to public restroom facilities that are appropriate to the aperson's gender identity. Like anyone else, transgender persons using restroom facilities are primarily concerned with relieving and grooming themselves, and with ensuring their own personal safety.

14. That the Department of Public Health conduct transgender sensitivity training for all personnel to ensure that transgendered persons are treated with respect and dignity, that their complains are taken seriously and acted upon with reasonable dispatch, that their physical health needs are not overlooked due to prejudice against transgendered persons, that transgendered clients and patients do not endure physical or psychological abuse in the process of obtaining services.

15. That the Department of Public Health continue to conduct inservice training covering the treatments, medications, procedures, and new medical, social, and psychological developments with respect to the transgendered community.

16. That medical service providers, including hospitals, clinics, and private practitioners, ensure that they and their support staff are adequately trained to handle transgendered patients, to protect their health, and to ensure that their programs eliminate all unnecessary forced disclosure of transgender status as a requirement for receipt of services, to ensure that transgendered persons are not disqualified from receiving services based upon transgender status or identity, or upon perceived transgender status or identity, and to ensure that transgendered persons are treated with dignity and respect regardless of what surgery or treatments they have had or have not had.

17. That the Department of Public Health and all other medical service providers refrain from treating transgendered patients and clients as if they are "on display" or otherwise objectify them or subject them to dehumanizing treatment, preserving the client or patient's dignity, privacy and confidentiality, and that they also require employees and contractors to comply with the non-discrimination policy.

18. That the Department of Human Resources ensure that its investigators are trained in transgender issues, publicize to City and County employees the rights of transgender persons, and ensure that transgendered persons are not disqualified from employment, or discriminated against by any City agency, based upon transgender status or identity, or upon perceived transgender status or identity.

19. That the administrators of homeless shelters, battered women's shelters, substance abuse treatment programs, rape crisis centers, and other providers of social services in San Francisco ensure that their staff is trained in transgender sensitivity, that their program eliminates forced disclosure of transgender status as a requirement for receipt of services, and ensure that transgendered persons are not disqualified from receiving services based upon transgender status or identity, or perceived transgender status or identity.

20. That private employers in San Francisco add "gender identity" to their lists of protected classes and provide sensitivity training, institute hiring outreach to the transgendered community by advertising in local transgender community publications, and ensure that their transgendered employees, customers, and their clients are treated with respect.

21. That the Lesbian, Gay, and Bisexual communities educate themselves concerning transgender issues and experience, and encourage their political clubs to more actively fight for transgender rights, and that Lesbian, Gay, and Bisexual businesses and organizations affirmatively encourage the participation of transgendered employees, clients and members.

22. That the transgender community continue and strengthen its efforts to educate others with respect to gender identity and its distinction from sexual orientation, and with respect to the empowering inclusivity that is uniquely the providence of the transgendered.

23. That philanthropic and grant-making organizations and individuals consider funding transgender-related projects and social services.

24. That insurance companies acknowledge that transsexualism is a medical condition for which medical treatment is warranted and for which insurance coverage should be available. To serve as a model for other insurance carriers, the Commission recommends that the Health Services System Board modify the City Plan to cover transsexual treatment and procedures.

25. That while the Commission does not intend to recommend that all transgendered persons be regarded as disabled, the Commission does recommend that if a transgendered person does become disabled, for instance as the result of transsexual-related treatment or procedures, or for any other reason, that treatment for the resulting condition should be covered under the Americans with Disabilities Act, and the Commission recommends that the City lobby Congress and the State Legislature to amend federal and State disability laws accordingly.

26. That the District Attorney budget an increased amount for Community United Against Violence (CUAV) to enable its administrators to hire additional staff to provide outreach, education, and client services involving transgendered persons.

27. That public and private school administrators ensure that the condition of being transgendered is presented as another aspect of human biology that occurs naturally throughout society, and provide support services and/or referrals to transgendered and questioning youth so they do not have to suffer in isolation.

28. That professional serving transgendered persons should be held to their professional ethics: it is one thing to avoid transgendered clients because of lack of expertise—it is discrimination to avoid them because of aversion to their condition. For example, attorneys should represent transgendered persons as they would anyone else, by seeking appropriate damages as they would in any other case in which the client has suffered injury. The Commission therefore also recommends that any State board or licensing agencies take the appropriate measures to prohibit discrimination against transgendered persons as patients or clients and as members of the associations.

29. That while there is a presumption of confidentiality by insurance companies, physicians, therapists, counselors, and social service agencies, etc., because of the potential consequences of involuntary disclosure of an individual's transgendered status it is doubly important that persons who are privy to such information about a client should respect the privacy and confidentiality of transgender persons and must not use knowledge of an individual's transgendered status to harm or control her or him.

30. That transgendered persons should not have to be certified by medical, psychological, or other service providers in order to enjoy the rights and privileges of society.

From the Perspective
of a Young Transsexual

Alexis Belinda Dinno

Chapter 13

The community of transgender folk and the professionals who help them are generally much older than I am. I hope I will not alienate the older children among you by "staking a claim" to issues as though they were relevant only to the younger segment of our population.

I like being a transsexual woman. I think I have had a fortunate transition so far, despite some of its miseries. Nonetheless, when I was approached by a friend who asked me for advice about a fifteen-year-old who was a closet crossdresser and who thought he would like to be a she, I recoiled. Oh my God, get him to a gender therapist and make sure he is not just confused! He does not want to hoe this row. Does he know what he is thinking? There are no words for me to convey what the experience of making a gender transition as a youth is really like.

My childhood and upbringing were far from ideal, but I got off well with a set of tools for dealing with people, a desire to seek myself, a smart head on my shoulders—in short, entitlements. Still, I do not quite understand just how I managed to weather the blows dealt me by coming out and watching the world I knew disintegrate and rise up in a new form before my eyes.

One might expect something like gender transition to involve very large and significant portions of anyone's life. But there are some things, at least in my experience, that make gender transition especially difficult on youth. A number of them spring to mind: safety nets, adult relationships, assumptions and stereotypes, and of course economics.

Young people who have not yet established independence rely on family, friends, employment, and social and school scenes. Without them, we start to lose our definition, for the distinctions of identity depend upon a world with which we are familiar enough to contrast ourselves. The love and nurturing of family and friends, even when lodged in the sickness of abuse and social disarray, still feed us.

Youth are not used to building these structures up. We are given our schools, with their attendant social settings. If we are fortunate, we receive parents who care enough to be concerned about those weird people we hang out with (whether or not they actually have a clue as to what is really going on). We are coached and taught how to get along with people, not how to get along without. And I am not talking about independence here, like the kind I had growing up always doing things my own way. No. I am talking about being cut off, like when one's only parent calls you up a week after you have done your best job to cushion the coming-out event (replete with offers to pay for group therapy), and she says, "You're a sick aberration of an aberration. As far as I'm concerned you're dead, and I don't ever want to see you again. Don't you dare tell your grandparents because they'll blame me, and your grandfather will try to kill you."

Now, this is not to suggest that older individuals making the journey from one expression of gender to another do not experience this kind of rejection. However, older people have had more time to practice building close relationships and more time to know themselves enough to understand just how and where they might turn should the faithful depart their lives. For the transgender or transsexual youth, this sort of rejection is especially catastrophic.

For transgender youth, the different strands of the support web can prove treacherous in unsuspected ways. Even aside from the shock of discovering who is supportive and who is not when coming out, there are so many ways we can be undermined and supported. For example, I once had an mentor, an employer. Our relationship was productive, and I learned a great deal. When I came out to her, she lost all confidence in me (granted, I was losing all confidence in myself at the time as well). My job came to little in the end. Yet I would not give it up because I was not banned from the premises for being myself—even when the price of that permission or "support" was open attack for being transsexual. In 20/20 hindsight I know that I should have left long before I did, but that is the problem with being young: there is not a lot of retrospect to go around. And there are a lot of doorways that promise shelter.

I suspect I'm luckier than many. There was a time when I was homeless. I spent many nights sleeping on people's sofas and floors; some of those floors were the floors of heroin and speed dens. Sometimes when I would come home late at night, I would see myself, but maybe even a few years younger, and she would be out pulling tricks at 4:30 A.M. in the Tenderloin. I never got sucked onto those paths, but there are many who do. It's no wonder some gender specialists ask how often you have prostituted yourself, rather than if you have at all.

Adults were difficult for me to relate to while beginning my transition. As an only child, I always got along with adults, even when very young. Much to my chagrin, they rapidly disappeared from my life when I came out. Many friends who had known me from birth left, expressing their concern and disapproval: "You're too young to make this decision, you'll know why when you're older." They vanished, and have only recently begun to resurface. I suppose they have to give me credit: I fairly pass, I play the game, and do OK. Lest I seem too gloomy, let me point out that there *are* sympathetic and understandingly wonderful people in the world.

Beginning the expression of one's transgender identity at the age when one is beginning the expression of one's entire identity is bad. Sucks, bites, lags, wanks. I remarked to my therapist recently that the thing that makes transition so frustrating (go on, read *dysphoric* if you must), is that what really amounts to a small part of a person's overall identity (gender) colors every other aspect of life and interferes with it. If you called me transsexual and expected to get a good understanding of me because the label fits, you would miss so much of what is important about me. While most people get to figure out gender relationships and sexuality, and ideas of being a success by whatever standards, and how to be a role model, and what-have-you, transgender youths have to deal with perplexing unaddressables: "You're not really Queer." By whose definition? The lack of a language to deal with these issues does not help. Nor does the fact that so much is couched in sexist and heterosexist terminology. "Oh it's a sexual thing right?" "But Alexis, you're so male!"

Other problems are the assumptions. Given that the language of transgender is often limited to the language of sexuality, it becomes easy to assume that gay and lesbian issues and resources are the same as the issues and resources of the transgendered. Another problem with language and conception is that the idea of transgender life, in whatever form, may not be available for youth. Our culture has a very strong sense of the gay or lesbian, and to a lesser extent bisexual, person. These are part of our cultural iconography or typology of persons. Whether or not they are presented in detail or as positive or negative, they are available for the developing youth to grasp and manipulate. However, transsexualism, not to mention any of the other transgender conceptions, are hidden and almost nonexistent.

Common to the folklore of the transgendered is the story of the individual who is hidden away from support for years because she or he wasn't aware that there was anyone like her or him, let alone people devoted to her or his support. As far as I can remember, these are the only contributions to my transgendered concept until I started to open up to what my gender was:

At the age of four or five I asked my mother why that lady had a beard on her face. I was told, "That was probably a transsexual." These were explained to be men who wanted to be women and lived shitty lives because they had to endure years of living as women while having men's bodies before they were allowed to become women.

At the age of eight I sat down to watch "Evening Magazine" on CBS with my grandfather. The intro mentioned something about a little girl born a few decades ago who was now the father in an all-American family. The TV was immediately shut off.

At the age of sixteen I "learned" that transsexuals were unhappy people who almost always ended up with their lives in ruins after they had surgery. This was from a high-school health teacher who had a decidedly odd adoration of the male high-school football athlete ideal.

How, I ask, are young transgender people supposed to develop a coherent understanding of themselves with this level of information? I suppose some of this is changing because of Oprah and "The Crying Game."

In my experience, transgender folk also assume that an understanding or sympathy of transgender issues implies having them solved. We do not realize just how deeply ingrained gender socialization is, and often assume that those around us are incredulous of our real genders when they inappropriately call us he or she. Some of the people most supportive of my transsexualism have had difficulty with the pronouns. It takes a while to learn that this does not reflect the individual's acceptance of one's gender of choice. I even find myself screwing up pronouns when introduced to those who are just beginning to "present" as a gender aside from their biological sex. This seems much more prevalent among younger people. Adults seem particularly sensitive—or maybe it's just the kids these days.

The assumptions and stereotypes surrounding transgender identity are something of a double-edged sword. Though coming to terms with one's various identities can be amazingly difficult for young transsexuals, we do not have to rebuild our identities in the way a forty-year-old who is beginning to make the change might. We rarely have careers, marriages, or children to contend with.

Economic handicaps for transgender youth are readily apparent, and are often compounded by parental or guardian restrictions on what can and will be done to the mind and body of the youth. Sometimes tough choices must be made. I have relied on financial aid to fund my way through school. However, such funding depends upon my status as poor. If I decided to find a job paying enough to save up for Genital Reassignment Surgery, however, the amount I would earn would disqualify me from receiving financial aid; hypothetically, since I made so much money, I must surely be able to fund my own schooling. I have been presented the choice of a wait of many years for surgery; or I could save for it in the short term, and postpone my education. I call this a lose-lose situation, and it has that character entirely because of money. This kind of dilemma can easily be called a fortunate situation, however, when compared to other instances in which one finds other instances in which the costs of therapy, hormones, even wardrobe are totally unaffordable. Youth are much less likely to have access to the resources needed for gender change. As a rule, we do not have health insurance, or careers, or savings, or connections.

This discussion really only begins to outline the special situations in which transgender youth find themselves. I have focused primarily on problems, and really only on those in my personal experience. There are positive aspects to a young gender transition, however. The effects of hormone therapy are more dramatic. Coming out and gender transition do not impinge upon the pursuit of one's career and family life, as they often do in later years. There is more time to play with ideas and self-discovery.

Somehow, despite the potholes in this journey's road, I manage to enjoy the process. Sometimes it even occurs to me that most people are *not* transsexual; that mine has been an extraordinary experience, and one to be happy with.

You Are Not Alone: A Personal Quest for a Support System

Ayme Michelle Kantz

Chapter 14

Self-empowerment emanates from within. It is the cognitive shift that any of us can make by letting go of shame and embracing our personal and collective power, by knowing deep within that we are worthy. Social change occurs when we enter the larger community with a feeling of worth and expect nothing less than equal and fair treatment. The relationship between self-empowerment and social change continues as positive gains occur in society and transgendered individuals benefit from the gains. Self-worth and social change feed each other.

—**Luanna L. Rodgers, 1995**

My parents were continually challenging and even provoking me to try new experiences and take leaps of faith. They were always there to catch me when I fell, assure me that if I tried my best then it was OK. They would dust me off and send me out to try again. Consequently, I have been blessed with a high level of assurance and confidence. I can (and will) do what I set out to do. As a result, I have a strong sense of self-worth and dignity. I am empowered and proud.

It can be a lonely road, though. Finding a support system was vital for my personal growth. It was only when I found others in similar situations that I really began to relate to my experiences and found the courage to share those experiences. Learning that I was not alone made all the difference.

Call it karma or incredibly good luck, but I was offered the opportunity to change my life in December 1990. Would I finish my divorce and continue working in a dead-end job, enduring the frustrating struggle of expressing my gender identity? Or would I leave it all behind and completely start my life over again in a revolutionary way? It took all of two minutes to weigh the consequences.

Two months later I found myself in Palm Springs, California, in a new line of work, with a new wardrobe and no experience whatsoever. This was my dream coming true. The time had finally come to live my life "in the truth," and express with my entire being what I was inside—a woman. And so I began crossliving full time. I earned my living as a waitress at an exclusive desert resort. Mind you, I had never done food-service work before, but I had the good fortune to meet some amazing friends who taught me a lot about the work I was doing, about how to present myself, about how I felt inside. I actually became pretty good at food service, if I may say so.

As one of the nation's largest gay and lesbian resort destinations, Palm Springs has a large resident population of people who are happy in expressing who they are. I made friends quickly. My clientele grew. Many would wait for my tables. I served and became acquainted with the elite of the local gay community and was invited to many important fund raisers and private functions. I was made to feel quite welcome, and I blossomed in their support. But I'm here to tell you that there are very few transgendered people living in the desert. I realize now that a lot of my success was based on my novelty. I was the resort's "gimmick," if you would. Despite an abundance of caring friends, I was alone.

After two years I had reached a high level of confidence. I was truly happy with who I was. But it was time to move on, time to begin paying more attention to my external presentation and bring my body in line with my soul. I knew there were others out there like me. I was well aware of the national support organizations at the time, but we're talking the Coachella Valley here— it's pretty much isolated from what's going on in the "real" world. I found only five others, separated by wide distances. My attempts at getting us together were perceived as well-intentioned, but not very practical.

Without realizing it, I was expressing my need for a support system, but being isolated as I was, it was difficult and frustrating. I wanted to play by the rules with documented medical therapy and support, but there were no resources available in my area.

Taking matters into my own hands, I solved my immediate problems with obtaining hormone therapy by making excursions to Tijuana. I was mindful of the dangers of unsupervised hormone use, but I was determined to do it anyway. I started with the smallest dose and increased it slowly in six- to eight-month intervals. It was a calculated risk, but as it turns out, one that was worth taking. And yet, the loneliness I was feeling made me realize that without connecting somehow with others in the same boat, I was going nowhere fast—and going there alone.

It was time again to move on, time for a break. I took a week's vacation in San Francisco. What an eye opener! Within ten days, I returned to The City with my cat and an overloaded U-Haul.

In most of the larger metropolitan cities around the country, there are alternative magazines and newspapers published that target minority communities, such as the gay/lesbian/bi/trans populations. In San Francisco, which has a large gay and lesbian community, there are at least a half-dozen such publications that list resources and contact phone numbers for a wide variety of interests: support groups, social organizations, therapists—you name it. Most, if not all, of these are vended on the street or are available at alternative bookstores, restaurants, and bars. Most of them free. It was a simple matter to acquire copies and start making phone calls.

And so I found an organization called ETVC and discovered all the resources and connections I could have hoped for. Here was an organization that existed to serve the educational, support, and social needs of all members of the gender community, and to assist the general public in comprehending transgender and transsexual issues and needs. It welcomed all members of the gender community, regardless of sexual orientation or gender preference, and their significant others, friends, family, or anyone else interested in the subject of gender. Mecca! At last, I felt like I had found a home.

It was inspiring to not only have access to a vast wealth of information but to be invited to participate in the organization itself, to actually help guide its mission. So now a new challenge: to not only learn, but to teach as well. In June 1994 I was elected chair ETVC's Education Committee, and, believe me, my hands were suddenly full, and my life enriched and fulfilled as a result.

And then, when I least expected it, I fell in love—with another MTF transsexual. It was unlike anything I've ever experienced with another human being. Together we forged a life and were quite visible as an out lesbian couple within our community. Our relationship was not without controversy, even in liberal San Francisco, but we drew strength from the notoriety and worked hard to further the education programs and media work we become involved in. I have moved forward from that relationship since, but my life remains complete and fulfilled. It's truly been a magic carpet ride.

And I owe it all to finding a support system. Parents and family provided the initial love, but they could travel with me only so far. When I was ready and found a network of like-minded people, it was truly like coming home. I was reassured. I found comfort. I found love. And I'm not so lonely anymore.

Change is happening. Transgender people are emerging and becoming more visible; our community is growing as more of us realize that it's OK to stop living the lie. It's OK to admit to our friends, family, and coworkers that we are gender-gifted. And it's OK to come out of the closet and loudly profess that, yes, we are special, yes, we are happy and productive people. And yes, we want those around us to understand and accept us for who we are, and not what we wear.

Those of us gifted with two spirits need to realize that the very thing that makes us misunderstood, reviled, and hated by society is the very thing that is the source of our strength and pride. We live and express the truths of our lives and are the better for it. As the saying goes, "Ignorance is Fear. Education is the Cure." Let us increase our diligence and improve our awareness, for our road is difficult to follow alone.

A Midlife Transition

Heather Lamborn

Chapter 15

It's two o'clock in the morning, and I am once again filling my pillow with tears. For many nights, I have been unable to sleep, as my mind is filled with a terrible grief. Grief for what? I have been grieving the loss of my identity, my spirit, my soul. I feel trapped, with no room to turn, no place to hide my obligations to my elderly mother and my children. I feel exhausted, without the strength to continue life.

These were the thoughts that were becoming more intense every day. It was like a dam that had burst. I was no longer able to suppress my emotions— emotions that I had been able to keep under control for most of my fifty-four years. I had never before allowed myself to love deeply, to hate with passion, to cry in misery, or to laugh with the sheer exhilaration of living. I had always kept myself busy in order to crowd out thoughts about myself. Now, all these defenses had crumbled, and I felt lost and frail.

Except for a brief period during my early childhood, I had spent my life trying to live up to the expectations of others. Their interests always seemed to be more important than my own. How could I tell anyone my deepest, darkest secret? How could I possibly tell anyone that for my entire life I have hated the male body of my birth. What a cruel joke nature had played on me by not giving me the female body for which I had longed since earliest childhood!

At the age of four, I was allowed to wear my cousin's old dresses and to play as a girl. When I started school, however, all that changed. I was no longer allowed to wear my cousin's clothes. At school I avoided girls so that I would not be called a sissy, but at home my closest friends were girls. At school, I was unable to identify with the boys and join in their rough play, and I couldn't play with the girls for fear of teasing by the boys. I felt so alone.

After puberty, things got worse. The girls were always talking about boys, which excluded me from their circle. The boys were rougher than ever, and seemed to talk only about sex, sports, and cars. I was interested in none of these things and had no male friends. I followed quieter pursuits, although my lack of interest in sex bothered me. Was I homosexual? I didn't think so, but if not, why did I have this overwhelming desire to be a girl? I was confused. High school was the loneliest time of my life.

Those years were the mid fifties, and transsexualism was a word that was not yet in common usage. I didn't think of myself as a transvestite either; I just wanted to be a girl. Christine Jorgensen had recently made the headlines, but I thought of her sex change as some kind of unique experiment. I felt that I was alone in the world. I believed that I must be suffering from some sort of insanity.

For the next twenty years I struggled to control my "insanity" and not let anyone find out about my true feelings. I joined the army and served two years in peacetime Korea. I married a Korean woman because my family expected that I should marry, and I was less intimidated by Korean women than by American women. I got a civilian job at the Naval Air Station in Oakland, California, where we bought a house and raised three children. To all outward appearances, I was moderately successful, and was living a normal, uneventful life. In my own mind, however, things were far from normal and uneventful. I was still under the assumption that I was suffering from some form of insanity. The act of love with my wife was possible only if I fantasized that I was a woman. I acted out the male sex role as a duty to my wife; I felt like a circus animal performing on command. I became a workaholic. I watched television until late hours. I did anything and everything to keep my mind occupied. It took all my effort to remain "normal."

Despite my efforts, I would, on rare occasions, dress up in feminine attire. When dressed in this manner, I could create the fantasy that I really was a woman. This activity also carried a heavy price—guilt. I had always felt guilt about my feelings of femininity, but when I succumbed to them and actually crossdressed, my feelings of guilt and shame were overpowering. I must have bought five or six outfits in my desire to be a woman, and thrown them away again because I felt guilty.

I was about thirty-five years old, and had been married for ten years, when I chanced upon a book at the public library. The author claimed that about five percent of men enjoy dressing up in women's clothing. What a revelation! The sexual aspects of transvestism didn't seem to fit my own situation, but I decided that I must be a transvestite. At least there were other men with similar problems, and that made me feel better. I still had not heard of transsexualism. I didn't want my family to find out, though. I was sure that my wife would not understand, and I didn't want to tarnish the image that I presented to my children, especially our youngest son.

In 1985 my wife and I divorced. There were several reasons for our divorce, but I believe that my discomfort with trying to fulfill the male sexual role was the root cause. It made me very sad to see our marriage of twenty years end this way. At least we are still friends and we see each other often.

In the years following the divorce, the talk shows began airing shows about transsexualism. Now here was something I could relate to! Every week I would scan the television listings to see which show was featuring transsexuals. The guests described their feelings and how they coped with life in the opposite gender role. I learned much about myself in this manner, but I was becoming more depressed with my own situation.

After my son graduated from high school and went away to attend college, I decided to take a bold step; I disclosed my lifelong secret to my family and some close friends. As I told my story to each in turn, the release from emotional tension was profound. The flood of tears seemed to wash away a lifetime of guilt and shame. Now the secret was out, and I was free to be myself!

One of my friends suggested that I seek professional help. I believe she thought that a therapist could return me to the person that she knew. She, along with many of my other friends, believed that I was following a path to self-destruction. When they tried to convince me to stop what I was doing, they were acting out of love and concern for me. I do not blame them for what they tried to do. There is no possible way for them to understand that I am not simply making a choice between being male or female. They must take it on faith that, in my mind, I have always been female, and that I have no choice but to live the remainder of my life in my true gender. To my delight, my entire family and all but one friend finally accepted me for who I am. Perhaps that one friend will someday accept me as well.

My sessions with the therapist were, in the beginning, always tearful. Here I was, late middle-aged and only now coming to terms with my own feelings. I cried with grief over the fact that I had not begun my transition much earlier in life. I mourned the lost years I had spent in my hated male gender role. I wanted to proceed with my transition as quickly as possible in order to make up for the years that I had lost. It took many months of therapy for me to shake this feeling of lost time.

I am now almost two years into my transition. I have changed my name to Heather Jean, and now go about my social and business life in the female gender role. People generally accept me as a woman, and I feel comfortable. I have a wider circle of friends than ever before, and my social life has taken a dramatic upturn. My friends tell me that they can see a difference in me; I have changed from a passive male to an assertive, happy female who stands up for what she believes.

I now realize that I am a mixture of the old and the new. I do not grieve what has been lost. My past life was good in many ways, and I have no regrets about what I have accomplished. I can now integrate the good from the past into my future life. I am still the same person that I have always been, but now life has opened up to present experiences and challenges that were previously beyond my reach.

I had Genital Reassignment Surgery prior to my fifty-sixth birthday. At my age, I have no grand illusions about getting married, although I do date. Now that my life experiences include passing through transition, I consider myself to be fulfilled and successful.

Insurance and the Reimbursement of Transgender Health Care

Lisa Middleton, M.P.A.

Chapter 16

Transgender individuals and those who provide health care to them regrettably too often find that public and private health care insurance systems are open to others and their needs, but are closed to the transgendered and their needs. The foundations of discriminatory practices can be found in case law, public policy, and private contracts. While such foundations are not easily undone, such undoing is not impossible. Changing discriminatory practices requires both an understanding of how they came to be and the informed will to effect change.

Standard Exclusionary Language

Most public and private health-care programs exclude transgender health care. I quote from two policies containing industry standard and commonly used exclusionary language.

(1) Kaiser Permanente, CalPers, HMO policy, August 1, 1994–Sec. 5-A, Exclusions from Coverage, 13. Services related to sexual reassignment.

(2) Take Care, CalPers, HMO policy , August 1, 1994–General Exclusions and Limitations, A. Plan Exclusions, (33) Sex Change. Any procedure or treatment designed to alter the member's physical characteristics to those of the opposite sex or any other treatment or studies relating to sex transformation.

This chapter is an abridged version of a paper presented at the International Conference on Transgender Law and Employment Policy, July 1994, Houston, Texas.

A reading of the contents of either policy raises questions as to the extent the exclusionary language contradicts other provisions of the policy contract—specifically, those sections relating to mental health coverage. Should an individual otherwise covered for evaluation or treatment under a policy be excluded because the condition originating such care is related to sexual reassignment?

What is meant by the terms *services related to* and *any procedure or treatment*? Such language is broad and sweeping. Is it intended to exclude initial psychiatric care and evaluation as called for by the Standards of Care of the Harry Benjamin International Gender Dysphoria Association (Walker, et al., 1990)? Do such exclusions extend to hormone therapy? Or do they relate only to genital-reassignment operative procedures and hospitalizations?

The appellate courts have not been called on to define what is an appropriate standard for specific transgender services that may be excluded by the standard exclusionary language. Absent uniform standards, similarly situated transgender individuals are often treated inconsistently by their individual insurance plans.

Transgender Reimbursement Legal Issues

In the late 1970s and early 1980s there were a number of important cases that addressed the issue of reimbursement for the cost of Genital Reassignment Surgery (GRS). In each case, the coverage was sought under a state-operated federally funded Medicare program.

Doe v. State of Minnesota

(257 NW2d, 816. 1977) The Minnesota Supreme Court in *Doe* found that the Minnesota Medicare plan, which provided for a total exclusion of transsexual surgery from eligibility for medical-assistance payments, was void as arbitrary and unreasonable. The court found that transsexual surgery was singled out for exclusion and therefore violated federal standards that called for the state not to reduce benefits solely because of diagnosis, type of illness, or condition. Additionally, the court ruled out a standard that would equate medical necessity with a guarantee of surgical success.

Rush v. Parham

Rush v. Parham, (440 Fed Sup, 383. 1977) is one case of two involving Carolyn Rush. Ms. Rush sought reimbursement for GRS under the Medicare plan for the state of Georgia. As had the *Doe* court, this court found that the expressed language of the state of Georgia, which barred all transsexual surgery, was arbitrary and contrary to federal standards.

This court noted the distinction between permissibly excluded "non-therapeutic elective procedures" and impermissibly excluded "necessary medical treatment" drawn by the U.S. Supreme Court in *Beal v. Doe*. The court did not find persuasive the state's argument that GRS was experimental, cosmetic, unsuitable, or unavailable.

On September 15, 1980, the U.S. Court of Appeals Fifth Circuit reversed the decision and remanded the case to determine, first, whether the state did have a policy prohibiting experimental services; and second, was its determination that transsexual surgery is experimental reasonable. The Appeals Court stated, "We caution, however, that if defendants simply denied payment for the proposed surgery because it was transsexual surgery, Georgia would now be required to pay for the operation."

Rush v. Johnson

Rush v. Johnson (565 Fed Sup, 856. 1983) is the single most important precedent case to the exclusion of transgender people in health care. The issue was whether Georgia had a reasonable foundation for ruling that GRS was experimental.

The court relied significantly on the *Diagnostic and Statistical Manual of Mental Disorders* of the American Psychiatric Association (*DSM*), referring to it as "an authoritative text which is an expression of the consensus of the psychiatric community as of 1980," and noting that the *DSM* finds "since surgical sex reassignment is a recent development, the long-term course of the disorder with this treatment is unknown."

Plaintiffs and defendants introduced conflicting expert testimony as to the efficacy of GRS as treatment for gender dysphoria. Prominent among those testifying for the state was Dr. John Meyer of the Johns Hopkins Gender Program. He argued for a "psychogenic origin" of transsexuality. He further found that his research (1971–1974) revealed little long-term distinction between those who had undergone surgery and those who had not. The court quotes Dr. Meyer in finding "substantial evidence presents a picture of growing concern in the medical literature over the long-term effectiveness of sex-reassignment surgery as a generally accepted form of treatment." The court concluded there was no consensus in the professional medical community.

Dr. Meyer's conclusions from Rush have over the past twenty years been invalidated by the scientific community and established medical practice. Nevertheless, within case law, they lack any superseding decision and remain the scientific basis of federal precedent.

Coincidental to the proceedings in the two Carolyn Rush cases, the federal government was active in the research of transgender health care. On the basis of two studies in 1979 and 1981, the Health Care Financing Administration (HCFA) found that GRS is experimental and issued guidelines barring reimbursement for GRS. HCFA has not addressed the issue of GRS or transgender-related health care procedures since 1981. The 1979 study was completed by two pharmacologists. They found: "There are no definitive standardized diagnostic tests . . . available for evaluating the transsexual." The effect of psychotherapy on transsexuals was found to be mixed, depending on the researcher.

Interestingly, since it is perhaps the only issue two pharmacologists might be considered qualified to address, they noted, "Hormonal treatment . . . appears to be successful in relieving suffering in the transsexual patient. . . . Complications of hormone therapy in transsexuals have not been reported to any significant extent in the literature."

They concluded, "The surgical component of the treatment of transsexualism remains, within the greater medical community, an experimental procedure. . . . At the present level of the state of the art of transsexual surgery, the potential for incapacitating complications of the surgical procedure represents a greater risk of prolonging disability compensation than the primary disorder itself. . . . There appears to be a greater incidence of complications for these procedures compared to the average incidence of overall surgical complications."

The 1979 state of the art for GRS remains the basis of federal reimbursement policy.

Pinneke v. Preisser

The Eighth Circuit U.S. Court of Appeals decision in *Pinneke v. Preisser* (623 Fed 2d, 546. 1980) remains one of the most important to transgender people receiving appropriate health care. The court found that the state, "without any formal rule making proceedings or hearings . . . established an irrefutable presumption that the procedure of sex reassignment surgery can never be medically necessary when the surgery is a treatment for transsexualism and removes healthy, undamaged organs and tissue. This approach reflects inadequate solicitude for the applicant's diagnosed condition." The court further quoted from *White v. Beal* (supra, 555 Fed 2d, 1152) "that the regulations permit discrimination in benefits based upon the degree of medical necessity but not upon the medical disorder from which the person suffers."

The Lackner Cases

G.B. v. Lackner (145, Cal Rpt, 555. 1978) and *J.D. v. Lackner* (145, Cal Rpt, 570. 1978) were companion cases decided by the First District Court of Appeals in California. They are significant in that they establish that GRS is not a cosmetic procedure. Cosmetic procedures are routinely barred under both private and public health care programs.

Doe, Pinneke, both *Rush* cases, and the two *Lackner* cases argue to the point that transsexualism as a condition cannot be excluded from coverage. The underpinning of the denial of GRS reimbursement found by the *Rush v. Johnson* court was, first, that the state was permitted to bar experimental procedures, and, second, that the state had a reasonable foundation for its determination that GRS was experimental.

The exclusion of GRS services has been commonly extended to exclude both GRS and non-GRS transgender health care.

Experimental Medicine Reimbursement Legal Issues

GRS has been deemed experimental. Meanwhile, in nontransgender cases, the courts and legislatures are increasingly addressing the question of the obligations of payers for experimental procedures. Private health care plans do permissibly make and interpret their own rules. Nonetheless, such practices are subject to judicial review. The legal standard in such cases is the question of "abuse of discretion."

The April 1993 edition of *JAMA* the *Journal of American Medical Association* reported in a survey of seventeen legal cases from 1980 to 1989 involving unproven and experimental procedures that the plaintiff was successful in fourteen of those cases. The appellate courts have not generally responded, however, with the degree of sympathy found in juries.

Barnett v. Kaiser Foundation Health Plan

In *Barnett v. Kaiser Foundation Health Plan* (1994 WL 400819 9th Cir.[Cal]) the issues were as follows: Mr. Barnett required a liver transplant. Additionally, he had e-antigen hepatitis. Kaiser denied Mr. Barnett on the basis that, first, liver transplants were experimental, and, second, that Mr. Barnett was medically inappropriate because of his hepatitis. In evaluating Kaiser's actions, the court used the standard of "arbitrary and capricious. . . . The touchstone of 'arbitrary and capricious' conduct is unreasonableness." Were Kaiser's actions unreasonable?

The facts of this case provide a model for judging payer actions. Kaiser was able to demonstrate that they had in place a medical advisory committee that reviewed all liver transplant requests, that the committee acted on protocols developed by the UCSF Medical Center, that Mr. Barnett's hepatitis was an absolute contraindication to transplant under the UCSF protocols, that the committee had authority to make exceptions and in 120 of 250 requested cases had approved liver transplants, and that the committee was effectively shielded from the financial impacts of their decisions.

One of the more interesting comments in the testimony was that of the head of Kaiser's Medical Advisory Committee, that their criteria was under constant review "based on changing literature and views of the profession." (Unfortunately such "constant review," of changing literature has yet to be applied to transgender health care.)

Boland v. King County Medical Blue Shield

In *Boland v. King County Medical Blue Shield* (798 Fed Sup, 638. 1992) the facts were these: Mrs. Boland was diagnosed with terminal breast cancer. She sought authorization and reimbursement for high-dose chemotherapy with autologous bone-marrow transplant. This is a procedure classified by Blue Shield as experimental. Blue Shield defined experimental procedures in their contract in an fashion standard to the industry:

> An experimental or investigational service or supply is one that meets at least one of the following:
>
> 1. Is under clinical investigation by health professionals and is not generally recognized by the medical profession as tested and accepted medical practice.
> 2. Requires approval by the federal Food and Drug Administration or other governmental agency, and such approval has not been granted at the time the service or supply is ordered.
> 3. Has been classified by the national Blue Cross and Blue Shield Association as experimental or investigational.

In deciding for Blue Shield, the court was persuaded that within limits of reasonable discretion, Blue Shield was free to determine medical procedures to be covered. The court relied significantly on findings that the Blue Cross and Blue Shield Association acted in accord with standards "generally recognized by the medical profession as tested and accepted medical practice."

Jacob v. Blue Cross and Blue Shield of Oregon

Jacob v. Blue Cross and Blue Shield of Oregon (92 Or.App, 259. 1988) is also a cancer case. Plaintiffs sought reimbursement for Gerson therapy received at a clinic in Tijuana, Mexico. (Gerson therapy is a generally unendorsed, unproven cancer treatment involving dietery restrictions and immuno-augmentive therapy.) The court found for Blue Cross and Blue Shield. The case is of note for the definition of medical necessity as defined by the insurer—within "accepted medical standards in our service area, it cannot be omitted without adversely affecting the patient's condition." Second, though finding for Blue Cross and Blue Shield, the court noted, "Blue Cross does not have unlimited discretion to decide what is and is not covered. In determining whether a claim falls within the exclusions, it must apply the objective standards set forth in the exclusions."

Cowan v. Myers

Cowan v. Myers (232 Cal.Rptr, 299. 1987) is a Medicare case. It is significant for its definition of medical necessity and its determination of who properly should determine medical necessity.

Plaintiffs argued that it is the individual physician who should determine in each case what is medically necessary for that patient. The court rejected that argument. "Regulations expressly permit the state to limit services on the basis of medical necessity. We are convinced the Act did not intend the physician to be the sole arbiter of medical necessity . . . such a rule [would] result in inconsistent and unfair applications based on variations between physicians."

California regulations had defined medical necessity as "that which is medically necessary to protect life or prevent significant disability." The court required California to conform to federal guidelines and include after "significant disability" the phrase "or to alleviate severe pain."

Medical Technology Assessment Practices

How can we judge whether a payer is acting reasonably in making its determinations? Payers, public and private, increasingly rely on what has come to be known as "Medical Technology Assessment Protocols." The practice of developing such protocols is a growing field employing medical, legal, and payer expertise.

In the late 1970s and early 1980s, when transgender challenges to reimbursement policies were finding their way into the courts, payers were called on only to answer a two-part question in determining whether a procedure was experimental: Is it safe? Is it effective? It was an orientation that was heavily weighted to the experiences of the provider. Providers and payers have come in the past decade to recognize the limits of such an analysis—most particularly, the limits it places on the experiences of the patient. Meanwhile, payers have certainly noted that new procedures with costs that are unlimited often have benefits that are quite limited.

In 1992 the U.S. Department of Health and Human Services sponsored a conference called "New Medical Technology: Experimental or State of the Art." The conference brought together a number of disciplines and sought to provide definition to the process of answering the question, Is it experimental?

"Safety and efficacy remains, but . . . [assessments] now encompass the measurement of effectiveness, considerations of the quality of life, and patients' preferences, and especially the evaluation of costs and benefits" (New Technology Assessment, 1990). As this statement indicates, the focus of new assessment practices is on the outcomes on the procedures applied—the clinical and financial outcomes and the quality of life that results from the application of the medical technology. A modern protocol includes the experiences of the patient:

> Although the health care system sometimes behaves as if the patient did not matter, the patient *is* the ultimate customer. . . . Two fallacies abound in the health care community concerning information from patients. The first is that patient derived data must be inaccurate or certainly not as accurate as information gleaned from a physician. The second is that the only information one can obtain from patients is their satisfaction with the service they receive. Both of these notions are patently untrue. (Goldfield, et al., 1991)

Blue Cross and Blue Shield uses the following five criteria to define experimental:

1. The technology must have final approval from a regulatory body.

2. There must be scientific evidence concerning the effect of the technology on health outcomes—that is, there must be some published evidence about the benefits and risks of using the intervention.
3. The technology must improve net health outcome. Does the person live longer? Is the quality of life better? Does it increase the ability to function?
4. Is the new technology as beneficial as current technologies?
5. Is net approval attainable outside of a research setting? We might stipulate that the technology should only be used in certain settings, but this will not stop the technology from being approved. Gleeson, 1997)

Individual Claim Strategies

Nothing here should be taken to replace or substitute for the necessary consultation with trained personal legal counsel.

- Rule 1: Don't take no for an answer. No is frequently just the beginning of a negotiation process.
- Rule 2: Make your request in writing; keep copies of your correspondence.
- Rule 3: Insist on answers in writing; retain for evidence purposes.
- Rule 4: For anything you pay for out of pocket, obtain a receipt and keep your receipts.

Does your policy contain the standard exclusionary language regarding GRS and related services? Look in the General Exclusions section of the policy contract. If not, congratulations! Your issue is now one of demonstrating the medical necessity of your desired procedure. Key findings that will indicate medical necessity to payer organizations are these:

- Diagnosis, treatment, and procedures conducted in accord with accepted and standard medical practice for this condition. Were the Harry Benjamin Standards of Care followed? If so, that's very important. It is indicative of accepted practice.
- The absence of this procedure will adversely effect the patient's condition.
- Procedure or service is necessary to protect life, prevent significant disability, or to alleviate severe pain.
- Alternative methods of care were attempted and unsuccessful—for example, psychotherapy failed to change the underlying condition. The requested care offers a greater opportunity for success than alternative care already delivered or now considered.

If your policy, like most, contains the standard exclusionary language, the issue of medical necessity remains. What is added is the burden of overcoming the expressed contractual exclusion. The strategy I am suggesting in response to the experimental designation of the procedure as experimental is to challenge the process used by the payer in reaching that designation. Can its designation process for transgender care be shown to be legally deficient in comparison with the practices engaged in by the payers and condoned by the courts in *Barnett v. Kaiser, Boland v. King County,* and *Jacob v. Blue Cross*?

Officials of the health care organizations should be asked the following:

Exactly what is being defined as experimental? Diagnostic examinations and testing? Therapy? Hormones? GRS? (If any procedure related to transgender health care is excluded, then that is beginning to sound very similar to a legally suspect exclusion by condition.)

How was the conclusion that it is experimental reached? On what evidence? When was the evidence last reviewed? What literature was reviewed? How timely is that literature?

What are the qualifications of the personnel responsible for making the experimental determination? What experience do they have in the diagnosis and treatment of transgender people? Was any medical analysis completed prior to the implementation of the exclusion? Was it an underwriting decision?

Are they familiar with the procedures requested? With the physicians who have performed or will perform the procedures? With their success and complications rates? Have they attempted to familiarize themselves?

Do they have a medical review committee? Was this request reviewed by the medical review committee? Why not? On what basis does the medical review committee become involved in an appeal?

Can and does the medical review committee make exceptions to the bar against reimbursement for experimental services? How often? On what basis? How often do they make exceptions where the patient is transgendered?

By what process does the payer's review procedures attempt to keep up with changes in medical practice? Has the paper used that process to track developments in transgender health care procedures?

Has a Technology Assessment Protocol of the requested procedure been completed? Insist on a copy. When was it done? Does it include patient experience as a criteria? Is there a plan to do an assessment protocol? If so, when, and on what basis are procedures denied while the protocol is being developed? Are the procedures and treatments sought "nontherapeutic and elective;" or are they "medically necessary and consistent with established medical practice"?

Conclusions

My conclusions, on the basis of the facts and cases reviewed, are as follows:

- Transgender people should not be denied reimbursement on the basis of their condition.
- The most controversial or at minimum the most litigated transgender procedure—Genital Reassignment Surgery (GRS)—has been held by Medicare officials and by most private health care plans to be experimental.

- Experimental procedures as a class of benefits may be permissibly excluded from coverage. That which is medically necessary may not be excluded.
- The extension of the coverage exclusion from GRS to non-GRS transgender health care procedures—for example, hormone therapy, psychological therapy—appears not to be founded on medical evidence or case law, but on unchallenged, arbitrary payer actions.
- The courts have given to the payers the responsibility for determining what is experimental and what is medically necessary. It is a responsibility that is subject to judicial review on the basis the reasonableness of the decision-making process. Payers may not act in an arbitrary or capricious manner.
- The courts have held, regardless of express exclusionary language, that to exclude GRS simply because it is GRS would be an insupportable, arbitrary action.
- Determinations of what is experimental and medically necessary should be based of medical evidence in accord with recognized medical practice.
- To achieve reimbursement for medical procedures, including transgender procedures, the patient must show that a body of medical evidence exists that defines accepted, standard, and proven medical practice for a given condition. That is not an argument for any or all of the specific Harry Benjamin standards; it is an argument for recognized standards in the application of medical services to transgender people.
- The Recommended Guidelines are to be applauded. Professionals providing transgender health care need to continue to study this issue and to publish the professional literature evidence that transgender health care treatment procedures can be reliably diagnosed and are clinically successful. There also needs to be published evidence that for both diagnosis and treatment, there exists an accepted consensus of what constitutes normative appropriate care, and that the medical complications of such procedures are, within accepted professional standards, both known and controllable.

References

Fuchs, Victor R., Garber, Alan M. 1990. New Technology Assessment. *New England Journal of Medicine* 323 (10).

Gleeson, Susan. 1997. Memorandum from Executive Director, Technology Management Department, Blue Cross and Blue Shield Association.

Goldfield, N., Pine, M., and Pine J. 1991. Measuring and Managing Health Care Quality: Procedures, Techniques, and Protocols. In *New Medical Technology: Experimental or State of the Art?* edited by Mary L. Grady. AHCPR Pub. No. 92 0057. Rockville, MD: U.S. Department of Health and Human Services, Agency for Health Care Policy and Research.

Walker, Paul A., et al. 1990 (rev.). *Standards of Care: The Hormonal and Surgical Sex Reassignment of Gender Dysphoric Perons,* Palo Alto, Calif.: The Harry Benjamin International Gender Dysphoria Association, Inc.

Facial Surgery for the Transsexual

Douglas K. Ousterhout, D.D.S., M.D.

Chapter 17

Anthropologists have identified various aspects of the skull that are different in the male and the female, but artists have appreciated the differences as well. Facial aesthetic surgery for the transsexual is primarily directed to making that individual look as feminine (male-to-female), or MTF or as masculine (female-to-male), or FTM as possible. The skull shape can be modified to take advantage of these skeletal differences.

Females have a more pointed chin and less nasal prominence than males. Males tend to have a broad chin and more of a nasal hump. The forehead is quite different, especially the areas of the brows and the mid-forehead. Males have brow bossing (fullness) with a flat area in between the bossing, while females tend to have a completely convex skull in all planes.

The shape of the skull affects the drape and contour of the skin. Changing the shape of the forehead, modifying the angle and the sides of the lower jaw, the chin, and the prominence of the cheeks can also help tremendously to change gender presentation and will assist in changing one's facial appearance from distinctly male to female or vice versa. Nasal surgery may be extremely important in this regard. The techniques used and the areas modified are individualized. Quite obviously, some MTF transsexuals are already much more feminine in appearance than others, and some FTM transgender individuals are much more masculine in appearance than others.

The majority of routine facial aesthetic plastic surgeries are performed to reduce the effects of aging: reducing wrinkles, lifting sagging skin, removing fat deposits. Facelifts, brow (forehead) lifts, blepharoplasties (cosmetic surgery of the eyelids), and removal of excess fat in the neck are the most frequently completed aesthetic facial soft tissue procedures. Such surgeries are also frequently desirable for the transsexual as well.

The decision as to what facial surgery to have is based upon a combination of skeletal and artistic evaluations, radiographs, anthropological measurements, asymmetry evaluations, facial masks, and photographs of the patient. Patient's self-assessment is also very important to surgical planning.

Surgical Procedures

Forehead

The forehead covers a very large portion of the face and thus is a very important part of facial aesthetics. As the male forehead is so different from that of the female, this may be one of the most important areas to modify. Depending on anthropological measurements, the size of the frontal sinuses (in the lower forehead above the nose and eyes), and the general contour of the orbits (eye sockets) and forehead, there are three different ways in which the forehead can be modified. The surgery varies from bony contouring to the most involved problem, in which the anterior wall of the frontal sinus must be placed in a more posterior position. Orbital rim contouring may be necessary and can be completed at the same time. A forehead lift can also be accomplished during the same operation, if indicated. The hair-bearing scalp can be brought forward to decrease forehead length and help to decrease areas of baldness.

The surgical approach to these procedures is all basically the same: that is, there is an incision in the scalp, either within the hair-bearing area or in the front of the hair, as indicated for each individual.

Nose

Noses vary tremendously from individual to individual. In general, small noses are not a problem in the male, but a nose may be quite masculine, though the individual is feeling quite feminine. If one has thin skin, a significant size reduction can generally be completed. If the skin is, however, quite thick (as is often the case in males), the contour can still be markedly improved, but there may be a limitation in the size reduction possible. However, contour changing alone greatly feminizes the basic nasal appearance. If breathing difficulties happen to coexist with an appearance deformity, breathing can generally be improved markedly at the same surgery.

Cheeks

Although the shape of the cheeks and their prominence, or lack of it, is not considered a female or male characteristic, it is generally very pleasing for both females and males to have full or prominent cheeks. Augmentation is therefore often very helpful in facial contouring. Cheek reduction can be completed, but its need is much more rare.

Cheek augmentations are generally completed by the use of an implant, but certain bone cuts (osteotomies) and bone segmental repositionings are useful in selected individuals. Various sizes and thickness of implants are available to fit individual differences and desires. The implants are most often placed with the patient under sedation and with the use of local anesthesia. The approach is usually through the mouth, so no skin incisions are made. Implants can also be placed through a lower eyelid incision. The implant is placed through a tunnel, under the soft tissue, and immediately overlying the cheek bones.

Chin

The bony chin varies markedly between the male and female, as the male chin is generally wide, while the female chin tends to be more pointed and narrow. The degree of masculinity or femininity can vary tremendously. The chin can be modified in numerous ways to improve facial appearance. It may require only a small implant, and possibly, bony cuts repositioning the chin and, on occasion, narrowing it. Various modifications to the chin can be made, depending upon the individual anatomy of the patient and the desired result.

Occasionally, even with bony osteotomies, various types of implants are additionally necessary to obtain the desired contour. The surgery necessary can vary tremendously.

Angle of the Mandible Surgery

Males tend to have more obvious mandibular angles, than do females. The contour in the male is usually due to heavy jaw muscle but particularly a lateral flaring of the bony angles. The female tends to have smaller muscles and a more gradual curve from the upper posterior border of the mandible to its inferior border. Modification can reduce some of the obvious aspects of masculinity and create a more feminine appearance. The opposite can be created in the FTM individual.

If there is a need is for a muscle reduction, the masseter muscle is reduced on its internal surface (the portion adjacent to the bone). The bone is almost always reduced laterally and the bony angle softened. Augmentation of the angle can be accomplished in several ways, but in most cases an implant is used. In all cases there are no skin incisions, as the surgical approach is through the mouth. Lateral mandibular reduction is also often indicated, especially in the MTF individual.

The oblique line of the mandible can be very thick, causing a very heavy lower facial appearance. This reduction can be combined with chin or angle-of-the-mandible modification, or both.

Soft-Tissue Modification

Various soft-tissue cosmetic procedures are available: facelift, forehead lift, blepharoplasty, hair transplants, suction-assisted lipectomy of the neck, breast augmentation, tracheal shave, suctioning of various fat deposits on the torso and upper and lower extremities, and abdominoplasty. All of these procedures may add significantly to overall feminine or masculine appearance.

Conclusion

I perform all of the surgeries I have described. I strongly feel that the result of all these procedures, when I have performed them on transsexual and transgender men and women, have been extremely beneficial for them, and that such surgeries can be a significant step in improving the quality of life of such individuals. Quite obviously, the procedures being completed need to be chosen on an individual basis, and not done cookbook style.

The result of surgery is of course helped tremendously by one's basic presentation. Cosmetic surgery, when properly selected and aesthetically completed in a patient who follows postoperative care instructions, can help considerably in improving that presentation.

What Is to Be Done? A Commentary on the Recommended Guidelines

Rachel Pollack, M.A.

Chapter 18

_____

Transgender people go to professionals for two reasons. First, our psychological society considers psychiatrists and psychologists to be the repositors of soul wisdom. Since many transgender people find their situation very troubling, or at least confusing, they may turn to these "experts" for understanding and assistance. Guidelines that help doctors and other counselors understand just what it is they are confronting will help them to serve the needs of the person asking for help. Such service may involve simply the assurance that questioning gender identity is a natural process (I prefer the term *natural* to *normal*, since *natural* implies a behavior that arises from our existence in the world, whereas normal simply means whatever society currently designates). The Guidelines (along with the work done by many other people, particularly in transgender support groups, activist organizations, and publications) help create a framework for specialists to give that valuable assurance. And if the clients themselves have access to the publication, the Guidelines can help give them the conceptual framework to judge their own needs, and whether or not the specialist is helping them.

The second reason for at least some transgender people to go to specialists is the desire to physically transform the body. This desire suggests that transgender issues will remain a question for the medical profession, even if we no longer consider transgender people to be in a pathologic state. Because the client comes to the doctor with a request for physical intervention, a great many ethical questions arise, particularly for the doctor. We will look more closely at some of these considerations in a moment.

The Guidelines include definitions of terms. In most sorts of discussions, such definition simply helps readers proceed on the same ground as the writer. But in may ways transgender issues are all about terms. Language, labels, pronouns—all these carry a great deal of power. The transsexual or transgender person seeks to re-create herself or himself; this re-creation involves physical changes, but it involves just as much, perhaps more: a name change, a change of pronouns, a change in social status, a change in communication. Outsiders may not accept these changes if they get stuck in their old perceptions. These perceptions become framed, even created, by language. "She" remains a "he" in the outsider's mind. "Joanne" is "really" still "Joe."

We cannot stress too strongly the importance of counselors' and other service providers' addressing transgender clients by their chosen name and congruent pronouns—whatever the client's hormonal or surgical status. To describe a transsexual woman as "he" or a transgender man as "she" not only strips away that person's (often fragile) identity, it also declares, "Nothing you say or do about yourself matters. All that matters is my perception of you."

And yet, we also cannot make any hard-and-fast rules about when to switch pronouns. If a physical male comes to a counselor with deep feelings of transsexuality but no experience of taking action, should we refer to this person as "she"? Most likely it would make "him" uncomfortable. However, I have known and counseled transsexual women who lived outwardly as men for various economic or family reasons, but whose inner female identity had developed to a point where they used a feminine name in counseling and support groups and clearly preferred the feminine pronoun. To make this issue still more complex, I also have known timid transsexual women who did not dare assert a female identity on their own, but responded very strongly when given the opportunity by others.

Clearly, the specialist needs some sensitivity, as well as experience. At the same time, those transsexual people who do present themselves unequivocally deserve to have their identities recognized in speech and writing.

The importance of language also arises in the various distinctions we make between different kinds of transgender behavior. As noted in the Guidelines, the umbrella term *transgender* has emerged recently, popularized by activist groups and publications. Its purpose has been to unite people. By implication, this brings together groups with historical differences and even hostilities, such as heterosexual crossdressers, butch lesbians, and transsexual women. As a political term, *transgender* suggests the idea "We are all violating society's rigid codes of gender, so why don't we all join together?" As a term for specialists, *transgender* helps map out a large and nebulous territory in which we can delineate some sharper distinctions.

People live within their distinctions. It may be true that it does not help people to identify completely with a narrow label, especially if they did not choose that label themselves but received it from either a doctor or a support group seeking to recruit new members. But once people come to some sense of who they are and what they desire, they may want some more precise term to describe the reality of their lives.

Whatever terms people use to describe themselves should not trap them. Many people who have gone through Genital Reassignment Surgery began by seeing themselves as transvestites, or butch lesbians, or drag queens, and only after experimentation decided they wanted something else.

It is no accident that the general expression *transgender* emerges at the same time as the proliferation of more and more names and groups. Both uses of language arise from a developing consciousness that seeks to name itself. Transsexual, transvestite, intersex, transgenderist, androgyne, drag queen, drag king, stone butch, high femme, hermaphrodite, crossdresser, maenad, galla, bi-gendered, pre-op, post-op, non-op . . . . The list goes on and on, becoming almost an incantation, with that useful word *transgender* giving a counterweight to all the variations and distinctions.

We also need to respect those who will not accept any label at all for themselves. People used to say that someone was a transsexual until they had surgery, and then they became a "real" woman or man and could join society. They were encouraged, even instructed, to leave "all that" behind and claim their place in the world. For some, this resulted in a damaging isolation, especially when they felt required to conceal their past history. Now, however, an opposite ideology has begun to develop, one that tells transsexuals and other transgender people that they remain "transgender" all their lives, and must not try to "deny" this fact about themselves. For some people, this is simply inappropriate. It does not answer their inner sense of who they are.

For some people, *transgender* or *transsexual* is a noun. This is the core of their identity. For many others, however, these words are adjectives. The noun, the true sense of self, is *man* or *woman*.

Language also figures in the issue of transgender "pathology." Louis Gooren, M.D., of Amsterdam's Free University gender clinic, has said that from the beginning he and his colleagues made the decision to refer to the people they saw as *clients* rather than *patients*. Such an attitude has begun to emerge in the United States as well. Those who own the language own the reality. The term *gender dysphoria* has always seemed to me to form a new level of pathologizing transgender experience. *Dysphoria* implies permanent unhappiness, a break with reality, and someone who acts out of misery alone. It does not allow for the sense so many transgender people have of knowing precisely who they are and what they want. Nor does it allow for the great joy, the euphoria that comes to transgender people when they start living as their real selves. Thus, I applaud the suggestion in the Guidelines that once an individual has self-identified transition goals or has established a self-defined transgender identity, he or she is no longer considered gender dysphoric and subsequently sheds that unnecessarily pathologizing label.

All this brings us to the central question: Is transgender experience pathological? Once someone makes such a claim, is there any way to "objectively" disprove it? The argument against pathology seems to rest on the transgender person's inner sense of rightness about her or his life, on the ability to function in society, and to some extent on the historical precedents of transgender people throughout human culture. None of this is really "objective."

On the other hand, those who argue for a pathology model also cannot really prove their case. To a large extent, they fall back on "common sense" arguments. "Of course a man cannot be a woman. How can he?" But this doesn't really say anything. Common sense is "common" only because it is commonly agreed upon.

If neither side can really prove its argument, we should remember that the burden of proof always lies on the person who makes the original assertion. If the medical profession, or common sense, wishes to label transgender people as sick, then it really is up to them to prove this. And in fact, no such proof has ever been found. Somehow, we have turned the situation around and required transsexuals and transgender people to prove that they are not sick—an impossible task, which no one should ever undertake.

Once we get past the insistence that all transgender experience is pathologic we find ourselves faced with ethical dilemmas. When people approach a doctor for hormones or surgery, how does the doctor determine what to do?

At this point we might look at the question of why people want medical treatment. In recent years, a segment of the transgender political community has challenged the desire for hormones and surgery, claiming that if society accepted transgender people for themselves, without any pressure to "pass" or otherwise conform, then people would not need to alter their bodies. Some have further suggested that the medical profession pushes people into unwanted physical changes.

From my own experience, and from talking with transsexuals, transgenderists, and others over twenty-five years, I do not believe for one moment that the desire to change the body is something imposed from outside. People want these things because they are possible. We must always remember that transsexuals and transgenderists seek out medical treatment. This is why they go to the doctors and clinics in the first place. They will go to great lengths to obtain this treatment and, if denied it, will often suffer serious emotional damage. Some will even mutilate themselves in an attempt at self-surgery (in this context, we should realize that at least MTF surgery has existed, in crude form, for thousands of years in a great many cultures, and continues to exist today, in such places as India).

However, the Guidelines make a very strong point that not all transgender people want medical intervention, and even more important, not all of those who want hormones also want surgery. There is something absurd about denying hormonal changes to a person unless she or he also accepts surgical changes. We also need to allow people the opportunity to take hormones, and then later on determine whether surgery is indeed a correct choice.

It is vitally important to allow people to make such decisions for themselves. We cannot say, on the one hand, that a transgender identity is not pathologic and, on the other, that only doctors or other "specialists" are capable of deciding what a person should or should not do with her or his own body. This is especially true with regard to hormones. Where we might argue that surgery is major and irreversible, this in not at all the case with estrogens, and even testosterone is not as extreme a change as surgery. The Guidelines suggest ways for a specialist to decide whether someone should receive hormones. This determination, apparently made solely by the specialist, comes after three months of counseling. Thus, the transgender person not only must surrender this life decision to someone else's judgment, he or she must also enter into a therapy relationship that may not be necessary or desired. Once again, all power remains with the specialist. The specialist even gets to decide if the person has shown enough "consistency," causing the situation we have seen too many times before, where the transgender person has to project the "correct" attitude in order to get a consent letter.

Am I suggesting "hormones on demand"? In a word, yes. I see no reason to take the power of this decision away from the transgender person himself or herself and turn it over to a specialist. Obviously, a responsible doctor will not want to give treatment to someone who appears to be psychotic or a drug abuser, or who does not understand the physical risks involved. But these are all extreme cases, and they would apply to any medical procedure of any kind (for instance, administering estrogen to a woman complaining of serious menopausal symptoms). To deny the transgender person her or his own choice on hormones ensures that the person remains in a state of subservience and pathology.

The situation with surgery is more complex simply because surgery is so consequential. Physicians have every right to want some assurance that they are fulfilling the first principle of medicine, to "Do no harm." And yet, much of what we have said about hormones also applies to surgery. On what grounds can we take away the right of a transsexual person to make his or her own decision?

The Guidelines call for the specialist's "actual opinion" that the surgery will enhance the person's "quality of life." Why should the specialist be the person to make this judgment? If we say to someone, your opinion about your life does not matter, only a "specialist's" matters, we are reducing that person to an infantile state of dependency. And how does the specialist make such a vague decision? Wouldn't this depend largely on the specialist's own prejudices about what makes a good life? Once again, we return to a situation in which transsexual people have to figure out someone else's standards and then work to satisfy them in order to get a consent letter. The transsexual client and the specialist thus enter into an adversarial relationship rather than a therapeutic one.

The situation becomes compounded by the requirement for a "supporting evaluation letter" with even more details than the primary. The Guidelines call for an "assessment of the individual's presentation"—in other words, whether or not the person satisfies this specialist's own conceptions of masculinity or femininity. Why should transsexual people have to meet someone else's beliefs, rather than their own?

And yet, no responsible surgeon will want to operate on just anyone who walks into his or her office asking for a "sex change." What, then, is to be done? If we wish to allow the transsexual person the power to decide, then the requirements need to focus on the idea of "informed consent" (actually, the expression is a misnomer, since it is usually the transsexual person who requests the surgery and the doctor who must consent to it).

Informed can mean several things. First, that the client is not psychotic. Again, this holds for a great many medical procedures (similarly, the surgeon bears the responsibility to determine if the person can physically sustain an operation). In most cases, simple observation and discussion can determine whether or not the person is in touch with reality. If the surgeon has genuine doubts, he or she may ask for an evaluation. But such evaluation should come only in particular cases, not as a matter of course.

Second, *informed* means a full discussion of the surgical technique, the risks involved, and recovery procedures. It also should include a discussion of such topics as the surgeon's follow-up, and the satisfaction or dissatisfaction of previous clients. The area of sexual functioning especially needs to be addressed. In the past, a number of surgeons have focused on cosmetic appearance and the ability to sustain intercourse, without enough concern for orgasmic sensitivity. If faced with a choice, the transsexual woman or man may indeed choose, say, appearance over orgasm. But he or she should know in advance if such a choice needs to be made. This, too, falls under "informed consent."

Finally, transsexual people need to be "informed" by their own experience. In other words, they need to go through a period of living in role, preferably for a year. However—and this is very important—the purpose of the year of living should not be to satisfy anyone else's criteria of "quality of life" or successful "presentation." It exists simply for the person to gain an understanding of what kind of life awaits her or him after surgery. If the transsexual person can demonstrate that she or he already has gone through a year or more of living in role, then the surgeon can consider this requirement satisfied.

Please note: "living in role" does not mean "passing." It may be true that a person who passes will live a happier life. It also may not be true. Many transsexual people find themselves much happier when they give up their concern with passing. The point is, this decision, too, must rest with the transsexual person himself or herself, informed by a period of living the new life.

Should counseling be available? Certainly. So should knowledge of support groups, activist organizations, and the possibility of one-on-one peer counseling with another transsexual woman or man. Available, yes. Required, no. Not everyone wants such things, or needs them.

Some people will argue that this plan invites abuse. Transsexual people might push their way through to surgery, only to regret it afterward. To this objection, I can only point to the abuses in the current system of gatekeepers and letters of approval. What harm does it do to someone not to have surgery? What does it do to wait years after deciding that surgery is what a person needs?

What harm do we do to people when we deny surgery because they express an unorthodox femininity or masculinity?

At some point, we must finally allow transsexual people the basic right to make their own decisions about their own lives.

Genital Reassignment Surgery: A Source of Happiness for My Patients

Eugene A. Schrang, M.D.

Chapter 19

O f all the conditions individuals must endure, gender-identity confusion or uncertainty must certainly be one of the most distressing, not because of great morbidity or mortality, but because the accompanying emotional conflicts can engender much unhappiness for the patient and her or his family, with possible later problems involving social activities and associations with colleagues at work.

The etiology of this condition is obscure, but I am personally quite certain that the problem occurs in utero and is therefore congenital and not genetic; that is, it is not something that is passed from generation to generation.

Management and treatment are difficult, since the mind's gender is immutable. We cannot change a person's gender no matter what we do; historically, we know of no case where a mind changed spontaneously from male to female, or vice versa. Compounding the problem are the varying degrees of severity which, from a practical point of view, simply means that Genital Reassignment Surgery is not for everyone.

Genital Reassignment Surgery is only for those individuals who have been assessed as transsexual, who have been properly screened and evaluated, and who have fulfilled the basic requirements for the operation. A most important additional requirement is that burning desire—that great emotional strength to stay the course and proceed toward the final goal in spite of the many negative expressions of other people. Without this deep motivation, a difficult and frustrating journey can easily become an impossible one.

It is well known that there are various methods of performing the transformation procedure, as well as a variety of techniques involved. Each depends on the operating surgeon's preferences and capabilities. Personally, I have always felt that the simplest method of doing things is usually the most beneficial and productive. Complicated and overly involved operations introduce additional and unnecessary risks. The less one does to accomplish an objective, the better the final result. This is why I have focused on making the genital-reassignment procedure as simple as possible by performing the penile inversion technique.

The inversion technique is an excellent operation, and the final result is hard to surpass. In terms of ease of performance, lack of complications, and patient satisfaction, penile inversion is the method of choice for most MTF transsexuals. Use of the sigmoid colon has been advocated and performed successfully by capable surgeons; however, it has been my experience that the results do not justify the extensive surgery, which involves another organ system and can result in such voluminous mucous flow that sanitary pads must be used almost continuously.

I have three objectives in doing the surgery: First, to bring to bear every plastic surgical technique that will result in a vulva which rivals the appearance of the genetic female. Unfortunately, this cannot be done with one operation, since the blood supply to the area would be severely compromised. Thus, a labiaplasty to enhance the femininity of the perineum is done no sooner than three months after genital reassignment in patients who desire it. On the other hand, many individuals find the shape and form of the area is so pleasing that they accept it without having more surgery.

During the labiaplasty, the superior portions of the labia majora are brought together over the previously created clitoris by the use of a double Z-plasty, with an attempt being made to form a hood over the clitoris. If the patient feels her clitoris is too large, it can easily be made smaller at this time. Because the clitoris is made from the same tissue as the urethra, there is an opening—a "connection"—between the top of the urethral opening and the bottom of the neo-clitoral opening. It is this fistula that I open as part of the labiaplasty, which results in an area of very feminine-looking mucous membrane rather than skin between the urethra and clitoris. Lastly, any other revision of the vulva, such as reshaping the labia, can be done along with ancillary surgical procedures of the face and breast.

I consider it important that after healing, patients should be able to experience comfortable, effortless, trouble-free sexual intercourse. This can be accomplished only if the dimensions of the neo-vagina are adequate. If the neo-vagina is short or has strictures and stenosis making penetration uncomfortable, the operation was not successful. A number of surgical principles must be carefully adhered to if the final result of the neo-vaginal construction is to be one of adequate depth and accommodating size with no contractures. Clearly, the operating surgeon must make the neo-vagina sufficiently deep to satisfy the requirements for intercourse. The dissection is carried out within the very narrow confines between the rectum and prostate gland as far posteriorly as Denonvilliers' fascia, which is virtually as far back as the intra-abdominal cavity. If this dissection is inadequate, the depth of the neo-vagina will be compromised; also, enough levator ani muscle must be divided for ample diameter.

Assuming that all dimensions of the neo-vagina are satisfactory, the opening must now be lined with epithelium—but remember that a seven-inch-deep neo-vagina cannot be lined with skin from a three-inch penis, and also keep in mind that it takes two inches of penile skin just to reach the opening of the neo-vagina. Obviously, if the penis is short, with little to contribute to the job of lining the entire shaft, additional epithelium must be obtained by the use of a skin graft, which is best obtained from the lower abdomen between the umbil-icus and the pubic hair. Experience tells us that this is a better donor site than the buttocks or thighs. It is easier to hide the donor site scar, and the grafts can be removed with greater facility than from anywhere else. Obviously, if the patient is not interested in future sexual intercourse, no graft is necessary, and we simply accept whatever depth we can get, which in some cases is virtually nothing.

If all this great effort is expended to create a functioning vagina but the patient does not experience warmth, excitement, and orgasmic feeling in the operated area, I do not believe that we have achieved all that we could from the procedure; it is this sense of sexual fulfillment that is my third objective. The mind is truly the most important sexual organ, but without proper nerve and blood supply to the reconstructed site, no amount of stimulation will cause arousal. For this reason I make every effort to preserve all possible nerve tissue.

The nerve of sex is the external pudendal nerve, which leaves the lower spinal cord and eventually passes through Alcock's canal, where it branches out to supply the entire genital and perianal areas. By making sure that this nerve's integrity is maintained and as many branches of the nerve are kept intact as possible, we can feel quite certain that the equipment necessary for orgasm is present and will function to the patient's satisfaction. This brings us to the basic surgical principle, which dictates that as much tissue as possible be preserved. The more experience I have with surgery—surgery of any kind—the less tissue I am inclined to sacrifice.

At one time, I removed most all of the corpora cavernosa. I no longer do this because I have found that by saving enough corpora to construct the neo-clitoris, we produce yet another source of pleasurable sensations. During sexual arousal, all erectile tissue in the genital area becomes engorged with blood, and it is this engorgement that causes some of the intense excitement experienced dur-ing intercourse. For this reason I construct the clitoris from the corpora cavern-osa rather than utilizing—as some surgeons have proposed—a small part of the glans penis, either as a skin graft or as an island flap, preserved on a long neurovascular pedicle that usually does not survive anyway. I believe that the entire intact head of the penis serves a better function inside the neovagina. At the conclusion of the operation, if all has gone well, we should have two—possibly three—potential sources of orgasmic sensation: the intravaginally posi-tioned head of the penis, the crus of the corpora cavernosa on either side of the urethra, and the clitoris constructed from the penile corpora cavernosa and corpus spongiosum.

So, excellence in the areas of aesthetics, function, and pleasure is my surgical goal for the transsexual patient. As the operation has developed in my hands, I have observed with great satisfaction the ability to routinely reproduce these objectives. Of course it is impossible to attain the same degree of success in everyone, but only in those individuals who have anatomical, physiologic (such as diabetes), or psychological problems do we fail to realize the full potential of the procedure. Also to be considered are the expectations of the patient. In those whose expectations are so high that they are unattainable, the outcome, as far as the patient is concerned, will be disappointing. My suggestion to anyone contemplating surgery of any kind is to keep your expectations within reason.

Do things always go well? No, this world is too imperfect for that. Problems and complications do occur from time to time, but fortunately not very often. Genetic males who take female hormones run the risk of forming thrombotic emboli that could be fatal. By discontinuing the use of hormones three weeks prior to surgery and by assisting blood flow in the lower extremities with intermittent pressure stockings during the bed-rest period after surgery, the likelihood of this is greatly reduced.

The most feared intraoperative complication is the inadvertent entry into the rectum while dissecting the neo-vagina. This could result in a rectovaginal fistula, necessitating a colostomy, with an eventual surgical attempt to repair the damage. Should this happen, the neo-vagina is invariably lost to scarring.

Severe postoperative bleeding requiring blood transfusions or gastrointestinal ileus calling for the use of a nasogastric tube to remove air from the stomach may occasionally be seen, and requires our immediate attention. Certainly, less significant problems can arise to bedevil us. As postoperative healing progresses, contractures of the neo-vagina can occur. These are usually due to lack of diligent neo-vaginal dilation by the patient. It is difficult to understand why anyone would neglect to dilate on a regular basis when it is so vital to the outcome of their surgery, especially after they have come so far, but it does happen.

Substandard craftsmanship can also result in a less than ideal cosmetic and functional outcome. I have examined and reoperated on patients done elsewhere who have had objectionable swelling in the neo-urethral area from retained bulbospongiosus and ischiocavernosus muscles that should have been removed. Once this excessive muscle is excised, the area becomes comfortable, with improvement in appearance as well. This retained muscle can also affect the urethra's normal function. Patients will complain of the "sprinkling can" effect, which, incidentally, can also be caused by scar that is present around the neo-urethral orifice; scar and urethral deformity occur because the opening was not sutured properly to begin with. Great care must be utilized when suturing the urethral mucosa to the neo-urethral opening, because it must be sutured internally, not externally. Attention to detail can make the difference between a superb result or one that will make a patient unhappy for a lifetime.

The future of genital reassignment is exciting. I see on the horizon a great deal of evolution and development: improvements in technique and the way the operations are done. For example, a great step forward will be a method to line the neo-vagina without the necessity for a skin graft. Clever and talented surgeons will come upon the scene, and they will make sensational things happen.

The sources for genuine human happiness are many and diverse. It is my sincere hope that Genital Reassignment Surgery in my hands has been, and will continue to be, a source of happiness for all. As far I am concerned, the development of the MTF genital-reassignment procedure is a never-ending search for excellence that has been both an adventure and a great source of satisfaction.

Over and Out in Academe: Transgender Studies Come of Age

Susan Stryker, Ph.D.

Chapter 20

Many nontranssexual professional academics* are beginning to catch on to what we transsexuals have known for a long time: Transsexuality encompasses a fascinating, complex set of phenomena that poses some radical questions about the way sexuality, gender, identity, and desire are instituted and maintained. It has much to teach us about the cultural processes through which individuals become intelligible to one another as persons, about relationships between the body and technology, and about the social construction of reality itself.

We've learned transsexuality's lessons the hard way—figuring out how to evade the cultural assumptions that work to prevent us from embodying and performing ourselves the way we need to, learning to exploit other assumptions that work in our favor. Nontranssexuals have generally learned about these issues from books about us written by other nontranssexuals, and have only recently begun turning to our own accounts and interpretations of what we've been up to. Over the last few years, however, a whole new body of interdisciplinary scholarship in the humanities, arts, and social sciences has emerged that has helped shift the concept of transsexuality out of the realm of psychopathology. The disease model no longer holds undisputed sway among most people who study transsexuality (apart from the medical/psychotherapeutic professions with a personal stake in the managing and regulation transsexual lives).

Increasingly, the us/them dichotomy is not a useful way of distinguishing between professional academics and transsexuals. I have been in personal contact with a dozen or so transsexual academics—art historians, economists, psycholo-

An earlier version of this essay appeared in *TNT: The Transsexual News Telegraph*, no. 4, (Spring 1995).

gists, librarians, biologists, mathematicians—whose professional career has nothing to do with transsexuality. There is nothing new, however, about transsexuals in academe; one of the essays in Green and Money's *Transsexualism and Sex Reassignment* (1968) uses the case of a MTF engineering professor who wanted to continue her career post-transitionally to discuss the process of changing name and sex designations on school records and other personal identification papers. What is new is that more openly transsexual people are entering academe than ever before; we are part of the process of changing how the sex/gender system operates in the academic workplace. Just as many Westerners have learned to turn to indigenous voices rather than Euro-American ethnographers and enthropologists when trying to understand non-Western cultures, and just as gays and lesbians are presumed to have greater insight into homosexuality than straight psychiatrists, transsexuals themselves are finally beginning to be seen as authorities on transsexuality.

Two international academic conferences marked the changing position of transsexuals and transsexuality in the academy. "In Queery, In Theory, In Deed: The Sixth North American Lesbian, Gay and Bisexual Studies Conference" drew about 3,000 people to the University of Iowa, November 17–20, 1994. One of the liveliest controversies at the conference had to do with how to draw the line between butch lesbian identities and FTM transsexuals. Dozens of other papers dealt with various aspects of queer gender. But even more important than the academic work presented was the fact that many transsexual academics from around the world were finally able meet and talk with each other face-to-face. Many of us knew a few other transpeople working on topics related to our own studies, but all of us met people in Iowa we'd never even heard of before. As a result, we organized the Transgender Academic Network, an electronic mailing list intended to keep members up-to-date on work going on in the field of transgender studies.*

The Iowa conference had its negative aspects as well, however. During the closing plenary session, someone from the floor asked why the title of the conference did not include the word *transgender*. Rather than answer the question, one of the panelists started talking about the need for multiracial diversity. After

Anthropologist Jason Cromwell of the University of Washington managed the TAN list until 1996, when it was taken over by Stephan Whittle of the Manchester Metropolitan University in England. The purpose of the Transgender Academic Network is to advance the state of transgender studies, both within the academy and without. Participation is open to anyone seriously interested in the study of transgenderism, whether or not they identify as transgendered, and whether or not they hold academic degrees, and regardless of self-identification, educational level, or professional status. However, we ask that the intent and purpose of the group be respected: It is designed as an informational resource for transgender people and others involved in transgender studies. It is neither a support group for individuals beginning to question their gender identity, nor a place for the nontransgendered to assume that they have an understanding of transgenderism superior to that of transgender people themselves. Individuals interested in joining the network may subscribe by sening e-mail to transacademic-request@mailbase.ac.uk. The list functions as an initial point of contact, a place to post announcements and ask questions. Lengthier discussions are carried out on the trans-theory list. trans-theory-request@mailbase.ac.uk.

a round of hissing and booing, someone else from the floor asked that one of the conference organizers please address the transgender question. One of the organizers did, saying that it had been hard enough to get a gay, lesbian, bisexual studies conference approved by a conservative university administration, and they didn't want to jeopardize the whole event by using the word *transgender*. The organizer's answer prompted a barrage of protest. An FTM got up and spoke eloquently about how transgender inclusion was necessary for queer politics, and how lesbian and gay studies that didn't address variable constructions of gender simply reproduced dominant cultural norms of proper masculinity and femininity. What was equally inspiring, however, was the number of nontranssexuals who rose to speak on behalf of transgender inclusion. Several of those who did so were young Asian dykes, suggesting that transgender status is beginning to be seen by some within the queer community as an important axis of difference that must be taken into consideration when working against other sorts of assumed privileges, such as those based on class or ethnicity.

On February 24–26, 1995, the Center for Sex Research at California State University at Northridge hosted "The First International Conference on Gender, Cross-Dressing, and Sex Issues: A Dialogue Between Professionals and Those in the Community." As the title of the event suggests, the organizers had little sense that the transgender community and the professionals who study it might possibly intersect or overlap. Still, the conference productively broke down these artificial barriers on several fronts—though not necessarily in ways intended by the organizers. For example, the management of the convention hotel posted signs on restroom doors asking participants in the conference to please use only the restrooms in that portion of the hotel where the conference was being held. Rather than challenge this blatantly transphobic act, the organizers agreed (not that it stopped most transgender people from relieving their bowels and bladders wherever it suited them to do so). As a result, many nontransgender professionals found themselves side-by-side at the urinals, stalls, and make-up mirrors with people they were much more accustomed to observing in a clinical setting.

The Northridge conference did signal that nontranssexual professionals who are interested in us increasingly recognize that they need to talk *with* us, and not simply *about* us—even if many nontranssexuals still don't have a clue how to do so without arrogance and condescension. Several nontranssexuals spoke up during sessions to counter some of the most offensively pathologizing statements made about us by other nontranssexuals. Everybody there at least paid lip service to the idea that a "new paradigm" was needed to account for the complexities of sex and gender in the late twentieth century, and that looking at transgender phenomena was a good way to start articulating that paradigm. Members of the committee responsible for revising the Harry Benjamin International Gender Dysphoria Association's Standards of Care for the hormonal and surgical treatment of transsexuals listened respectfully to transgender people's concerns and dissatisfactions—though there is no sign that HBIGDA will relinquish without a struggle its position as a gatekeeper for access to transsexual embodiment technologies.

Transsexual people presented by far the most innovative work at the Northridge conference in legal studies, the arts, literary analysis, and anthropology. And once again, as in Iowa, transsexual academics and activists had a chance to come together and further consolidate the growing professional networks that have emerged among us over the last few years. These networks are an important part of the community-building process, and they work to further the development of cogent, intellectually sound interpretations of transgender experience that do not rely on ideas of sickness, dysfunction, abnormality, or deviance.

The Guidelines and, indeed, this whole book also represent a shift in this direction. I appreciate the hard work, thoughtfulness, and compassion evident in Gianna Israel and Dr. Donald Tarver's efforts, and I share with them the desire to improve the quality of care and services available for transgender individuals, particularly transsexuals. I appreciate, too, their interest in having me serve on the advisory board for this project and their willingness to accept some of my suggestions for revision along the way. I most appreciate, however, their inclusion of this essay in *Transgender Care*, in that I strongly dissent from one of the underlying assumptions informing the entire work. Because I consider transgender identification to be neither a physiological nor a psychological disorder, I therefore believe that psychotherapeutic professionals have no business regulating transgender access to surgical and hormonal gender-reassignment techniques. The disproportionate number of essays in this addendum that address the need to depart radically from the existing standards of care endorsed by HBIGDA underscores both the depth of feeling on this issue in the transsexual community as well as the seriousness of the situation. Until transsexuals believe they are being treated as equal partners in the process of transitioning from one gender to another, the trust and faith in the service provider which are so necessary for quality health care will simply not be possible. What is at stake here is who has the power to determine how one's body is treated. There is no middle ground; either one has this power oneself in any given situation, or one doesn't. As transgender medical services are currently delivered in the United States, it is the psychotherapist, not the transsexual, who ultimately determines what will happen to the transsexual's body. This is an unacceptable situation.

In the next few years, scholarly work on transsexuality that contests the pathologization of our identity, done by transgender academics and sympathetic allies, will become increasingly common. How this will translate into meaningful gains for our community remains to be seen. One thing is certain, though—we are becoming increasingly able to define the meaning of our own lives. This cannot help but advance the cause of transgender liberation.

Reference

Green, Richard, and John Money, eds. 1968. *Transsexualism and Sex Reassignment.* Baltimore: Johns Hopkins University Press.

Transsexuality, Science, and Prophecy

Max Wolf Valerio

Chapter 21

I've donated my body to science. How many people have had the experience of living both as a man and as a woman? Of experiencing the hormonal surges, wearing the skin and muscles, the shifting moods, the social, spiritual, and historical onus of both sexes?

Transsexuality is a phenomenon. Awesome with cloaked paradoxes, unknowable, ranging far from accepted cultural beliefs and practices, instigating reexaminations of identity and of the methods and practices that enable us to know or perceive identity. Identity as willed, as having the agency to restructure the very body that it's perceived to inhabit.

Transsexuals are agents provocateurs on the edges of a culture hurtling headlong into a century where technology will interface on an escalating basis with our bodies. We are the furthest, most extreme expression of manipulation of the body, almost as though that body, that human stretch of flesh, were a piece of plastic, or some other nearly synthetic, malleable substance. We restructure our glands, our body fluids, skin, nerves, and genitals. We are thieves of technology for the will of an inscrutable and delicious fate. Some call it choice, others call it destiny. Our lives recovered by science, the oblique point of reference for an expanding arc of transformation.

Because we have lived the impossible, a transformation that was previously only dreamt about but never accomplished, we must demand to be known and understood as precursors, explorers, brave, poignantly human men and women. Prophets of a richly complex net of perceptions, dialogues, radically violent instrumentalities of transformation concerning sex, gender, body modification and identity. Ancient archetypes whisper or sing to us that we are connected to archaic, abiding images of man and woman in our essence, even from within our seeming contradictions. We intensify the archetypes of maleness and femaleness in order to see through them, to live past them, to fully and completely reconfigure their meaning.

By becoming a man, I became all men. I developed a new compassion for maleness and femaleness as it's lived in this culture. What previously seemed to be sexist posturing or empty role playing took on the texture and vulnerable complexities of a passionate panoply, richly lived, real. *Real* as in abiding, reasonable, rooted in experience that is lived, not conspired, not counterfeit. A reality with contradictions, genuine feeling and insoluble, although difficult meaning. I've come to a more complete understanding of why people act in the ways they do. I'm not as quick to judge men or, for that matter, women. I no longer have a subtle feeling of superiority because of being on a "politically correct" side (in my case, the feminist side). I'm not as dogmatic or defensive. I feel so much more human now, although I am actually stranger than ever before (since I'm someone who's had a "sex change"). I feel so much freedom, now that I've done my deepest will and shattered my old life in the course of it.

Because of my transformation, I have had to increasingly reexamine my assumptions concerning sex, gender, human culture, and motivations. This is one of the great opportunities that this transition brings to transsexual people, if we are equal to taking it on. Freedom, knowledge and the ability to participate in mystery. The mystery our lives become once we've changed our sex and therefore eluded all conventional expectations of how and who we are; and the mystery that we find the world to be, as we take part in it from the vantage point of complete strangers, alien to and yet intimately familiar with each sex, knowing that just as we are not simple, nothing and no one else is either. The world is a stretching, shaking net wild with biologically rooted instinct, flashes of intuitive, abstract thought forms encoding and creating culture, inchoate dream sequences, yearnings that search and destroy all assumptions, all dogmatic wishful thinking. A jungle and we're in it, alive with the certainty of hounds in a war zone.

■ ─────────

> We need rites of passage.
>
> Rites of passage that empower.
>
> That lead us into our dreams.

There should be guidance, communication, the conferring of understanding from one transsexual to another. People need information and places to safely discuss and explore all options and issues relating to gender. Once an individual has determined that he or she wishes to alter his or her biological sex, that individual should be able to with a minimum of problems. To achieve this, we need to create places within our communities where transsexual and transgender people can find each other and talk, share anecdotes, process information.

More of us need to come out of the woodwork and stay out. We have to arrive at a deeper, more complex understanding of what it is to be transsexual or transgender. We need to insist on our humanity, our basic, simple identities as man and woman, although this simplicity appears to contradict the apparent complexity of our history and perceptions.

We have changed our sex. Future generations of transsexuals will only do it more thoroughly, more completely, as technology becomes more refined. The previously unthinkable range of that transformation has actually wed us more deeply to the more ordinary strands of humanity. On the margins, the periphery, is where the middle expanses are most easily viewed.

Hormones

Delia van Maris, M.D.

Chapter 22

For the transsexual, the most significant aspect of therapy is the administration of steroidal drugs to assume the secondary sex characteristics of the opposite gender. As a therapy, it cannot stand by itself, and this point is endorsed by the Guidelines.

The focus on surgical intervention should be anticlimactic, and indeed, increasing numbers of transsexual and transgender individuals elect not to go through with a surgical procedure. Others do not feel that transition is complete until a surgical alteration of external sex organs is completed.

The surgical procedures are focused in time, cataclysmic, often painful, and followed by troublesome complications; they are not reversible. They have a finality that is an emphatic mark of the end of a journey. On the other hand, the effects of hormonal therapy are not immediately seen, and for some do not appear fast enough. Overdosing with increasing amounts of drug is not the answer. Hormonal therapy must be represented as a gradual opportunity for change. The therapy must be judiciously given, consistent, monitored both for effect and for side effects, and combined with other aspects of supportive care. Over a two-year period, as hormonal effects develop, there is the opportunity to make a transition in other ways. Dealing with emotional issues (some of which may be due to hormone therapy), employment problems, and personal relationships can be accomplished concurrently. The final goal should be not only hormonal manipulation, but socialization into the new gender role, often referred to as "living full time."

To some degree, hormonal therapy is reversible. The alterations do not carry the finality of a surgical procedure, but unfortunately, we do not know to what extent the changes can be reversed if the individual has a change of mind and direction.

When goals are met and the transition is well done emotionally, psychologically, and in terms of physical appearance, most of the task is completed, since this is the person that will be perceived by the outside world. Final alteration of external sex organs and their functional capacity is an element of these changes that is usually seen by only a few people, most often in intimate relationships.

For the FTM transsexual, the results of hormonal therapy can be quite remarkable. Phenotypic development is always female in the absence of testosterone, or in the absence of testosterone receptors (testicular feminization). Embryological development depends heavily on the introduction of testosterone at the appropriate time. One way to view this therapy in these patients (and with the undertaking of the administration of these drugs, I always refer to them as *patients* to emphasize the seriousness of the endeavor) is the alteration of a relatively undifferentiated anatomic state. Testosterone given to the female causes the development of male secondary sex characteristics in a relatively short time. There is beard growth, growth of body hair in general, changes in voice character, and the development of male-pattern baldness. There is marked muscle growth, particularly in the arms and shoulders, and clitoral hypertrophy. The latter is quite variable. The FTM transsexual often has two significant complaints, neither of which can be altered by hormonal or surgical manipulation. One is stature, since epiphyseal closure has long occurred and has determined height. The other is lack of the socialization process during the teenage years. Locker room humor, elements of adolescent male interaction, and interaction with other females are temporal experiences that cannot be replaced.

For the MTF, the problems are different. Here, the development of the male secondary characteristics are to be reversed rather than established. Keeping this in mind, one targets the secondary goal as gentle encouragement of female secondary sex characteristics. With estrogen therapy, body hair will not markedly be diminished. Removal of the beard must be mechanical (electrolysis), as existing facial hair is unaffected. Male-pattern baldness and male voice characteristics will not be reversed. Breast development will approximate the genetic potential and can be estimated by analyzing maternal phenotypes and female siblings. Even though the changes in breast tissue may be significant, because of the limb-shoulder size, the breast may be perceived as inadequate, as it is "lost" and minimized by the larger skeletal frame. In many cases, the desired changes are not effected until castration, with the estrogenic effect unopposed by testicular testosterone.

Currently, the one advantage that the MTF does have is in the final surgical procedure. The creation of a neo-vagina, satisfactory is appearance and function, has to date been more successful than the creation of a penis capable of tumescence.

The approach to transsexual and transgender individuals is complex. The effects of administration of sex hormones vary among individuals. Dosing and effect for the FTM and the MTF must also be considered on a separate and individual basis, and this includes the occurrence of side effects and complications.

Hormonal therapy must be considered in perspective, and as only one element of transition. With proper medical care and monitoring, it can be done safely, and can lead to a satisfactory result. The recognition of the complexity of the problem, and the necessity to mobilize resources and provide a multidisciplinary approach, is the strength of the Guidelines.

The Therapist versus the Client: How the Conflict Started and Some Thoughts on How to Resolve It

Anne Vitale, Ph.D.

Chapter 23

The role of the therapist in working with gender-dysphoric individuals is unique in the profession of psychotherapy. This is due to the elusive nature of the disorder, the psychological profile of the individuals presenting, and what is often construed as the "gatekeeper role" of the therapist.

From the beginning of formal treatment, the relationship between the gender community and the therapist has been contentious. There are signs that the situation is improving, but to this day, far too many therapists are justifiably accused of being autocratic, under- or ill-informed about the disorder, and financially exploitive. How did we get into this mess, and how do we fix it?

Although what the *Diagnostic and Statistical Manual of Mental Disorders* (4th edition) calls "Gender Identity Disorder" (302.85, *DSM*-IV) appears to occur at random in all cultures and populations, those presenting to the therapist are likely to be extraordinary high-functioning and accomplished individuals. It is not unusual for the clients to be strong-willed, independent, and very well read on the medical aspects of gender-identity disorder. They may be deeply afraid of what may be in store for them because of the immensity of having to change one's sex, but to their credit, they are generally determined to live normal lives.

The "gatekeeper" function refers to the client's need for referral letters from the therapist for hormone therapy and, eventually, Genital Reassignment Surgery. Given their desire for these letters, the clients are ready, if need be, to take on the therapist in a battle of wits.

This contentious relationship was initiated by the medical profession. With the noted exception of the writings of Harry Benjamin and Christian Hamburger, most of the early medical literature (of the 1960s and 1970s) on gender-identity disorder seemed more intent on showing just how sick gender-dysphoric

251

people are than to expand and critically evaluate treatment techniques. The tenor of the times can be summed up in a statement made by Howard J. Baker in the *American Journal of Psychiatry*, chastising those who treated transsexuals:

> We also find in the literature such terms and phrases as "psychotic," "delusional confection," "psychopath," "delusional quest," "masters of the art of self-deception and of deceiving others," "psychopathic personality," "paranoid," "neurotic," "schizophrenic," "borderline psychasthenic," "intricate suicidal dynamics," and "so-called transsexuals," all of which amounts to little more than psychiatric name calling and contributes little to our understanding of the disorder. (Baker, 1969, p. 1415)

Baker goes on to say:

> My experience leads me to believe that the literature is actually quite constrained in its expression of disdain for these persons. Visits to medical, surgical, and psychiatric wards on which these individuals have been evaluated and treated have demonstrated clearly to me how physicians and nurses alike hold them up to ridicule. Is one paranoid in a delusional sense when he is in fact treated with ridicule, contempt, disdain and sometimes overt hatred by those from whom he seeks assistance, as well as being harassed by society in general? (Baker, 1969, p. 1416)

Even though the current literature is more objective, there are still far too many therapists who fail to understand and appreciate the complexity and the seriousness of the problem they are treating. Very few therapists have experienced similar situations in their lives. Unlike grief, or depression, or even a drinking problem, with which they may be personally familiar, most therapists have no first-hand experience with gender dysphoria. Some have difficulty imagining the persistent, intense anxiety caused by gender dysphoria. For others, it is all but impossible.

A second problem is negative countertransference. For example, a therapists may have a gut-level disgust for feminine men or masculine women and may openly cringe at the thought of having them "mutilated" by surgery. Or a therapist might not have as visceral a reaction about the surgery, but might be bothered by feelings that the individual is trying to avoid his or her obligations as a member of the original gender, especially if both the therapist and the client are married and have young children. Negative thoughts of the prospect of the psychotherapist's father, mother, husband, wife, daughter, or sons crossdressing or changing sex can and often do get in the way of good psychotherapy.

Therapists, like most people confronted with an uncomfortable issue, are likely to avoid talking about an issue with which they feel uncomfortable—gender reassignment. Some therapists will instead try to "cure" the client by looking for and then "fixing" something they find it easier to deal with. The American Psychological Association's ethics code (APA, 1992) (1.04a, 1.04b) is quite clear: psychotherapists are required to refer clients who present with problems they're not qualified to work with. Unfortunately it's far easier and much more profitable to consider gender dysphoria as a symptom of benign midlife crisis or some other condition. In this case, the client would be treated with care and sympathy, but most certainly would be diverted from looking closely at feelings about gender expression.

Another common alternate diagnosis, especially among psychiatrists, is borderline personality disorder. Unfortunately, there is some overlap in diagnostic consideration to justify this thinking. For example, persons with borderline personality disorder often make recurrent suicide threats or gestures of self-mutilation, and they experience significant and persistent identity disturbances. In addition, both gender identity disorder and borderline personality disorder seem to peak when the client is in the thirties and forties. This resemblance is especially problematic for the gender conflicted because persons with borderline personality disorder are notoriously thought of as unreliable, manipulating, and demanding. They are routinely referred to as among the most difficult clients to work with. This is probably the origin of the "gender clients are master manipulators" myth that is still negatively impacting the proper treatment of gender-identity disorder.

Another and far more insidious problem occurs when the gender-conflicted person, realizing he or she needs the help of a specialist, applies for treatment at a "gender clinic." As one might expect, most clients apply for entry to gender clinics trusting, first, that the staff in the clinic is sympathetic, and, second, the clinicians know what they are doing. They may be wrong on both counts. For example, most gender clinics are attached to medical schools whose primary reason for existing is to train new clinicians and surgeons. Both the clinical staff and the students are in constant turnover, so very little subjective judgment regarding the client is allowed. Instead, every applicant is subjected to standardized interviews and a battery of expensive psychometric examinations. If the client fits the profile the clinic is looking for, the individual is diagnosed as transsexual and assigned a timetable and a series of tasks to perform. Typically, if the client who doesn't fit the profile is told that he or she is not transsexual and is dismissed from the program. In the latter case, the individual is out hundreds, perhaps thousands, of dollars, and leaves more confused than ever and completely demoralized. It's a black-and-white approach to a many-shades-of-gray disorder.

Fortunately, there are many highly qualified therapists who feel comfortable and even enjoy working with this population. These people generally refer to themselves as Gender Specialists. They tend to work independently, maintaining a dependable referral list for the nontherapeutic aspects of their work. The actual therapeutic orientation varies from therapist to therapist.

Some therapists are noted for being very accepting and motherly. Although this works for some people, some gender clients complain that this approach eventually leads to feelings of being demeaned or patronized. Another common approach is Jungian. Clients sometimes complain that Jungian theory seems theoretical and peripheral to what actually occurs in their everyday lives.

Having been through transition myself, I am a strong advocate of empowering the individual by using a supportive, responsible, down-to-earth existential-humanistic approach. In my opinion, the role of the therapist in helping an individual with gender-identity disorder is to be very clear about the physiological and psychological ramifications of the disorder and to serve as a guide in aiding the individual through the morass of possibilities leading to his or her own resolution.

A hopeful and relatively new element in treating gender-identity disorder is that more and more transgendered people are getting involved in its treatment. I was pleasantly surprised to see a significantly high percentage of transgendered mental health professionals at the October 1993 meeting of the Harry Benjamin International Gender Dysphoria Association in New York City. A similarly high percentage of transgender professionals were present at the first International Congress on Gender, Crossdressing, and Sex Issues, which met in Van Nuys, California, in February 1995. This meeting, sponsored by California State University at Northridge, was billed as "A Dialogue Between Professionals and Those in the Community." What we are finding is that there is a lessening distinction between the two.

As a first step in resolving our difficulties, I suggest we start with a more clearly defined idea of what constitutes a qualified gender therapist. I believe a Gender Specialist should be a licensed professional with sufficient training and supervision to handle this extremely debilitating disorder. The individual should be ready to accept crossdressing and sex or gender incongruity as a psychologically unalterable, congenitally attributed, natural phenomenon. As long as the client is not showing signs of a thought disorder such as schizophrenia or multigendered personalities of a multiple personality disorder, the therapist should have nothing invested in the direction in which the client searches to find his or her true self.

Every individual has the right to be whatever sex he or she wishes to be. The therapist's primary duty is to see that the client works diligently and thoroughly through the issues and that the client is capable and accepting of full responsibility for his or her actions. With the exception of the minimum twelve-week evaluation required by the Harry Benjamin Standards of Care (Walker, et al., 1991) for hormone therapy, the therapist should give the client all the time necessary to come to his or her own resolution. That resolution might be a low-impact one, such as coming to feel comfortable about crossdressing, with perhaps some mild hormonally induced feminization or masculinization. If a more drastic and higher impact change is required, that resolution might include a complete alteration of secondary sex characteristics, with or without Genital Reassignment Surgery.

A good Gender Specialist should be independent of organizational oversight, leaving him or her free to individualize care. The better therapists I know take a case-management approach. As needs arise, a good therapist must not only be able to ease the client's anxiety but also able to educate, support, and provide a wide variety of professional referrals.

A good gender therapist knows other good gender therapists for general referral and consultation. He or she should also be familiar with the professional record, medical orientation, and demeanor of several endocrinologist, psychiatrists, and surgeons.

A good gender therapist can help his or her clients express themselves socially in the new gender role. This can range from providing passing letters and legal referrals to consultations with relatives and employers. And, yes, there are many times when straightforward psychotherapy is required. Who knows? Maybe, eventually, even the negative appellation of *gatekeeper* can be changed to something closer to *gate watcher.*

It all boils down to a matter of trust. I believe that the gender community has tried hard to be patient. It is now up to the medical and psychological professions to earn that trust and make it all work.

References

American Psychologicasl Association. 1992. Ethical Principles of Psychologists and Code of Conduct. *American Psychologist* 47: 1597–1611.

Baker, Howard J. 1969. Transsexulism: Problems in Treatment. *American Journal of Psychiatry* 125: 118–124.

Walker, Paul A., et al. 1991 (rev.). Standards of Care: The Hormonal and Surgical Sex Reassignment of Gender Dysphoric Persons. Palo Alto, Calif.: The Harry Benjamin International Gender Dysphoria Association, Inc.

Appendix: Resources for Transgender Individuals, Families, and Professionals

National and International Organizations and Agencies

AEGIS—American Educational Gender Information Service

P.O. Box 33724, Decatur, GA 30033-0724
(770) 939-2128 (Administration)
(770) 939-0244 (Hotline)
(770) 939-1770 (FAX)
Internet: aegis@mindspring.com
FTP, AEGIS-List, see listing or inquire.

AEGIS is a nonprofit membership organization providing education and resource information for all transgender people, their families, and professionals who work with them. Membership is $36.00 a year. Members receive two issues of *Chrysalis,* four issues of *AEGIS-Quarterly* newsletter, membership card, and 10% discount on all AEGIS products. Nationally sponsors affiliates. AEGIS maintains the National Transgender Library and Archives. Sample issues of *Chrysalis* are $9.00 (postage paid).

IFGE—International Foundation for Gender Education

P.O. Box 367, Wayland, MA 01778
(617) 899-2212 Administration/Information
Internet: IFGE@world.std.com
Homepage: Http://www.transgender.org/tg/ifge/index.html

IFGE is a nonprofit membership organization providing information and educational resources for the transvestite and transsexual community, family members, and professionals. Holds "Coming Together" convention at a new city each year. Publishes *Transgender—Tapestry,* $40.00 annually or $12.00 single issue. IFGE also publishes pamphlets and books, including Dr. Sheila Kirk's book, *Hormones*. Membership with IFGE helps support national outreach to organizations, professionals, and the general public. Basic membership is $25.00 annually, giving members a right to vote for Board of Directors, subscription to a quarterly newsletter, and special discounts from some venders, advertisers, and IFGE products. Inquire about other membership levels.

Renaissance Education Association, Inc.

987 Old Eagle School Road., Suite 719, Wayne, PA 19087
(610) 975–9119
Internet: bensalem@cpcn.com
Homepage: Http://www.ren.org

Renaissance is a national nonprofit organization that sponsors local support groups so that individuals can find a safe space to learn about transgender behavior. It has four chapters and thirteen affiliates in nine states. The Renaissance philosophy is open, non-discriminatory membership for everyone. Renaissance publishes a monthly 24-page newsletter, *Renaissance News & Views,* which provides an open forum for discussion of gender-related social, political, and legal issues, as well as basic information about events in the transgender community. The annual subscription is $20 if you are not a chapter member. A complete list of monographs, papers, and community outreach bulletins is available upon request. Renaissance's operates a speaker's bureau and is a founding member of the Transgender Alliance for Community, which promotes community projects; it is also a founding member of GenderPAC.

Creative Design Services (CDS)

P.O. Box 61263, King of Prussia, PA 19406
(610) 640–9449 (Orders)
(610) 648–0257 (FAX)
Internet: Info@cdspub.com
Homepage: Http://www.cdspub.com

CDS is an independent publishing resource that carries numerous publication titles, videos, and other resources regarding crossdressing and transgender issues. CDS' *Who's Who Guide to the Transgender Community* is the most thoroughly researched and respected referral resource for transgender persons and support professionals. Updated annually, it is available for $10.00 plus 2.00 for shipping and handling. CDS also publishes *Ladylike (TM) Magazine* for crossdressers, containing glossy color photography with informative articles and real life stories. *Ladylike Magazine* is available for $10.00 a single copy or $32.00 quarterly (postage paid). Upon request, CDS will fax or e-mail its current catalog.

ICTLEP—International Conference on Transgender Law and Employment Policy

P.O. Drawer 35477, Houston, TX 77235-5477
(713) 723-8452 (Administration)
(713) 723-1800 (FAX)
Internet: ICTLEP@aol.com (keyword "ICTLEP")

ICTLEP is a nonprofit organization that sponsors an annual international law conference dealing with a wide range of legal, employment, and medical policies affecting transgender persons. Publishes conference proceedings; available at $65.00 per subject title.

ETVC (Educational Transvestite Chapter)

P.O. Box 426486, San Francisco, CA 94142-6486
(510) 549-2665 (Hotline)
(415) 334-3439 (Voice Mail)
BBS: 2400 Baud, (415) 239-8467

ETVC is an active support organization for transvestites, transsexuals, and other transgender persons. Annually holds the world-renown Miss ETVC Cotillion. Membership is $20.00 per year, and members receive *ETVC Newsletter.* ETVC maintains a lending library and holds various support groups for transgender persons and significant others.

The Brothers Network in San Francisco

973 Market, Ste 650
San Francisco, CA 94103
(415-356-8140)

National Black Gay and Lesbian Leadership Forum

1219 La Brea Avenue
Los Angeles, CA 90019
(213) 964-7820

The San Francisco Human Rights Commission

25 Van Ness, Suite 800
San Francisco, CA 94102
(415) 252-2500
(415) 431-5764 (FAX)

FTM International

5337 College Avenue, No. 142
Oakland, CA 94618
Homepage: http://www.ftm-intl.org/

FTM International is a not-for-profit educational organization providing specialized information on FTM issues. Publishes the *FTM Newsletter* quarterly ($15.00 annually for individuals; $20.00 international subscriptions; $25.00 for professionals). Sponsors an annual FTM conference, welcoming professionals and transgender persons. Sponsors local support group meetings in San Francisco and Oakland.

Ingersoll Gender Center

1812 East Madison, No. 106
Seattle, WA 98122-2843
Homepage: Http://www.halcyon.com/ingersol/iiihome.html

Provides MTF and FTM support groups and local newsletter. Publishes *Information for the Female-to Male Cross-Dresser and Transsexual,* by Lou Sullivan.

HBIGDA—The Harry Benjamin International Gender Dysphoria Association

3790 El Camino Real, No. 251
Palo Alto, CA 94306
(415) 322-2335
(415) 322-3260 (FAX)

HBIGDA is a professional membership organization of gender-specializing counselors, psychotherapists, psychiatrists, surgeons, and researchers. Holds biennial professional-level conferences at international locations. Publishes "Standards of Care" for transsexual medical and psychological treatment. Annual memberships available for professional practitioners, for interns and students, and for organizations. Members receive HBIGDA newsletter and periodic bulletins, plus an international membership directory.

Internet Resources

Transgender News Groups

alt.transgendered
soc.support.transgendered
alt.personals.transgendered
alt.sex.trans

Discussion Lists

Discussion lists are discussion groups that are linked by e-mail. They are easy to join. Send an e-mail message to the address listed below, placing the message indicated within the body of your e-mail (not on the subject line). Do not worry about making a mistake; discussion lists are automated and typically send a help message by e-mail to you, should you make a mistake. Print out any instructions sent to you, for later reference.

AEGIS-List
Address: majordomo@lists.mindspring.com
Message: Subscribe aegis-list <*your e-mail address*>

Tg-Spirit
Address: Listserv@listserv.aol.com
Message: Subscribe tg-spirit <*your name*>

Tgs-Pflag
Address: majordomo@mtcc.com
Message: Subscribe Tgs-Pflag <*your e-mail address*>

Transactive-1
Address: Listserv@netcom.com
Message: Subscribe transactive-1 <*your e-mail address*>

Transgen
Address: Listserv@brownvm.brown.edu
Message: Subscribe transgen <*your name*>

Tsmenace

Address: Majordomo@zoom.com
Message: Subscribe tsmenace *<your e-mail-address>*

Bisexu-l

Address: Bisexu-l@brownvm.brown.edu
Message: Subscribe bisexu-l *<your name>* to listserve@brownvm.brown.edu

GLB-News

Address: GLB-News@listserv.aol.com
Message: Subscribe glb-news *<your name>* to listserv@listserve.aol.com

IRC (Internet Relay Chat) Sites

#Transgen
#Crossdress

America Online (AOL) Trangender Community Forum

Type "Go TCF"

Anonymous FTP (File Transfer Protocols)

ftp.mindspring.com/users/aegis
ftp.netcom.com/pub/os/osprey

Gopher

gopher.casti.com:70/11/gaystuff/QRD/trans

World Wide Web (WWW)

There are literally hundreds of WWW sites of interest to transgender persons. Visit any
webcrawler or web search site such as Yahoo (http://www.yahoo.com). Type in the search
word of your subject choice, such as "transgender," and your search begins!

About the Authors

GIANNA E. ISRAEL was born in Phoenix, Arizona. She developed interests in mental health, medicine, education, ethics, and cultural diversity early on in life. In private practice as a Senior Gender Specialist since 1988, she provides individual and relationship counseling, nationwide telephone consultation, evaluations, and case consultation. Ms. Israel has had the opportunity to work with over a thousand transgender men and women, and also is a member of the transgender community.

Ms. Israel stays up to date on gender-identity support issues and parallel mental health and medical information. She is continually refining her counseling and evaluation expertise through ongoing peer-consultation with psychotherapy and medical providers. This has included two and a half-years of individual and group psychotherapy training and consultation with Jerry Exel, Ph.D., in Portland, Oregon. Additionally, she has received suicide and crisis-intervention certification from the State of California, is a member of the Harry Benjamin International Gender Dysphoria Association (HBIGDA), and is a founding member of the Board of Directors for the American Education Gender Information Service (AEGIS).

Outside her private practice, Ms. Israel has extended her skills at Berkeley's Pacific Center for Human Growth, at San Francisco's Women's Building, and at the City and County of San Francisco's Center for Special Problems (CSP). As a Gender Identity Program Associate at the CSP since 1992, in collaboration with Jeff Gold, Ph.D., and Donald Tarver M.D., she has been instrumental in the start-up of a self-help and peer counseling process for the center's clients. Additionally, she has provided training and exchanges ongoing consultation with the CSP's Gender Identity Program staff. Nationally, Ms. Israel hosts regular conferences on America Online's Transgender Community Forum. These conferences reach a broad audience and focus on such issues as coming out, relationships, and employment and discrimination.

As an author, Ms. Israel is published nationally and internationally on mental health and transgender issues. She was also one of the first authors to initiate awareness regarding HIV, homelessness, and cultural-diversity issues in the transgender community. Prior to writing her 1988 series on HIV and AIDS, including an article featured in *NNTN Bulletin,* no national transgender publication had ventured to address this issue or include safe-sex material.

Currently, Ms. Israel is a regularly featured columnist with IFGE's *Transgender–Tapestry* ("Ask Gianna"), with *TV-Connections* ("Educational Reflections"), with the Internet's *TG-Forum Magazine* and on American Online's Transgender Community Forum. Internet users can also read her writings at the "Gianna E. Israel Gender Library" hosted by Ms. Diane Wilson found on the World Wide Web. Ms. Israel is also printed internationally, including in the Dutch language publication *Transformatie.* Her regular column, which features essays such as "De Transgenderist: Als Zelfidenticatie Het Opneemt Tegen T&T-stereotypen (8/96)," has informed European readers of the specialized needs of various subpopulations within the transgender community. Currently she is working on a Swedish-language gender-issue book, *Fraagestaellningar Kring Koensidentiteten,* which will provide mental health, medical, and social support information (in press 1998, Foereningen Benjamin, Stockholm).

Ms. Israel feels honored working with and writing for transgender and professional communities. In each endeavor she is noted for developing forums that promote non-pathologizing social, psychological, and medical principles, and that are mindful of individual self-determination rights, consumer-protection safeguards, and inclusive of culturally diverse needs. In her role as principal author of and project administrator for *Transgender Care,* she has made every effort to further these principles as well as establish a forum that facilitates effective professional and consumer dialogue, collaboration and contribution.

Ms. Israel initiated her gender transition in the early 1980s. During this time she found herself with limited gender-support resources, even though she resided in "liberal" San Francisco. She simply went about the business of building her self-identity, settling into a presentation that suited her needs as well as surrounding herself with friends and a new, adopted family capable of respecting her life journey. In her private life Ms. Israel enjoys spending time with her loved ones and interacting with people from all walks of life. She considers her relationships and skills to be blessings. Jazz, humor, and spirited reflection are key elements she uses to balance her challenging professional life.

DONALD E. TARVER II, M.D., is a public sector and private practice psychiatrist in San Francisco. Dr. Tarver received an A.B. degree in biology from Harvard University in 1982 and then received an M.D. degree from the University of Cincinnati College of Medicine (UCCM) in 1987. He has distinguished himself professionally as the recipient of the Community Psychiatry Award (UCCM) and an NIMH-sponsored American Psychiatric Association Minority Psychiatric Fellowship in Public Service.

During his residency in psychiatry at the University of California–San Francisco, he cofounded the Minority Residents Association and later joined that institution's clinical faculty. As a resident trainee of the Black Focus Program Unit at San Francisco General Hospital (SFGH), Dr. Tarver was cochair of the Black Task Force; he distinguished himself among staff and patients as a physician concerned about the human rights of marginalized populations. During his tenure there he is noted for establishing policies that were sensitive to these population's special needs yet maintained psychiatric protocol. Dr. Tarver continues to train others about African American psychiatric issues and cross-cultural competency.

His interest in gender-identity issues was sparked by his observation that transgender individuals and other marginalized populations were frequently subjected to discriminatory treatment by staff and patients alike. As a result of his work at SFGH, an annual award for the outstanding trainee of the Black Focus Program Unit has been named in his honor. From 1992 to 1994 Dr. Tarver served as a staff psychiatrist at the Center for Special Problems (CSP), where as Program Coordinator for the Gender Identity Program, in collaboration with Gianna E. Israel and other experienced staff, Dr. Tarver further developed experience as a Senior Gender Specialist.

At CSP Dr. Tarver conducted individual and group psychotherapy, supervised psychiatric medication and sex hormone administration, taught staff and trainees, and conducted case consultation. During his tenure as Program Coordinator he promoted non-pathologizing principles in the support of the center's transgender clients, no easy task in the atmosphere of a city mental health clinic. In this capacity he provided cofacilitation of the Transgender Peer Support Group, networked with transgender community resources, provided consultation on gender issues to outside community agencies, and served on a panel at the Amercian Psychiatric Associations' 1992 San Francisco conference. While transgender activists vehemently demonstrated outside the facility, Dr. Tarver was inside educating and advocating to his peers about his understanding that having a trangender identity was not itself a pathologic condition.

Currently Dr. Tarver serves as Medical Director of New Leaf (a mental health, substance abuse and social support center for lesbian, gay, bisexual, and transgender individuals and families), and Psychiatric Consultant to Baker Places, Inc. Dr. Tarver served as Medical Director of Westside Crisis and Outpatient Clinic, then Medical Director of Westside Community Mental Health Center, from 1993 to 1997. He maintains a private practice and spends time providing training to other medical and mental health institutions. Dr. Tarver continues to advance psychological and medical professional practices that are inclusive of human rights. Dr. Tarver was a founding member and past cochair of Lesbians and Gays of African Descent for Democratic Action (LGADDA), as well as a founding member of the Umoja Strategy Group (working to overcome gender and sexual orientation discrimination in the African American community). Additionally, he has served as a board member of Forensic Health Care, Inc., Gay and Lesbian Alliance Against Defamation (GLAAD/SF), The Brothers Network, and Operation Concern.

About the Reviewers and Contributors

BARBARA F. ANDERSON, PH.D., L.C.S.W., was born in New York City and educated at Queens College and Columbia University School of Social Work. She spent the next twenty years raising a family and working first as a social worker in agencies and then as a therapist in private practice in a Philadelphia suburb. As her career developed, she focused more on working with individuals, couples, and families with sexual, relationship, and gender concerns. She became licensed both as a marriage counselor and social worker and certified as a sex therapist.

In 1984 she enrolled in a doctoral program at the Institute for the Advanced Study of Human Sexuality in San Francisco. Upon graduating in 1987 she began to focus her interests even more sharply and developed a practice serving the many needs of the transgender community and its friends and family. In 1993 she relocated to San Francisco and establiId a clinical social-work and sex-therapy practice that includes providing consultation to colleagues in the areas of gender counseling and ethical professional practice. She also coordinates Gender Identity Treatment Program at the Center for Special Problems, a city-sponsored mental health agency. Additionally, she is a member of the Harry Benjamin International Gender Dysphoria Association and serves on the Transgender Task Force of the Human Rights Commission of San Francisco and the Ethics Committees of the American Association of Sex Educators, Counselors and Therapists and of the Society for the Scientific Study of Sex. She is also an adjunct faculty member of the City College of San Francisco, teaching in the Older Adult's Program.

LARRY BRINKIN has been an activist in San Francisco for over thirty years. He was a member of the Society for Individual Rights and a cofounder of the Bay Area Gay Liberation, the Lesbian/Gay Labor Alliance, and the Gay and Lesbian Alternative Dispute Resolution Service. He has long been active in working for civil rights in the lesbian, gay, bisexual, transgender, and HIV communities, and on the behalf of women and people of color. He was a pioneer in the struggle for domestic partner benefits. Currently, he is the Coordinator of the Lesbian Gay Bisexual Transgender and HIV Unit

264

of the San Francisco Human Rights Commission, and he played a major role in the recent passage of legislation in San Francisco protecting transgender persons from discrimination.

MILDRED L. BROWN, PH.D., is a well-respected clinical sexologist and therapist who has maintained a private practice in Los Gatos, California, for the past fifteen years. She received a Ph.D. in Human Sexuality from the Institute for Advanced Study of Human Sexuality in San Francisco, where she has been an Associate Professor of Clinical Sexology since 1980. As an accomplished professional, she is board certified as a sex therapist by the American Association of Sex Educators, Counselors and Therapists (AASECT), as a clinical sexologist and clinical supervisor by the American Board of Sexology (ABS), and she has held membership with the Harry Benjamin International Gender Dysphoria Association (HBIGDA) for the past fourteen years.

Dr. Brown began her private practice when few resources existed for transgender individuals in northern California's San Jose area. As a Gender Specialist, she has helped crossdressers, transsexuals, and other transgender individuals in resolving gender-identity issues and in building healthy, supportive resources. She conducts group therapy for transsexuals; workshops and support groups for spouses, significant family members, and children; and provides consultation to various corporations on gender issues.

She has participated in panel discussions on transsexualism and has been interviewed by numerous newspapers, magazines, and radio shows. Dr. Brown also has appeared on national television programs such as "People are Talking" and the Home Box Office (HBO) special "What Sex Am I?" She has published articles in the *Medical Aspects of Human Sexuality* and in the *Journal of Sex Research* and is coauthor of *True Selves,* which features professional insights and personal reflections based on her experiences supporting transgender individuals (Jossey-Bass, Publishers). "Millie" is an avid tournament bridge player, and she enjoys traveling and spending time with her husband and two children.

DONNA COLVIN, was born in Fresno, California, in 1952 and graduated from Clovis High School in 1970. She began her transition during the early 1970s, proceeding to live full time in role, and she initiated hormones in 1972. During 1974 she provided counseling in the Hollywood Gay Community Center with Shannon O'Hara; later that year she moved to San Francisco and became an original member of Electra Theater, a local, primarily transgender, women's theater and dance group. Since the late 1970s Ms. Colvin has held a variety of employment positions, including apartment manager, Army medical records department technician, data processing, and medical transcriptionist. Finding herself isolated from the transgender community while living in central California (the Valley) from 1987 through 1992, she moved to San Diego. The transgender community there was lacking, so in 1993 she decided to return to San Francisco where she reinitiated her involvement with the Electra Theater group and became involved in Transgender Nation. Since July 1994 she has been cofacilitating the Transgender Support Group at the Center for Special Problems and providing administrative assistance for the Recommended Guidelines project, working with Gianna E. Israel. Presently she is studying to continue in her counseling career. She firmly believes that having a transgender identity does not constitute having mental illness.

JASON CROMWELL, PH.D., is a long-time community member and has facilitated support groups at Seattle's Ingersoll Gender Center for the past thirteen years. He holds a doctorate in cultural anthropology and is a former board of directors member with the International Foundation for Gender Education (IFGE). Currently, Dr. Cromwell is a member of the board of directors of the American Educational Gender Information Service (AEGIS) and the newly formed FTM Conference and Education Project.

ALEXIS BELINDA DINNO was born Alexis David Dinno during the last days of the 1960s to Catherine Anne Dinno, a single, self-supporting mother. She was raised among the burgeoning technological edifices in Silicon Valley by a flower-child, university intellectual, ex-Roman Catholic of a woman, ostensibly to embrace the diversity of life, and to help it when she could. Ms. Dinno graduated from Mountain View High School in 1988 and promptly entered the De Anza and Foothill Community College. After two years she broke free of the event horizon that is the South Bay and landed at the University of California at Berkeley, where she is now completing her bachelor's degree in interdisciplinary studies with focus on social theories of global political economy. During her time in the East Bay she dropped out of school twice. On the first occasion she computerized a small clothing company and began her outward transition from male to female. on the second occasion she worked as a peace activist for SANE/Freeze (now Peace Action).

SISTER MARY ELIZABETH, SSE, is founder and systems operator of the AIDS Education Global Information System (AEGIS). Her multidisciplinary background includes more than twenty years' service with the U.S. Navy, U.S. Naval Reserve, and U.S. Army Reserve, where she held the rank of chief petty officer and sergeant first class, respectively. She holds a bachelor's degree in liberal studies, an associate degree in human services, and an associate of science degree in electronic engineering technology. In 1976–1978 she lobbied for the passage of California's birth certificate and driver's license name change for transgender persons. She also lobbied the U.S. State Department Passport Office to establish standardized procedures for issuing passports to both pre- and postoperative transsexuals. In 1980 she founded the ACLU's Transsexual Rights Committee, and in 1986 she established J2CP information services taking over the Janus Information Facility founded by Paul Walker, Ph.D. In 1988 she cofounded the Sisters of Saint Elizabeth of Hungary and made vows in the Episcopal and Franciscan traditions. Since 1990 she has operated AEGIS as the order's primary community-service activity. Sister Mary Elizabeth is also the author of "Legal Aspects of Transsexualism" (published by IFGE).

DONNA FREEMAN and JULIE FREEMAN. Julie was born in Cleveland, Ohio, and Donna in Los Angeles. They met while both were undergraduates at the University of California at Berkeley. Julie still has an active career as a teacher, and Donna retired recently after thirty years at IBM. They have been married for thirty-one years and have two daughters, both college graduates. Donna has been a crossdresser for as long as she can remember. In early 1987, at the age of forty-five, she felt she could no longer keep her crossdressing a secret and told Julie. After an unsuccessful search for information from several mental-health hotlines, they finally found Tri-Ess and then ETVC. They have both been very active in the Bay Area gender community since July 1988. Donna was secretary of ETVC for two years and membership coordinator for five, and she was their Member of the Year in 1993. In May 1991 she co-founded the Diablo Valley Girls, a social support group in Walnut Creek, and continues to perform most of the administrative functions for the group. Julie has been a focal point for significant others support in the Bay Area for many years. Together, they have provided counseling and support to many couples seeking help with transgender issues.

AYME MICHELLE KANTZ was born July 9, 1956, in Encino, California and raised in Granada Hills. Her father was choir director and organist at their church, so she was recruited into a singing career at the early age of eight. She has a sister and brother, both younger. The family moved to Santa Monica in 1968, and she graduated from high school there in 1974. After a year of city college and two at Arizona State University studying architecture, she ultimately graduated from the Institute of Audio Engineering (Hollywood) and began working in the recording arts industry in 1978. From there, she has held a creative assortment of jobs in office admininstration, media coordination, art direction, print buying and selling, typesetting, and marketing. Through it all, she has continued singing and has enjoyed a professional vocal career spanning twenty-six years.

Ms. Kantz lived with her parents until she was twenty-three. In 1989, though, she met a woman, and they soon moved in together, getting married five years later and surviving for another five. By 1990, she was divorced and in a dead-end job, but was finally exploring her sexual and gender identity. As a creative outlet, she joined the Gay Men's Chorus of Los Angeles, and during a Christmas concert weekend with them in Palm Springs, she was offered a transgenderist's dream, a job as a woman. She left Los Angeles and moved to the desert, where she spent the best three years of her life.

She was inspired to move to the Bay Area during a week's vacation in September 1993, and she currently resides in San Francisco in a house that she shares with her lover, Tyrrell, and two gay men, both cherished friends from Palm Springs. She found ETVC and was impressed with the scope of their mission and soon became involved at their Executive Committee level; she was elected to chair the Education Committee in May 1994. She is a project administrator for a major bank and has now been crossliving successfully as female for four years.

HEATHER LAMBORN is a transgender woman residing in Oakland, California. She leads an active life as a businesswoman and enjoys interacting with friends, who may be transgender or not. During 1995 I was a contestant in the ETVC Cotillion. Ms. Lamborn serves as a role model to the community, particularly demonstrating that individuals can successfully transition during their later years. More information about her experiences may be found in her essay (see Chapter 15).

STEPHANIE ANNE LLOYD was born Keith Michael Hull in 1946. Trying hard to conform to the male stereotype, Keith married and had three children while advancing to become sales and marketing director of one of the biggest companies in the United Kingdom.

Finally facing the alternatives of either committing suicide or coming to terms with transsexuality, Keith was transformed completely into Stephanie in 1983. A sex change by such a prominent individual dominated the front pages of the British tabloids for weeks and resulted in the loss of her career, home, and family.

Penniless and alone, she struggled to set up transformation. Later she met and then married a millionaire. Today she runs the Albany Gender Identity Clinic, Transformation shops, and, with her husband, a chain of food supermarkets. More than anyone else in the United Kingdom, she has campaigned tirelessly and very publicly for the rights of all transgenderists.

Ms. Lloyd lives with her husband on a farm in Wales surrounded by dogs, cats, peacocks, chickens, ducks, geese, and she, of whom she says of fondly: "They all just accept and love me for who I am—no subjective judgments, no complaining about being owned by a transsexual—if only people could be more like animals!"

VICTORIA LYNN has been learning to adapt to and develop her feminine side for over two decades. Born in northern New York state, she now lives in Syracuse, with her wife and daughter. Both of them are fully aware of her special needs and support her one-hundred percent in every endeavor.

In addition to acting as an editor for *Transgender Care*, Victoria is a well-known author within the gender community, and she has had a number of fiction and nonfiction works published across the country.

Locally, Victoria is very active in gender issues, serving as a board of directors member and treasurer for EON as well as leading the effort to create a medical-care support collective for transgender people in the central New York area. Although she is employed in the entertainment industry, Victoria hopes to eventually write full time. She also hopes to someday extend the scope of her femininity via hormone treatments to bring her physical appearance more in line with her emotional and spiritual self.

LISA MIDDLETON, M.P.A, is a transsexual woman working and residing in San Francisco. Her undergraduate education was completed at UCLA. She holds a master's in public administration from the University of Southern California. She has been employed for over twenty years in the insurance field, specifically, in workers' compensation. She has held both claims management and policy-making responsibility. Ms. Middleton has testified and lectured on insurance reimbursement practices and policies on numerous occasions before business forums and medical, legal, and governmental bodies. Her current duties include senior corporate responsibility for reimbursement and payment guidelines and practices, preferred-provider contracting, and medical protocol policy oversight.

She encourages, and believes critical to the progress of our community, a substantially improved dialogue and cooperation between legal, medical, and insurance professionals concerned with transgender health care.

Her essay is abridged from a version written for the International Conference on Transgender Law and Employment Policy (ICTLEP), to whom she is deeply indebted. Information on the ICTLEP can be found in the Appendix.

DOUGLAS K. OUSTERHOUT, D.D.S., M.D., was educated at the University of Colorado, Boulder, the Minerva Institute in Zurich, Switzerland, and the University of Michigan, Ann Arbor, where he received his dental degree in 1961 and medical degree in 1965. While there, he was inducted into several honor societies, including the Dental Academic, Medical Historical, and Medical Academic Honors fraternities.

He continued at the University of Michigan as a resident in general surgery after serving as a captain in the U.S. Army Medical Corps from 1966 to 1968. He completed his residency in plastic surgery at Stanford University Medical Center, where he held the position of Chief Resident from 1971 to 1972. From there, he trained in Paris as the first American to assist Dr. Paul Tessier in the techniques of craniofacial surgery.

Upon returning to the United States, Dr. Ousterhout was certified by the American

Board of Plastic Surgery in 1974 and has been in the practice of plastic surgery in San Francisco since then. He is actively associated with eighteen medical societies, including the American Society of Plastic and Reconstructive Surgeons, American Society for Aesthetic Plastic Surgery, Société Française de Chirurgie Plastique Recontructrice et Esthetique, American Society of Maxillofacial Surgeons, the Harry S. Benjamin International Gender Dysphoria Association, and the International Society of Craniofacial Surgery.

Dr. Ousterhout has served on the boards of many plastic surgery societies and in 1994–1995 was President of the American Society of Maxillofacial Surgeons. He helped found one medical journal and has been on the editorial board of four plastic surgery journals. He holds staff memberships at several hospitals, including Davies Medical Center, Saint Francis Memorial Hospital, California Pacific Medical Center, but particularly with the University of California, San Francisco, where he is clinical professor of plastic surgery, participating with a panel of internationally known experts at the Center for Craniofacial Anomalies. He has operated in many countries outside the United States.

Throughout his career, he has presented dozens of scientific papers, both nationally and internationally, at major medical meetings. He has published over one hundred scientific articles, most of them having to do with various aspects of facial surgery, particularly contour changing in the transsexual. He is the author of a medical textbook, *Aesthetic Contouring of the Craniofacial Skeleton,* published in 1991 by Little, Brown and Company. It covers all the aspects of bony contour change, including facilitating both the MTF and the FTM transsexual transition.

RACHEL POLLACK, M.A., was born in Brooklyn in 1945. She received her bachelor's degree from New York University, and her master's degree from Claremont Graduate School in California. Early in 1971 she came out as a transsexual, publicly declaring her female sense of identity and beginning her full-time life as a woman. At the same time, she also came out as a lesbian, a concept almost unknown at that time.

In the summer of 1971 she moved to Europe, first to London, where she started hormones, then to Amsterdam, and in 1976 she had surgery from Dr. Philip Lamaker. For neither the hormones nor the surgery did she undergo extensive counseling. The psychologist who approved her surgery was a man who knew her from her attendance in a support group he ran. They spoke for some twenty minutes, during which he told her that she obviously knew what she was getting into, and that she knew herself much better than he could ever hope to know her.

After surgery, Ms. Pollack pursued her career as a writer. She has written twenty books, including *Unquenchable Fire,* which won the Arthur C. Clarke Award in Britain for the best novel of the year. In addition to her five novels, her work includes nonfiction books and several collections of short stories. Her books have been translated into nine languages.

In the past few years she has lectured and written on transsexual and transgender issues. In 1993 she spoke before the forty-nation Council of Europe. In that year she also addressed the International Conference of the Harry Benjamin Association. One of her primary concerns in writing about transsexuality is to set the subject in a context of mythology and crosscultural traditions from history and around the world. In 1995 "Aphrodite: Transsexual Goddess of Passion," based on a speech she gave in France in 1993, appeared in the *Journal of Archetypal Psychology.* She is currently working on *Daughter of Belief,* a book on the passion of transsexual people.

EUGENE A. SCHRANG, M.D., was born in Milwaukee, Wisconsin, on October 27, 1931, to Edmond J. Schrang, a practicing architect and Agatha Schrang. Both parents of central European origin. Dr. Schrang's education includes four years at Marquette High School in Milwaukee and four years at the University of Notre Dame, where he received his bachelor of science degree. His doctorate in medicine was earned at Stritch School of Medicine of Loyola University in Chicago. His surgical residencies consisted of two years at Albany Medical Center in Albany, New York, and two years at St. Mary's Hospital in San Francisco, six months of which he taught general surgery at the Sacramento County Hospital in Sacramento, California. His three years of plastic surgery residency was spent with the world-renowned Truman G. Blocker, Jr., at the University of Texas in Galveston. He is board certified by the American Board of Plastic Surgery and is an active member of both the American Society and International Congress of Plastic and Reconstructive Surgeons. He has been in medical practice since 1965, and his professional interests are centered in cosmetic and reconstructive plastic surgery in addition to MTF genital reassignment.

JOY DIANE SHAFFER, M.D., after earning a bachelor of science degree at the California Institute of Techonolgy, underwent MTF Genital Reassignment Surgery in 1979, despite authoritative professional advice that doing so would doom her career. In 1981 she was admitted to the Stanford Unviersity School of Medicine and quietly became the first postoperative transsexual person known to have enrolled in medical school. Dr. Shaffer is now board certified in internal medicine. In January 1995 she founded Seahorse Medical Clinic in San Jose to focus on improving transsexual care through teaching and research. Her interests include expanding reproductive options for transsexual persons, investigating new therapies to optimize reassignment outcomes, and gender studies of the brain.

GAIL SONDEGAARD is one of the founders and currently the sole publisher and editor of *Transsexual News Telegraph,* a left-wing transsexual magazine of art, cultural commentary, and politics. Reticent and shy, she works by day as a legal secretary. Her nights are her own. She made the transition to full-time living almost ten years ago and has never regretted it.

SUSAN STRYKER, PH.D., is an MTF transsexual who earned her Ph.D. in U.S. history at the University of California at Berkeley in 1992. She was a founding member of Transgender Nation and currently serves on the board of directors of the International Foundation for Gender Education (IFGE). She contributes regularly to the transgender community press and writes on transgender issues for a broader academic audience. She currently teaches feminist theory and history of sexuality in the Women's Studies Department at UC Berkeley, and she is completing the manuscript of *A Critical Gender: Transsexuality in Theory and Practice* (forthcoming from Oxford University Press in 1999).

SHARON ANN STUART is a bi-gendered person who has been expressing both masculinity and femininity alternately since early childhood. A lawyer and former law professor and law librarian, Ms. Stuart is a veteran of the U.S. Marine Corps and a former instructor at the U.S. Naval Justice School. Noted as a civil rights activist and theoretician, she has participated in the 1993 March on Washington and the Stonewall 25 March (1994). She is currently active in efforts to establish a political and educational activist coalition in the gender community.

Ms. Stuart is vice-chair of the board of the International Foundation for Gender Education (IFGE) and a charter member of the board of the International Conference on Transgender Law and Employment Policy (ICTLEP). She is a coauthor of the International Bill of Gender Rights (IBGR), director of ICTLEP's IBGR Project, and also serves as the director of ICTLEP's Military Law Project.

A long-time Tri Ess member, Ms. Stuart serves as president of Lambda Chi Lambda, a Tri Ess chapter. She is also active as a member of the National Lesbian and Gay Law Association (NLGLA) and is a local contact person for Parents and Friends of Lesbians and Gays (PFLAG).

Born in Kansas City, Missouri, in 1940, Ms. Stuart now resides in a small upstate New York village where I devotes her time to gender advocacy and activist cause and to writing and speaking about gender issues.

MAX WOLF VALERIO is a poet, writer, performer, and transsexual activist. In his previous life, he wrote an essay for the prize-winning feminist anthology *This Bridge Called My Back* and published a poetry chapbook, *Animal Magnetism* (e.g. press, 1984). His work has been praised by Adrienne Rich and Robert Creeley. Max is hard at work on a definitive collection of his poetry. In 1992 he appeared in the film *Female Misbehavior* and in the short feature *Max,* directed by Monika Treut. *Female Misbehavior* is available in video stores nationwide. Currently, he's writing a book about his perilous, eye-opening, and politically incorrect transition from lesbian feminist to heterosexual man. This book will be published in 1998 by William Morrow/Avon.

DELIA VAN MARIS, M.D., is a transgender physician with a long history of experience with the transsexual and transgender community. In the late 1960s she was associated with two academic health centers that provided endocrinologic therapy for transsexuals in preparation for their surgery, both for FTM and MTF patients. Since that time she has been a vocal advocate of rational, consistent, and medically monitored hormonal therapy. Implicit in this advocacy is that such therapy is only part of a spectrum of care necessary to achieve desired individual goals. Education of the transsexual and transgender person who assumes the role of client or patient and education of the care givers has been her recent point of focus. She has a particular interest in patients that in medical jargon have been "lost to follow-up" after Genital Reassignment Surgery, or who have chosen not to take this final step. Still active as a practitioner and a medical educator, Dr. van Maris is married, the father of five, a grandfather, and currently resides in the Southeast United States.

ANNE VITALE, PH.D., was born July 4, 1937 in Endicott, New York. She holds advanced degrees in engineering, art, and psychotherapy. Although she continues to practice all three disciplines, her primary profession and interest is psychotherapy.

She received her doctorate in counseling psychology from the Professional School of Psychology, San Diego, in 1982. She joined the staff of the D Street Counseling Group, San Rafael, California, in 1985. She continues to be associated with the group in private practice. Her postdoctorate studies, since 1984, have been with Jim Bugental, Ph.D.

Her psychotherapeutic orientation is existential-humanist with a specialty in the search for gender authenticity. She maintains a full client load of pre-, non-, and post-operative individuals, seeing them in individual and group sessions. She is completely open to helping her clients find their own authentic place in the broad spectrum being human allows.

Her interest in gender authenticity are rooted in her own lifelong sex and gender integration needs. Resolution for her came through a prolonged transition (1975–1980) and MTF Genital Reassignment Surgery on January 10, 1980.

She is a member of the Association for Existential Inquiry, the Harry Benjamin International Gender Dysphoria Association (HBIGDA), and a founding member of the Bay Area Gender Associates (BAGA). In addition, she is the author of "T Notes," a regularly appearing column in the *Cross-Talk* journal and CD Forum, an online bulletin board available through the Internet.

SHERRI WEBB was a native of the San Francisco Bay area. The late Ms. Webb was an outstanding African American transgender woman. She had Genital Reassignment Surgery during 1989. Working at the Tenderloin AIDS Resource Center (TARC), she provided outreach to people of color and to transgender and HIV-positive individuals. She specialized in providing counseling, referrals, and HIV education, frequently making home and hospital visits to those individuals who were unable to visit her office. Ms. Webb served as a talent competition judge for the 1995 ETVC Cotillion and was interviewed by numerous publications about her work.

KIKI WHITLOCK is a Filipina-American postoperative transsexual and bisexual woman. She is a health education specialist with the Asian AIDS Project (AAP) in San Francisco, where she is the Transgender Program coordinator providing HIV/AIDS and STD-prevention information and health education targeting Asian and Pacific Islander transgender people. She is currently a member of the HIV Prevention Planning Council and a former board member of the Tenderloin AIDS Resource Center.

For the past five years, Ms. Whitlock has been a transgender advocate and educator lobbying for transgender people's rights and providing workshops on transgender issues to public-service organizations in the Bay Area. She regularly attends national conferences on HIV/AIDS to coordinate and facilitate panel discussions on transgender issues. In April 1994 she became a member of the San Francisco Human Rights Commission's Lesbian, Gay, Bisexual Transgender Advisory Committee, and she serves as chair of the Transgender Task Force to that committee. In May 1994 Ms. Whitlock became the first self-identified transgender person to receive a community service award from the Harvey Milk Lesbian, Gay, Bisexual Democratic Club of San Francisco.

Index